READINGS IN DEVELOPMENTAL PSYCHOLOGY

READINGS IN DEVELOPMENTAL PSYCHOLOGY

Edited by
Dr. Lancy D' Souza
Professor
Department of Psychology
Maharaja Degree College
University of Mysore
Mysore, Karnataka
(INDIA)

DISCOVERY PUBLISHING HOUSE PVT. LTD.
NEW DELHI-110 002

Published by:
Tilak Wasan
DISCOVERY PUBLISHING HOUSE PVT. LTD.
4383/4B, Ansari Road, Darya Ganj
New Delhi-110 002 (India)
Phone : +91-11-23279245, 43596064-65
Fax : +91-11-23253475
E-mail : parul.wasan@gmail.com
discoverypublishinghouse@gmail.com
web : www.discoverypublishinggroup.com

First Edition: **2012**
ISBN: 978-93-5056-116-4

Readings in Developmental Psychology

Printed at:
Shree Balaji Art Press
Delhi

Preface

This book is devoted to articles related to the field of developemental psychology. It is a collection of articles originally published in various issus of Asian Journal of Development Matters Journal (Mysore, Karnataka). This book contains around 25 articles on diverse fields of psychology from cognitive domains to spirituality to sports domain!

We are highly grateful to the authors who responded to the call for papers and cooperated to make this effort meaningful. We hope that the articles published in this issue will help readers in appreciating the nuances of recent trends in Psychology, stimulate research and promote relevant and fruitful research. Lastly, we are grateful to ROAD TRUST® for providing me an opportunity to edit this issue on this topic.

Earliest, we would like to Solute *Shri Sai Baba* for his blessings. We would like to thank all the Editors of various Journals, Books and Periodicals. We are very thankful to our friend, guide and philosopher Dr. Steven wind (USA). Next, we are most grateful to Prof. Annapurna M, Dr. Anjali Kuranee, Dr. Hari Mohan Mathur, Dr. Shiva Prasad, Dr. R.S. Reddy, Jyothi Lakshmi S, Dr. Srivatsa, Dr. Manjula for their logistic help. I owe a deep sense of gratitude to to my wife for her vital role. Some how, we could not contact few authors. Hence we greatly acknowledge their articles. Heartful thanks to *Artha Journal of Socials Sciences*, Christ College, Bangalore, and India and to our parents also. Further, we extend my acknowledgement to the research staff of our Institute sharing their knowledge.

—Editor

Contents

1

Nutritional Status and Cognitive Performance of School Children

Shekhara Naik R[1]
Jamuna Prakash[2]

ABSTRACT

Malnutrition has significantly correlations on cognitive development in childhood that reduces the work capacity (Wachs, 1995). Children from urban and rural do have little difference with socio-economic status but nutritional both area children have one or other kind of malnutrition on deficient of nutrients in their diet. Therefore to assess the nutritional status and cognitive performance of school children from Mysore taluk was designed. The study recruited 1093 children, 575 male and 518 female for the cognitive performance (RCPM) test and measured the nutritional status according to the weight for height (waterlow). Study revels that, cognitive test scores among children of normal nutritional status scored 8.6, 11.44, 15.46, 20.55 and 7.93, 10.72, 14.08, 21.27 whereas malnourished status children scored 10, 10.75, 13.19, 15.77 and 7.64, 9.826, 12.34, 13.42 male and female respectively in the following age groups 4-6, 6-8, 8-10, 10 & above. As the children age proceeds the cognitive scoring increased among both sex, male children were shown higher cognitive scoring than the female, the better nutritional status children shown superior cognitive scores than malnourished.

1. **Department of Studies in Food Science and Nutrition, University of Mysore, Mysore, Karnataka (India).**

2. **Reader, Department of Studies in Food Science and Nutrition, University of Mysore, Karnataka (India).**

Introduction

School age is the most active stage of growth and lots more activities performed during this age. Malnutrition in Indian children is more or less 50 per cent, about a half of the children are underweight and 40 per cent are stunted. There is no gender bias with respect to nutritional status of females (NNMB Report-2000). Recent studies indicated the relations between indexes of malnutrition and development is inconsistent. The significant correlations between Anthropometric measures thought to be indexes of chronic mild malnutrition and measures of cognitive development in childhood. Modest associations were also demonstrated between measures of Anthropometry (particularly weight) and activity (work capacity) (Wachs, 1995). Urban packets of children population are look like better in health but still they need attention towards better nutrition; improve their nutritional status that intern perform better in the cognitive and scholastic developmental activities, the rural packet of the population is socioeconomic and health is worst than urban areas. Therefore to assess the nutritional status and cognitive performance of schoolchildren from urban and rural areas Mysore is designed.

Methodology

1000 schoolchildren were recruited in the study; 500 each from urban and rural area and there are between 4 to 10+ years age groups studying in 1st standard to 4th standard. The selection of schools and subjects was done in accordance with random sampling technique from both areas. Selected children Anthropometry observation was recorded with the help of standard measuring tools; nutritional classification done according to water lows qualitative cut off for the nutritional status. Each children cognitive performances of was recorded with the help of Raven's colour progressive matrices (RCPM).

Raven's Colour Progressive Matrices

Raven's Coloured Progressive Matrices have been used extensively as a 'culture-fair' test of intelligence. They measure the ability to reason and solve problems. The battery of test book consisting of 3 sets i.e. *A*, *Ab* and *B*. each test set consisting of 12 visual problem in the form figures and the subject is shown a visual pattern with a missing section and is required to select 1 of 6 alternative sections to complete the overall pattern (each problem having six answer figure, among six one of figure solves the problem) as the test proceeds, the problems become progressively more difficult. The test is not timed, and the subject continues until satisfied with the choice made. The score is the number of correct items selected. Each correct answer were considered scored with one; finally total score of each child from three set was considered for Raven's classification; it was done based on percentile of score acquired within the age group. The percentile was calculated by taking the score of the within each age group; maximum score of the within the group was considered as cent percentile and calculated rest of the score for interpretation and reporting (Ravens CPM -1998). The data was statistically analyzed for the signification by SPSS10 version package.

Results

Table 1.1: Nutritional status and cognitive performance (RCPM score) of school children according to Waterlow's classification from Mysore taluk

Water low's Classification		Normal		Malnourished		Over all	
Age Group	Sex	Mean	SD	Mean	SD	Mean	SD
4-6	Male	8.6765	4.8513	10.0000	5.0166	8.8889	4.8708
	Female	7.9348	4.9008	7.6471	3.5697	7.8571	4.5538
	Total	8.3772	4.8634	8.6667	4.3417	8.4375	4.7463
6-8	Male	11.4444	5.3258	10.7500	5.4432	11.3320	5.3400
	Female	10.7233	4.7664	9.8261	4.3783	10.5595	4.7023
	Total	11.0847	5.0613	10.2558	4.8946	10.9419	5.0379
8-10	Male	15.4655	8.0753	13.1957	8.2748	14.9909	8.1510
	Female	14.0809	7.3907	12.3409	6.8095	13.6556	7.2731
	Total	14.8581	7.8005	12.7778	7.5636	14.3900	7.7871
10+	Male	20.5556	9.7873	15.7778	9.1348	18.9630	9.6734
	Female	21.2727	7.1287	13.4167	7.3911	17.1739	8.1556
	Total	20.8276	8.7426	14.4286	8.0534	18.1400	8.9625
Over all	Male	12.8908	7.2036	12.1204	7.1783	12.7461	7.1989
	Female	11.8371	6.3879	10.8067	5.8661	11.6004	6.2813
	Total	12.4053	6.8561	11.4317	6.5418	12.2031	6.8006

According to the Waterlow's classification the children were classified as normal and malnourished (stunted, wasted and both form of malnutrition were combined), the average cognitive (rcpm) score among nutritionally normal children of Mysore taluk were 8.37, 11.08, 14.85, 20.82 and 12.40 among 4- 6, 6-8, 8-10, 10 & above and overall age groups respectively.. The mean cognitive (RCPM) score by the malnourished children were found with 8.66, 10.25, 12.77, 13.4 and 11.43 among 4-6, 6-8, 8-10, 10 & above and over all year's age groups respectively; it indicated that the malnourished children cognitive (rcpm) score was less than the normal children in all the age group except 4-6 year age group. In accordance with the gender; male children cognitive score was 8.6, 11.44, 15.46, 20.55 and 12.89 but female children score was 7.93, 10.72, 14.08, 21.27 and 11.83 among 4-6, 6-8, 8-10, 10 & above and over all age group were shown in normal cases, whereas malnourished male children score was 10, 10.75, 13.19, 15.77 and 12.12 whereas female children score was 7.64, 9.826, 12.34,13.42 and 10.43 among 4-6, 6-8, 8-10, 10 & above and over all age groups in the study area; the finding shown that, normal nutritional status of both sex children shown higher cognitive score than the malnourished children in all the age group, as both normal and malnourished nutritional status children of male gender had upper hand than the female gender except in 4-6 years age group. All together nutritional status children's mean cognitive (rcpm) score of male was 8.88, 11.33, 14.99, 18.96 and 12.74 whereas female were with 7.85, 10.55, 13.65, 17.17 and 11.60 among 4-6, 6-8, 8-10, 10 & above and over all years age groups; in all the age group male children cognitive score was greater than the female children. On combine both gender cognitive (rcpm) score was 8.43, 10.94, 14.39, 18.14 and 12.20 among 4-6, 6-8, 8-10, 10 & above and overall. The finding clearly indicated that, as children age proceeds the cognitive (rcpm) scoring increased among both sex with significant difference, male children were shown higher cognitive (rcpm) scoring than the female, the children of better nutritional status associated with superior cognitive scores than malnourished.

Discussion

School children of the urban and rural Mysore were assessed for their nutritional status and cognitive performance. The cognitive performance and normal nutritional status of the school children from Mysore taluk, were assessed with cognitive performance test, the mean score of the test to be 8.6, 11.44, 15.46, 20.55 and 12.89 score among male and 7.93, 10.72, 14.08, 21.27 and 11.83 among female children of 4-6, 6-8, 8-10, 10 & above and over all years age group. The malnourished status of male children cognitive scores are 10, 10.75, 13.19, 15.77 and 12.12 and female children score 7.64, 9.826, 12.34, 13.42 and 10.43 among 4-6, 6-8, 8-10, 10 & above and over all years age groups in the study area; the finding shown that, normal nutritional status of both sex children shown higher cognitive score than the malnourished children in all the age group, as both normal and malnourished nutritional status children of male gender had upper hand than the female gender except in 4-6 years age group. All together nutritional status children's mean cognitive score of male was 8.88, 11.33, 14.99, 18.96 and 12.74 whereas female were with 7.85, 10.55, 13.65, 17.17 and 11.60 among 4-6, 6-8, 8-10, 10 & above and over all years age groups; in all the age group male children cognitive score was greater than the female children. On combine both gender cognitive score 8.43, 10.94, 14.39, 18.14 and 12.20 among 4-6, 6-8, 8-10, 10 & above and overall years age group. The finding clearly indicated that, as children age proceeds the cognitive (rcpm) scoring increased among both sex with significant difference, male children were shown higher cognitive (rcpm) scoring than the female, the children of better nutritional status associated with superior cognitive scores than malnourished. The cognitive performance of children is associated with nutritional status of children shown significant, the relations between indexes of malnutrition and development is inconsistent; significant correlations between Anthropometric measures thought to be indexes of chronic mild malnutrition and measures of cognitive development in childhood, modest associations were also demonstrated between measures of Anthropometry and activity (Wachs. 1995).

M.D. Niehaus and co worker (2002) the early child hood diarrhea is correlated with reduced cognitive function among children, Pollit and *et al* (1998), poor nutrition among schoolchildren has adverse effects on attention and memory processes effects that may be mediated by metabolic changes in plasma glucose regulation in the brain.

Conclusion

School children of the growing stage, the physical activities are more and pressure on mental activity too follows. Cognitive performance of the children is the active development of brain that promotes the brain cells to cognize the events observed and retain in the memory to recall depending on the circumstances. The cognitive performance associated with nutritional status of the children, as children age proceeds the cognitive performance increase among both sex with significant difference, male children were shown higher cognitive scoring than the female, the children of better nutritional status associated with superior cognitive scores than malnourished. Therefore, the cognitive performance of the children is associated with the nutritional status of children.

REFERENCES

Mark D. Niehaus, Sean R. Moore, Peter D. Patrick, Lori L. Derr, Breyette Lorntz, Aldo A. Lima, And Richard L. Guerrant, Early Childhood Diarrhoea is Associated With Diminished Cognitive Function 4 To 7 Years Later in Children in A North-east Brazilian Shantytown. *Am. J. Trop. Med.* Hyg., 66(5), 2002, pp. 590-593.

Michael B Zimmermann, Kevin Connolly, Maksim Bozo, John Bridson, Fabian Rohner, and Lindita Grimci. Iodine Supplementation Improves Cognition in Iodine-deficient School Children in Albania: A Randomized, Controlled, Double-blind Study1-4. *Am J Clin Nutr* 2006; 83:108 -14.

NNMB Survey Report, NIN, ICMR 2000.

Pollitt Ernesto, Santiago Cueto, and Enrique R Jacoby, Fasting and Cognition in well and Undernourished School children: A Review of Three Experimental Studies. *Am J Clin Nutr* 1998;67(suppl): 779S-84S.

Raven, J., Raven, J.C., and J.H Court. Raven Manual: Section 2, *Coloured Progressive Matrices*, CPM49-51, 1998 Edition, Published by Oxford Psychologists Press, Oxford.

Wachs T.D., Relation of Mild-to-moderate Malnutrition to Human Development: Correlational Studies. *J. Nutr*. 125: 2245S-2254S, 1995.

Wechsler D. Wechsler Intelligence *Scale for Children*. WISC-III UK. London, United Kingdom: Psychological Corporation, 1992.

2

The Relationship Between Mother's BMI, Child's Sex and Malnutrition in Children Under Five Years of Age

Sadat Zohreh MS.[1]
Abedzadeh Masoomeh MS.[1]
Saberi Farzaneh[1]

ABSTRACT

Objective: Malnutrition is one of the important risk factors for morbidity and mortality in children aged five years and below. The present study was conducted, in health centes in Kashan, Iran, to evaluate the association between mother's BMI and child's sex as Risk factors for malnutrition.

Methods: In a case-control study, by using cluster and random sampling, 125 children under five years of age with malnutrition, based on weight for age using 2 standard deviations criteria NCHS (Case group) and 125 children without malnutrition (control group), were enrolled during the study period. Mother's BMI and child's sex was compared in two groups. Results were judged with Chi-square and t-test.

Results: Results showed that the baselines were similar in two groups. Mean mother's BMI was significantly different in two groups with (25.5 ± 5.1) in the case group and (27.5 ± 5.1) in the control group (P<0.02). Also results demonstrated that child's sex was related to malnutrition (p<0.02). Odd's ratio and confidence interval for effect of BMI<22 and female sex on malnutrition were (OR=2.1, C1=3.74-1.16 and OR=1.81 C1=3.05-1.07) respectively.

Conclusion: This study showed low mother's BMI and female sex increased the risk of malnutrition in children less than five years.

Key words: Child's sex, malnutrition, mother's BMI, risk factors.

1. **Faculty Member, Department of Midwifery, Kashan University of Medical Sciences, Kashan, (Iran).**

Introduction

Malnutrition is one of the leading causes of morbidity and mortality in children aged five years and below. Physical growth and development is a major concern in the field of pediatrics. A child's normal growth and development not only impacts a child's general health and well-being but also affects the society as well. During infancy and early childhood children grow rapidly, any barrier to prevent the normal process can leave irreversible damages to the child's physical and emotional well-being. National Centre for Health Statistics classifies a child as malnourished when a child's weight for age is 2 or more standard deviation below the mean in the comparison standard[1]. Malnutrition has had a significant effect on physical growth and cognitive development. Malnutrition and repeated infection is prevalent in developing countries, where they account for 45-54 per cent of death rate for children less than 5 years old[2]. A study in Birjand found 18.5 per cent of children were malnourished[3].

Factors contributing to malnutrition are many and varied. The major causes of malnutrition as conceptualized by several authors relate to socio-economic status of the family, child's sex, mother's Body Mass Index (BMI), child's poor health and repeated infection, weight at birth, unsatisfactory food intake, and also whether the child has been breast-fed or bottle fed. Other factors include psychological and emotional state of the family members, birth orders, and the age difference between the child and the previous child[4,5,6,7,8].

Studies in different countries have revealed different factors contributing to malnutrition. A study in Africa found a relationship between child's malnutrition and mother's low BMI, female sex of the child, and family socio-economic status. Another study in Brazil found a relationship between mother's low BMI and child's malnutrition while some other studies revealed no relationship between mother's BMI and child's malnutrition. Studies in Birjand and Boushehr found a relationship between child's sex and malnutrition. Studies in India and China revealed no relationship between child's sex and malnutrition. Due to controversies in the etiology of malnutrition, mother's BMI and child's sex, a study was conducted in Kashan, Iran, in 2002-2003, to determine the role of mother's BMI and child's sex on malnutrition of children younger than five. All children had been referred to 10 different health centers in Kashan.

Materials and Methods

This study was a case-control study using cluster-random sampling from May of 2002 to June of 2003. Sampling took place in ten different health centers in different parts of Kashan following the approval of the research protocol by the institutions' ethics review boards. 125 children who were malnourished based on weight for age using -2 standard deviations criteria

NCHS (Case group) and 125 children without malnutrition (control group) were enrolled during the study period. Two groups were matched in confounding variables including birth weight, age, infant' feeding practice (whether the child was breast-fed or bottle-fed) during the first year, time of weaning off breast feeding, birth order, mother's employment, mother's age, and education, the age difference between the child and previous child (birth interval), and unwanted pregnancies. Excluded criteria were child's illnesses, respiratory infections, and diarrhea in the previous two weeks and low birth weight. Anthropometric measurements, height and weight, were taken by standardized scientific tools and procedures by trained individuals following interviewing mothers. The measurements were documented in the forms previously developed by the researchers. At the end, mother's BMI and child's sex were compared in two groups. Chi square and t test were utilized for statistical analysis.

Result

The study found a relationship between malnutrition and mother's BMI<22 (P<0.02) as demonstrated in Table 2.1. Also the study revealed child's sex was related to malnutrition (P<0.02) as shown in Table 2.1. Odd's ratio and confidence interval for the effect of BMI <22 and female sex on malnutrition were (OR=2.1 C1=3.74-1.16 and OR=1.81 C1=3.05-1.07) respectively. Further, Results showed baseline factors were similar in both case and control groups (Table 2.2). Mother's BMI was significantly different in both groups with (25.5 ± 5.1) in the case group and (27.5 ± 5.1) in the control group (P<0.002).

Table 2.1: Mother's BMI and Children's Sex in both case and control groups

	Groups	Case Group	Control Group	P
Mother's BMI	≥ 22	85 (68)	102 (81.6)	0.02 (Highly Significant)
	< 22	40 (32)	23 (18.4)	
	Total	**125 (100%)**	**125 (100%)**	
Children's Sex	Boys	37 (29.6)	54 (43.2)	0.02 (Highly Significant)
	Girls	88 (70.4)	71 (56.8)	
	Total	**125 (100%)**	**125 (100%)**	

Table 2.2: Baseline characteristics in both case and control groups

Characteristics	Case group	Control group	Results
Birth weight in gram (X±SD)	3130 ± 373.9	3216 ± 370	P<0.1
Child's age in month (X±SD)	28.6±14.2	28.7±15.4	P<0.8
Mother's Education: Elementary and less	74 (569.2)	70 (56)	P<0.8
Middle and High school	45 (36)	50 (40)	
Higher Education	6 (4.8)	5 (4)	
Infant feeding practices in the first year:	106 (84.8)	110 (88)	P<0.6
Breast fed	19 (15.2)	15 (12)	
Bottle fed Start of complementary feeding in month	5.9±2.06	6.02±0.96	
Birth Order: First	53 (42.4)	49 (39.2)	P<0.8
2nd and 3rd	58 (46.4)	61 (48.8)	
4th and after	15 (12)	14 (11.2)	
Mother's age in years Birth interval in years (X±SD)	29±5.5 6.2±3	29.3±5.2 6.3±2.8	P<0.8
Unwanted pregnancy Yes	36 (28.8)	29 (23.2)	P<0.4
No	89 (71.2)	96 (76.8)	
Mother's employment Employed	7 (5.6)	5 (4)	P<0.5
Housewife	118 (94.4)	120 (96)	

P value demonstrated baseline characteristics were similar in two groups.

Discussion

This study's result demonstrated that mother's mean BMI in both control and Case group were (27.5+5.1) and (25.5+5.1) kg/m^2 respectively, and by using t-test were significantly different (P<0.002). Also the study revealed a significant relationship between mother's BMI<22 and malnutrition in children (P<0.02). This study also found a relationship between malnutrition and female sex (P<0.02).

Multiple studies investigating relationship between mother's BMI and child's malnutrition have been conducted in different countries that have revealed different findings. The study of 4923 children younger than 36 month by Aqueh *et al* found a positive relationship between mother's anthropometric measurement and those of the children. Also another study in Kerala by Sarma *et al*[2] India, found a relationship between mother's BMI, child's birth weight and child's malnutrition in children under 3 years old. Amigo *et al*[8] in a case control study on 153 children who were between 7-8 years old found a relationship between mother's height (OR=1.8), socio-economic status (OR=9.8), poor nutrition (OR=2.8), low birth weight (OR=2.1), and smoking during pregnancy (OR=1.8) and child malnutrition. Eelpout *et al.* in another cross-sectional study in Africa revealed family's socio-economic status and parents' marital relationships were considered factors in malnutrition in children under 6 years old. Anthropometric measurements of 2373 children and 1512 mothers were analyzed in that study. Although multiple factors were significant in developing malnutrition but when child's height and weight at birth were not considered, socio-economic status was an influencing factor in low weight for height but not for low height for age.

A study was conducted in Bangladesh by Islam *et al.* to investigate the impact of mother's BMI and socio-economic status of the family on malnutrition in children younger than 36 month. Their study which was a case control group included 125 children with less than 55 per cent of standard weight for age and for the control group 125 children who were matched with case group based on sex and health history were selected. The information was obtained through interviews with mothers and Anthropometric measurements. Results of their study revealed that dried milk feeding, mother's BMI, poor socio-economic status, polluted water, and mother's employment had a relationship with malnutrition but different analytical analysis found a strong relationship between dried milk feeding, mother's poor education and malnutrition with a risk factor of 4 times stronger. Other risk factors like mother's BMI needed further studies. An investigative study of nutritional circumstances of children under 5 in Kenya by Kogi-Malakau et al. was conducted. At this study, 14 perceived contributing factors to malnutrition including mother's BMI were investigated. None of the factors alone found to have a relationship with malnutrition. Peney *et al.* in California found different results; Three groups of children were selected for the research project:

1. Normal birth weight and high socio-economic status.
2. Normal birth weight and low socio-economic status.
3. Low birth weight and low socio-economic status).

All the children were breast-fed and were under one year old. The results demonstrated a relationship between birth weight and normal growth but no relationship between mother's BMI and child's growth.

Multiple studies have investigated the relationship between child's sex and malnutrition in children. Baily *et al.*[6] in investigating the effect of socio-economic status on inadequate protein-energy intake in children between 3-36 month found mother's young age (15-25), child's sex ($P<0.03$), single babysitter, and father's inappropriate employment to be significant risk factors. Heywood *et al.*[7] in another study in Indonesia on children under 5 years found a relationship between child's sex, mother's education, and low socio-economic status and malnutrition. A cross-sectional study in India on 600 children under five years of age found 46 per cent of them malnourished with the majority of them to be under 2 years old. In that study researchers found a relationship between malnutrition and child's sex, education and age of parents, vaccination, religion, and treatment of diarrhoea[4]. Another study in Benin investigated different factors causing malnutrition in 492 children. Child's malnutrition by assessing the score of weight for height was 5.7 per cent and height for age was 22 per cent. Also malnourished considering the score of height for age in boys, 25.1 per cent while that score for girls was 18 per cent ($P<0.0001$). Mahapatra *et al.* in Kerala, India investigating the causes of malnutrition, variables such as mother's health, feeding conditions, sex and age of the children were evaluated. Statistical analysis did not reveal any relationship between malnutrition and child's sex, age, or feeding condition in that study[2]. Another study on 75 children under 5 in India found no relationship between child's sex and malnutrition.

In the present study compound variables were matched in both case and control groups and only mother's BMI and child's sex was the focus of the study. In other studies, as presented, multiple variables were being investigated at the same time along with mother's BMI and child's sex. In such studies the results could be influenced by other variables. Another effect could have been cultural influences on child's sex and malnutrition. It is suggested to researchers to conduct another empirical study with more population to investigate the impact of mother's BMI, and child's sex on malnutrition when other variables are not the focus of the study.

REFERENCES

1. Alavi Naeini, S.M. Causes of Malnutrition in Children under Five in Health Centers in Birjand. *Journal of University of Medical Sciences in Birjand*; (1): 99-104.

2. Akumar S, Misra R. Epidemiology of Undernutrition. *Indian J Pediar*. 2001, Nov; 68(11): 1025-1030.

3. Baily RC. Wainan F, Bloos E. Prevalence and Predictors of Underweight, Stunting, and Wasting Among Children Aged 5 and Under in Western Kenya. *J Trop Pediar*. 2004, October; 50 (5): 260-261.

4. Baily RC, Wainana F, Bloos E. Prevalence and Predictors of Underweight Stunting, and Wasting Among Children Aged 5 and Under in Western Kenya. *J Trop Pediatr*. 2004, October; 50 (5): 262-270.

5. Delvarian Zadeh, M; Keshavarz, A; Jazari, A. Invsetingating the Influencing Factors in Appropriate Nutrition in Children Under 2 Years Old. *Journal of Knowledge and Health*, 1999, 42-45.

6. Delpeuch F, Traissec P, Massamba JP. Economic Crisis and Malnutrition: Socio-economic Determinants of Anthropometric Status of Pre-school Children and Their Mothers in an African Urban Area. *Public Health Nutr*. 2000 3, 39-47.

7. Veghari G R. Physical Growth Conditions of Children Under Five in Rural Areas of the City Gorgan. Journal of Gorgan *University of Medical Sciences*, 1999. 1, 6-10.

8. Peney KLG Cross. Cultural Pattern of Growth and Nutritional Status of Breast-feed Infants. *AM J Clin Nutr*. 1998, 67, 7-10.

3

Influence of Academic Performance, Gender and Area on Emotional Intelligence of Young Adults

Madhu Ramdurg[1]
K. Rajasekhara Reddy[2]

ABSTRACT

The present study reports the influence of academic performance, gender and area on emotional intelligence of young adults. A total of 320 (189 male + 131 female) young adults studying in urban and rural areas were randomly selected for the study. They were administered Emotional Intelligence Scale developed by Hyde, Pathe and Dhar (2001). Statistical techniques like 't' test and One-Way ANOVA. Results revealed that male and female young adults had statistically similar emotional intelligence scores. Area wise comparison revealed that young adults from rural areas were more emotionally intelligent than urban young adults. However, academic performance of the young adults did not influence emotional intelligence of the young adults.

Key words: Emotional Intelligence, Academic performance, and young adults.

Introduction

Emotional intelligence refers to the capacity for recognizing our own feelings and those of others, for motivating ourselves and for motivating emotions well in us and in our relationships. It is the ability to perceive

1. Human Resource Management, Stonebridge Associated Colleges, Cornwall- EX23 8ST, (United Kingdom).

2. Reader, Department of Studies in Anthropology, University of Mysore, Mysore, Karnataka (India).

accurately, appraise and express emotions, generate feelings that facilitate thoughts and an ability to regulate emotions to promote growth. It is also defined as an array of non-cognitive capabilities competencies and skills that influence one's ability to succeed in coping with environmental demands and pressure. According to Goleman, emotional intelligence has five elements: self-awareness, self-regulation, motivation, empathy, and social skills. With the dawn of 21st century, the human mind added a new dimension, which is now being held responsible more for success than intelligence. This is termed as emotional intelligence and is measured as EQ (emotional quotient). Over the past several years the term emotional intelligence has received much attention as a factor that is useful in understanding and predicting individual's performance at work, at home, at school etc. The concept of emotional intelligence was first introduced by Salovey and Mayer in the early 1990's and made popular by Daniel Goleman with publication of his book: "Why it can matter more than IQ" in 1995. Emotional intelligence is the capacity to create positive outcomes in relationships with others and with oneself. According to Mayer and Salovey (1993), emotional intelligence is the ability to monitor one's own and others' feelings and emotions, to discriminate among them, and to use this information to guide one's thinking and actions. Thus, emotional intelligence is an umbrella term that captures a broad collection of interpersonal and intrapersonal skills. Interpersonal skills consist of the ability to understand the feelings of others, empathise, maintain and develop interpersonal relationships and above all our sense of social responsibility. On the other hand, intrapersonal skills comprise of the ability to understand one's own motivation. Emotional intelligence plays a key role in determining life success. It becomes more and more important as people progress up the career ladder of their life. Emotions are our feelings; hence, emotional intelligence is our life. Emotional intelligence does not only measure emotions or intelligence. What it does is to open up a new way of looking at how our thinking and behaviour could be seen intelligent.

Review of literature on emotional indicated following aspects. Harrod and Scheer (2005) found that emotional intelligence levels were positively related to females, parents' education and household income. Amirtha and Kadhiravan (2006) found that gender, age and qualification influenced the emotional intelligence of schoolteachers. The main aim of education is the all round holistic development of the students. Devi and Uma (2005) found that the parental education, occupation had significant and positive relationship with dimensions of emotional intelligence like social regard, social responsibility, impulse control and optimism. McDowelle and Bell (1997) found that lack of emotional intelligence skills lowered team effectiveness and created dysfunctional team interactions and most effective performers lost the best networking skills.

Tapia and Marsh (2001) found an overall significant main effect of gender and two-way interaction of gender - GPA on emotional intelligence. Annaraja and Jose (2005) found that rural and urban B.Ed., trainees did not differ in their self-awareness, self-control, social skills and emotional intelligence. Though studies are done in northern region of India, we do not find many studies in the south, especially on young adults. The present study aims at studying the influence of academic performance, gender and locality on emotional intelligence of young adults in urban and rural areas of Young adults.

Sample

A total of 320 students were included in the present study. In the total sample there were 189 male participants and 131 were female participants. Of the 320 sample selected from the study, 130 were from rural area, and remaining 190 were from urban area. The age of young adults ranged from 19 to 23 years.

Tool Employed

The Emotional Intelligence Scale (EIS) developed by Hyde, Pathe and Dhar (2001) was used to measure EI. This instrument is made of 34 items and provides an indicator of the levels of perceived EI. The sub factors of the scale included self-awareness, empathy, self-motivation, emotional stability, managing relations, self-development, value orientation, commitment, and altruistic behaviour. Respondents are asked to rate their degree of agreement of the items on a 5-point Likert- type scale ranging from 1 (strongly disagree) to 5 (strongly agree). The reliability of the scale was determined by calculating reliability coefficient on a sample of 200 subjects by split-half method and was found to be .88. The validity of the scale assessed through content validity, which was sufficiently high.

Procedure

The tests were administered in a group of 3-5 subjects in a single session for about 25-30 minutes. Initially, rapport was established with the subjects and they were asked to introduce themselves. The purpose of the study was made clear to them. Then they were administered the emotional intelligence scale. They were given appropriate instructions and the questions were read out to them. They were asked to indicate their responses in the respective sheets given to them. Whenever the meaning of certain words was not clear to the students, they were made clear to them by one of the test administrators. Later the questionnaires were scored according to the manual and a master chart was prepared for statistical analysis.

Once the scores were arranged, they were subjected to statistical analysis like Independent samples 't' test and One-way ANOVA using SPSS for

Windows (version 11.5) software. To see the gender and area difference 't' tests were employed and to see difference between academic performance levels one-way ANOVA was employed.

Results

Table 3.1: Mean total emotional intelligence scores of male and female young adults hailing from urban and rural areas with different levels of academic performance and test statistics

Variables		Mean	S.D	Statistical Inference	Significance
Gender	Male	136.74	13.61	't'=0.933	P=.352 (NS)
	Female	135.35	12.21		
Area	Urban	132.69	12.49	't'=14.827	P=. 000 (HS)
	Rural	140.75	12.42		
Academic performance	Distinction	139.48	10.67	F=1.573	P=. 181 (NS)
	I Class	135.04	13.85		
	II Class	136.04	12.21		
	III Class	140.40	11.44		
	Fail	134.15	10.67		

Gender and Emotional Intelligence

Gender comparisons revealed that male and female young adults had statistically equal emotional intelligence scores (136.74 and 135.35 respectively). Further, t-test revealed a non-significant (t=.933; P=.352) difference between mean scores of male and female young adults.

Area and Emotional Intelligence

Surprisingly, rural young adults (mean 140.75) had higher emotional intelligence scores compared to urban young adults (mean 132.69) and 't' test revealed a significant difference (t=14.827; P=.000) between mean scores of rural and urban young adults.

Academic Performance and Emotional Intelligence

Academic performance of young adults did not have significant influence over emotional intelligence of the young adults as the obtained F value of 1.573 was found to be non-significant (P=.181). In other words, young adults having different levels of academic performance from distinction to fail had similar emotional intelligence scores.

Discussion

The main findings of the present study are:

1. Male and female young adults had similar emotional intelligence scores.
2. Rural young adults were more emotionally intelligent than urban young adults.
3. Academic performance of the young adults did not influence the emotional intelligence scores.

The results of the study are in quite contrary with the other studies. The findings of studies reported by Bhosle (1999), King (1999), Sutarso (1999), Wing and Love (2001) and Singh (2002) found females to have higher emotional intelligence than that of males. However, study by Chu (2002) revealed that males have higher level of emotional intelligence than that of females. The present study did not reveal differences between male and female young adolescents.

As far the relationship between academic achievement and emotional intelligence is conodered, the opinions are diverse. Pool, the senior editor of Educational Leadership, stated in an article she wrote in 1997 that emotional well being is a predictor of success in academic achievement and job success among others. Finnegan (1998) argues that schools should help students learn the abilities underlying emotional intelligence. Possessing those abilities, or even some of them, "can lead to achievement from the formal education years of the child and adolescent to the adult's competency in being effective in the workplace and in society". In January 2000, Coover & Murphy conducted a study that examined the relationship between self-identity and academic persistence and achievement in a counter-stereotypical domain. The study revealed that the higher the self-concept and self-schema, the more positive the self-descriptions, the better the academic achievement at 18. The study also showed that self-identity improves through social interaction and communication with others, which would enhance achievement.

One important aspect of the present study was that rural young adults had higher Emotional intelligence compared to urban young adults. The probable reasons would be that the rural young adults can understand, empathize and ability to deal effectively than urban young adults.

This study is only a starting point in the area of emotional intelligence. Emotional intelligence requires much more in depth research work, especially in India. An understanding of all these aspects will provide a better insight into the success equation required in life. This research study will prove beneficial for psychologists, educators, parents, counselors etc. for providing better knowledge about this vital component of success and its important predictors.

REFERENCES

Amirtha, M. and Kadheravan, S. (2006) Influence of Personality on the Emotional Intelligence of Teachers. *Edu Tracks* 5, 12, 25-29.

Annaraja, P. and Jose, S. (2005) Emotional Intelligence of B. Ed. Trainees. *Research and Reflections in Education* 2, 8-16.

Bhosle, S.1999: Gender Differences in EQ. In: http:// www. megafoundation.org/ ultralHIQ.HIQnews/Gender Differences (1999).

Chu, J.: Boys Development. *Reader's Digest* 94-95 (2002).

Coover, G.E., & Murphy, S.T. (2000). The Communicated Self. *Human Communication Research*, 26(1), 125-148.

Culver, D. (1998) A Review of Emotional Intelligence by Daniel Goleman: Implications for Technical Education. Retrieved from http://fie.engrng.pitt.edu/fie98/papers/ 1105.pdef

Devi, U.L. and Uma, M. (2005) Relationship Between the Dimensions of Emotional Intelligence of Adolescents and Certain Personal Social Variables. *Indian Psychological Review*, 64, 01, 11-20.

Dhull, I. and Mangal, S. (2005) Emotional Intelligence its Significance for School Teachers. *Edu Tracks*, 4, 11, 14-16.

Finegan, J. E. (1998). Measuring Emotional Intelligence: Where we are today. (Clearinghouse No. TM029315) Montgomery, AL: Auburn University at Montgomery, School of Education. (ERIC Document Reproduction Service No. ED426087).

Harrod and Scheer (2005). An Exploration of Adolescent Emotional Intelliegence in Relation to Demographic Characteristics. *Adolescence*, 40, 503-512.

Goleman, D. (1995). *Emotional Intelligence: Why It Can Matter More Than IQ*. New York: Bantam Books.

King,M.: Measurement of Differences in Emotional Intelligence of Pre-service Educational Leadership Students and Practicing Administrators As Measured by the Multifactor Emotional Intelligence Scale. Dissertation Abstracts International, 60(3): 606 (1999).

Mayer, J. D., & Salovey, P. (1993). The Intelligence of Emotional Intelligence. *Intelligence*, 17(4), 433-442.

McDowelle, J. O. & Bell, E.D.(1997). Emotional Intelligence and Educational Leadership at East Carolina University. Paper Presented at the Annual Meeting of the National Council for Professors of Educational Administration. Retrieved from Internet on 27th June 2005 via ERIC Document reproduction service. Clearinghouse Identifier: He030690

Pool, C. R. (1997). Up with Emotional Health. *Educational Leadership*, 54(8), 12-14.

Singh, D.: *Emotional Intelligence at Work: A Professional Guide*. Sage Publications, New Delhi (2002).

Sutarso, P.: Gender Differences on the Emotional Intelligence Inventory (EQI). Dissertation Abstracts International (1999).

Tapia, M. and Marsh, G. (2001) Emotional Intelligence: The Effect of Gender, GPA and Ethnicity. Paper Presented at the Annual Meeting of the Mid-South Educational Research, Association Mexico. (ED 464086)

Wing, E. and Love, G.D.: *Elective Affinities and Uninvited Agonies: Mapping Emotions With Significant Others Onto Health. Emotion, Social Relationships and Health Series in Affective Science*. Oxford University Press, New York (2001).

4

Play Peers and Time Involvement in Children with Mental Retardation

Afsaneh Khajev Khoshali[1]

ABSTRACT

The present study uses cross sectional observation and key informant interview techniques to elicit data on play behaviours in a group of 140 children with mild and moderate mental retardation. Their chronological ages ranges between 6-14 years. The sample included 71 males and 69 females. For the purpose of this study, three schedules were used: 'Child Survey Schedule', 'Daily Activity Log Schedule' and 'Play Behaviour Survey Schedule'. In distribution of play peers for children with mental retardation, the results indicate that, the range of play peers for children with mental retardation varies from same age peers (N= 40; 28.6%) to younger age peers (N= 35; 25.0%), senior citizens (N= 27; 19.3%), pets (N=25; 17.9%) and adults (N= 19; 13.6%). Sizeable segment children with mental retardation in this sample are reported to be without playmates and left to play alone (N= 33; 23.6%). However, these trends appear to be similar irrespective of the age, gender or diagnostic condition of the child (P>0.05). But in terms of the actual extent of time involvement by different play peers with these children, it is seen that there are no statistically significant differences (P >0.05). On an average, the play peers spend more time with younger children (age range 6-11 years) and mild degrees of mental retardation without associated problems than children above 11 years or those with moderate mental retardation having associated problems.

1. Department of Studies in Psychology, University of Mysore, Mysore, Karnataka (India).

Introduction

Play is an important medium for social development in young children. It is a 'voluntary activity' engaged for the enjoyment it gives without consideration of the end result (Piaget, 1962). Play is also a medium through which the child is 'instinctively prepared to take up the role of adulthood' (Jeffree *et al*, 1977). For younger infants and toddlers, play may be simply means of 'expending surplus energy a method used by children to relieve certain powerful experiences and thus come to terms with them' (Lansdown, 1985). Play activities can serve as recreational as well as propaedeutic task (Peshawaria, Menon and Reddi, 1991). There are many types of play observed in children depending on their age/developmental levels (Venkatesan, 2004b).

For the child, the primary goal when playing is to have fun. There is an intrinsic enjoyment derived by the child during play. Besides, it facilitates social adjustment, development and related skills. It improves physical health, language and cognitive development. Participation in play contributes to the overall well being of the individual or groups of children. For many children with special needs play becomes simply an opportunity to release their unspent or pent up energies in a constructive fashion (Fine, 1982).

The children with special needs are no exception in their penchant for play-even though the nature of their play might be different owing to their primary condition or due to circumstances surrounding them (Venkatesan, 2000). In a related study, it was found that all children with mental retardation showed some form or type of play. No case of child with mental retardation was reported as 'never plays' even though such an item existed in the interview schedule. It was another thing that these children indulged more in solitary than social play and/or toy or pet play like their normal aged peers. The preponderance of solitary play was explained as due to their skill deficits, non-acceptance of these children into play situations by others, non-availability of peers/play fellows, presence of problem behaviours in the child, etc.

Venkatesan (2004) studied a sample of 140 preschool children diagnosed as cases of 'developmental disabilities'. The investigators undertook information on hour wise engagement of each child. The results showed that the greatest part of the days schedule is spent by this sample of children on 'sleeping' (43.24%), followed by time spent at 'school' (for school going kids only) (14.41%), on 'feeding' activities (10.34%) and 'watching television' (9.61%) respectively. The amount of time spent on needed activity like 'playing with peers' (4.12%) was meager. In the case of autistic children, the amount of time spent on sedentary or exclusion activities like 'watching television' (21.23%) or 'playing alone' (14.6%) almost doubled and 'paying with peers' (1.74%) was almost reduced to half.

In another investigation on activity log of preschool children diagnosed as 'developmental disabilities' including 'autism spectrum disorders', it was reported that only 4.12 per cent of a day's schedule is spent on playing with peers. This was against 7.9 per cent of the time spent on playing alone and 9.61 per cent of time spent on watching television (Venkatesan, 2004a). These studies have given initial leads into the problem of play behaviours in children with special needs. There is a need to delve into the depths of the problem of play behaviours of children with mental retardation.

Aims and Objectives

It was the aim of this study to:

- Discover the nature of play peers for children with mental retardation.
- Explore the nature, type, number and amount of time spent by play peers for a typical day in the activity schedule of children with mental retardation.
- Study the relationship of play peers to specific organism variables like age, gender, associated conditions and/or severity of mental retardation and family variables (such as, type of family, socio economic status, parent age and education) as well as their choice of pay peers respectively.

Material and Methods

The study was carried out on a sample of 140 children diagnosed as mental retardation. A part of the sample was taken from various special schools in Mysore and Bangalore while others were also from the cases routinely seen at All India Institute of Speech and Hearing, under Ministry of Health and Family Welfare, Government of India, located at Mysore. The sample included 71 males and 69 females with mental retardation in the age range of 6-14 years. (Mean Age: 10.43; SD: 3.64). Within the sample, there were 69 cases diagnosed as 'mild mental retardation' and 71 cases with 'moderate mental retardation'. Of the overall sample, 89 children had one or the other associated problems like epilepsy, hearing or visual difficulties, etc. The remaining 51 children did not have any associated problems.

The procedure for data collection involved use of cross sectional observation and key informant interview techniques along with two schedules developed exclusively for the purpose of this study. The 'Child Survey Schedule' covered queries on personal details, diagnostic condition and health status of each child included in this study. Another 'Play Behaviour Survey Schedule' was used to record details on the 24-hour activity agenda of each child, their types of play activities, play preferences, toys/materials used by them during play, amount of time or money invested on play by significant others and so on. Open ended questions and non-directive interviewing techniques were used to gather as much information about commonly activities and/or situations of play in each child with mental retardation as reported by their parents or teachers. Wherever possible, several examples of reported play were collected to substantiate the declarative statements of parents or caregivers.

A simple 'Daily Activity Log Schedules' was also designed to elicit information about each child's hourly engagements during a typical day. For every hour in the 24-hour log schedule, data was elicited on the child's and others activities in terms of the time spent on sleeping, ablution, watching television (or playing computer and video games), playing alone, playing with peers, feeding, attending school (if any), home teaching and others. The total time spent by a given child and/or the significant family members under these activity heading were totaled and rounded off to the nearest minute. Wherever information was reported on the child's simultaneous involvement in two or more of the above-mentioned activities (such as, feeding while watching television or playing alone while the television is on), they were recorded as such. Thus, there could be less/more than the 24-hour schedule for some children, when totaling the reported activities for a given day or for all the children taken together in this sample. Data was collected and compiled in Microsoft Excel format and subject to statistical analysis by using freely downloadable statistical software/calculators on the web.

Hypothesis

Specific Hypothesis Investigated under this theme

1. The volume, variety, duration and length of time spent on play activities, or nature of play peers seen in children with mental retardation differ significantly with respect to child variables (such as, age, gender, presence/absence of problem behaviours, associated conditions and severity of mental retardation), family variables (such as, type of family, socio-economic status, parent age and education) as well as their choice of pay peers respectively.

Results and Discussion

The results of the study are analyzed and discussed under following headings:

(a) Distribution of Play Peers

It is seen that the range of play peers for children with mental retardation varies from same age peers (N= 40; 28.6%) to younger age peers (N= 35; 25.0%), senior citizens (N= 27; 19.3%), pets (N= 25; 17.9%) and adults (N= 19; 13.6%). Sizeable segment children with mental retardation in this sample are reported to be without playmates and left to play alone (N= 33; 23.6%) (Table 4.1).

Table 4.1: Distribution by Number of Play Peers of Children with Mental Retardation

Activity	Gender		Age			Severity		Associated Condition		Total	%
	Male	Female	6-8	9-11	12-14	Mild	Moderate	Present	Absent		
N	71	69	34	69	37	69	71	89	51	140	100.0
Same Age Peers	25	15	15	17	8	18	22	27	13	40	28.6
Younger Peers	19	16	14	14	7	14	21	25	10	35	25.0
None	13	20	7	17	9	15	18	24	9	33	23.6
Senior Citizens	13	14	9	11	7	15	12	19	8	27	19.3
Pets	15	10	7	13	5	13	12	16	9	25	17.9
Adults	7	12	7	6	6	12	7	13	6	19	13.6
Chi square	6.460		5.426			3.625		0.669			
P	>0.05 (NS)		>0.05 (NS)			> 0.05 (NS)		> 0.05(NS)			

(b) Distribution of Time Involvement:

In terms of the actual extent of time involvement by different play peers with these children, it is seen that there are no statistically significant differences ($P>0.05$). The involvement of all the peers appears to be more or less similar. The differences emerge only in terms of age, severity or associated condition of mental retardation for the actual amount of time spent by the play peers ($P< 0.05$). On an average, the play peers spend more time with younger children (age range 6-11 years) and mild degrees of mental retardation without associated problems than children above 11 years or those with moderate mental retardation having associated problems (*See Table 4.2 on next page*).

The following section highlights the types and distribution of time spent by different play peers for children with mental retardation in terms of gender, age groups, severity and presence or absence of associated conditions and presence or absence of problem behaviours respectively.

(i) There are a variety of play peers during play as reported to be available for children with mental retardation. The range of play mates vary from it aged peers (40 out of 140), younger peers (35 out of 140) and others (32 out of 140). Sometimes the child has older peers (27 out of 140) and elderly persons (19 out of 140). There are also instances where these children are left to play with pets (N=25 out of 140) or all alone by themselves (N=33 out of 140).

(ii) In relation to gender variable, it is seen that there is no statistically significant difference in the choice of play peers for children with mental retardation depending on whether they are males (N=71) or females (N=69) ($X^2= 0.384$; $P > 0.05$; NS).

(iii) In relation to age variable, however it is seen that there is a statistically significant difference in the distribution of types and duration of time spent by different play peers for children with mental retardation. It is seen that children between 6-8 years (N=34), 9-12 years (N=69) and 12-14 years (N=37) show differences in their types of play peers. ($X^2= 6.716$; $P<0.05$; S).

(iv) In relation to severity of mental retardation, there is no difference between the choice of play peers for mild (N=69) and moderate (N=71) cases of the sample included in this study ($X^2=0.384$; $P< 0.536$; NS).

(v) The presence or absence of associated conditions in children with mental retardation influences the choice of playmates. This is evidenced by the observation that children without associated conditions (N=51) have a greater variety of play peers as compared to children with associated conditions along with their primary condition ($X^2=29.578$; $P< 0.01$; HS).

Table 4.2: Mean and SD Distribution of Duration of Time Spent by Play Peers and Caregivers of Children with Mental Retardation

Activity	Gender		Age			Severity		Associated Condition		Total	%
	Male	Female	6-8	9-11	12-14	Mild	Moderate	Present	Absent		
N	71	69	34	69	37	69	71	89	51	140	100
Same Age	36.9	43.3	40.1	45.0	25.6	54.7	26.7	34.1	50.0	39.3	18.7
Peers	±24.8	±16.0	±17.1	±26.2	±15.0	±19.1	±15.0	±17.0	±27.4	±21.9	
Younger	35.5	27.2	26.8	31.1	42.9	27.1	34.8	27.8	41.5	31.7	15.1
Peers	±20.5	±13.8	±13.2	±16.8	±25.5	±15.8	±20.5	±14.2	±23.2	±18.0	
None	36.5	26.7	25.0	30.9	34.2	22.9	16.1	33.3	23.1	30.6	14.6
	±20.5	±15.5	±13.5	±19.3	±19.1	±16.1	±18.0	±18.4	±15.2	±18.0	
Senior Citizens	29.6	41.1	29.4	44.1	30.0	42.7	26.7	33.7	40.0	36.6	17.4
	±27.4	±21.6	±18.3	±26.0	±29.4	±27.8	±17.8	±21.7	±32.3	±24.8	
Pets	46.3	24.0	32.9	40.8	35.0	26.2	50.0	32.2	46.7	37.4	17.8
	±29.0	±22.3	±14.1	±34.1	±30.8	±19.0	±32.4	±27.8	±28.4	±28.3	
Adults	35.7	33.5	26.4	55.8	22.0	20.2	58.6	30.8	42.0	34.3	16.4
	±19.7	±26.5	±19.7	±20.1	±17.7	±13.8	±15.5	±18.9	±32.4	±23.6	
Chi square	10.743		22.268			41.098		6.509			
P	> 0.05 (NS)		< 0.025 (S)			< 0.001 (HS)		> 0.05 (NS)			

(vi) The presence or absence of problem behaviours in children with mental retardation emerges as a statistically significant variable in influencing the types and duration of time spent by significant others during play (X^2= 5.161; P< 0.023; S). It appears that children with problem behaviours have fewer companions in the form of same aged or younger aged peers than children without problem behaviours.

The following section highlights the types and distribution of time spent by different play peers for children with mental retardation in relation to various socio-demographic variables:

(i) In relation to the type of family, it is seen that there is a statistically significant difference in the choice of play peers for children with mental retardation depending on whether they are hailing from nuclear families (N=89) or joint families (N=51) (X2; 6.488; P< 0.01; HS).

(ii) In relation to SES, it is seen that there is a statistically significant difference in the choice of play peers for children with mental retardation depending on whether they are hailing from high SES (N=26), middle SES (N=87) or low SES (N=27) (X^2; 11.611; P<0.01; S).

(iii) In relation to parent education, there is no difference between the choices of play peers for children whose parents are school educated (N=68) and children whose parents are college educated (N=72) (X^2= 1.923; P>0.05; NS).

(iv) In relation to parent age, it is seen that there is a statistically significant difference regarding the choice or variety of play peers for various age groups ranging below 29 years (N=36), between 30-39 years (N=68) and those above 40 years (N=36) (X^2= 80.654; P< 0.001; HS).

REFERENCES

Fine, A. (1982). Therapeutic Recreation: An Aspect of Rehabilitation for Exceptional Children. *The Lively Arts*, 4.

Jeffree, D.M., Mc Conkey, R., & Hewson, S. (1977). *Let Me Play*. London: Souvenir. pp. 17-19.

Lansdown, R. (1985). *Child Development Made Simple*. London: William Heinmann.

Peshawaria, R., Menon, D.K., and Reddi, S. (1991). *Play Activities for Young Children with Special Needs*. Secunderabad: NIMH.

Piaget, J. (1962). *Play, Dreams and Imitation in Childhood*. New York: Norton.

Venkatesan, S. (2001). Parents Opinion on Prevailing Practices in Preschool Education. *Journal of Indian Education*. February. 57-63.

Venkatesan, S. (2002). *Building Bridges: An Analysis of Not for Profits for Disabled in India*. (in Press).

Venkatesan, S. (2004a). Activity Log of Preschool Children with Developmental Disabilities and Autism Spectrum Disorder. *Asia Pacific Disability Rehabilitation Journal*.16.1.

Venkatesan, S. (2004b). *Children with Developmental Disabilities: A Training Guide for Parents, Teachers and Caregivers*. New Delhi: Sage Publications.

5

The Role of Emotional Intelligence in Relation to Traits of Anxiety

Batool Pashang[1]
Mridula Singh[2]

ABSTRACT

The present study examines the role of Emotional intelligence, as measured by Emotional Intelligence Scale (EIS), in relation to Traits of anxiety (Emotional instability, Suspiciousness, Guilt proneness, Low integration and Tension), as measured by Anxiety Scale (IPAT). A total of 600 adults, between the ages of 20 to 50 were asked to complete the questionnaires. The mean score on total anxiety verified that the highest level of EI tolerated the lowest anxiety, which was followed by subjects with medium and low levels of EI. The results of the Low self-control (Q3) and Emotional Instability(C) traits, displayed that the highest level of EI yielded the lowest scores on those traits. The findings reported that the trait of Suspicion was tolerated same among the groups. On the other hand both the Apprehension and Tension traits pushed up on the high level of EI. In the case of medium level of EI, people were engaged with all of the traits on an average but the Apprehension was increased in this group in comparison to the other traits.

Introduction

The concept of emotional intelligence has received an increasing amount of attention in a variety of literature over the past several decades. According

1. **Department of Studies in Psychology, University of Mysore, Mysore, Karnataka (India).**
2. **Department of Psychology, Maharaja's College, University of Mysore, Mysore, Karnataka (India).**

to Salovey et al (1999) emotional intelligence proposes a new perspective in the study of emotions. They proposed EI is a vital phenomenon of human being, which provides helpful information for solving daily problems. In fact while considering this approach, we would essentially make use of emotions to aid our physical and psychological adaptation. General life stresses are found to deepen generalized anxiety. The individual who does well at work and receives a sense of achievement from it, all of a sudden begins to find that work has become drudgery. If for instance the work (or any other situation in daily life) is perceived as a negative environment, with the person no longer feeling fulfilled, then worry would take over in this situation. This could lead to the strengthening of anxiety in the workplace. The study by Gohm *et al* (2004) described that emotional intelligence is potentially helpful in reducing stress for some individuals but unnecessary for others. Another study by Extremera and Berrocal (2006) reported that high emotional attention is positively and significantly related to high anxiety. However they found that the high levels of emotional clarity and mood repair were related to low levels of anxiety. Petrides and Furnham (2004) showed that the trait of emotional intelligence plays an important role in personality, clinical, and social psychology, often with increasing effects over the basic dimensions of personality and mood. Furthermore they emphasized that emotional intelligence and self-efficiency are effective in determining occupational stress. Although each of the variables contributed significantly to the prediction of occupational stress with self-efficacy making higher contribution to the prediction of occupational stress (Adeyemo & Bolaogunyemi, 2003). The relationship between a measure of EQ, subjective stress, distress, general health, morale, quality of working life and management performance was examined by Slaski and Cartwright (2002). They realized a significant correlation in the expected direction indicating that managers who scored higher in EQ suffered lower stress and experienced better health and well-being; they also demonstrated a better management performance. The purpose of the present study is to explore the role of emotional intelligence in relation to the traits of anxiety. The traits of anxiety are emotional instability, suspiciousness, guilt proneness, low integration and tension. The present study aimed at investigating the role of emotional intelligence on traits of anxiety. It is hypothesized that emotional intelligence plays a significant role on traits of anxiety.

Measures

The following assessment instruments were employed in this study:

The Emotional Intelligence Scale (EIS) developed by Hyde, Pathe and Dhar (2001) was used to measure EI. This instrument is made of 34 items and provides an indicator of the levels of perceived EI. The sub factors of the scale included self-awareness, empathy, self-motivation, emotional stability, managing relations, self-development, value orientation, commitment, and altruistic behaviour. Respondents are asked to rate their degree of agreement of the items on a 5-point Likert- type scale ranging from 1 (strongly disagree) to 5 (strongly agree). The reliability of the scale was determined by calculating reliability coefficient on a sample of 200 subjects by split-half method and was found to be .88. The validity of the scale assessed through content validity, which was sufficiently high.

The other instrument was an Anxiety Scale (IPAT) developed by Cattel, Krug and Scleier in 1976. IPAT is a 40 items Questionnaire and provide a convenient and practical measure of anxiety traits. Traits of anxiety namely: Emotional instability, Suspiciousness, Guilt proneness, Low integration and Tension. Dr. A.W Bending has made use of Kuder-Richarson formula 20 and found the homogeneity values +. 60, +.63.and +.63 for the twenty items of the covert subscale; +.75, +.79 and +.76 for the twenty items of the overt subscale. The actual dependability (retest) reliability figures from data on 70 cases in IPAT scale files give a value of +.89 and + .82 for the covert and overt subscales, respectively. (A.W.Bending).

Participants and Procedure

A sample of 600 adults (male=300 & female=300), between the ages of 20 to 50 were selected randomly from students, teachers, housewives and shopkeepers in Mysore City (Table 5.1). The emotional intelligence scale (EIS) and anxiety scale (IPAT) were administered to them together. Maximum care was taken to see that no item was omitted and respondents were assured that their individual results would be kept confidential. Analysis of variance (ANOVA) was employed to find out the differences on emotional intelligence and anxiety among the adults.

Table 5.1: Distribution of sample characteristics

Groups	N	Male	Female
Students	300	150	150
Teachers	150	75	75
Housewives	75	–	75
Shopkeepers	75	75	–
Total	**600**		

Results

In order to verify the stated hypothesis, analysis of variance (ANOVA) technique was employed. Table 5.2 presents the descriptive statistics as well as results of ANOVA. The analyses of variance (ANOVA) revealed that EI levels

Table 5.2: Summary of results showing the difference among EI levels on Anxiety and Traits of anxiety

Anxiety	EI Levels	Mean	SD	F
Low self Control (Q3)	High	3.20	1.76	400.3*
	Medium	6.25	1.89	
	Low	9.67	2.91	
Emotional Instability (C)	High	3.54	1.97	269.43*
	Medium	5.59	1.78	
	Low	8.58	2.51	
Suspicion (L)	High	5.57	1.82	.13
	Medium	5.65	1.74	
	Low	5.64	1.78	
Apprehension (O)	High	8.34	2.89	14.93*
	Medium	9.13	2.99	
	Low	7.41	3.36	
Tension (Q4)	High	8.50	2.92	18.62*
	Medium	8.47	2.94	
	Low	6.84	2.90	
Total Anxiety	High	5.72	.96	167.30*
	Medium	6.82	.89	
	Low	7.41	.86	

Note: N=599; p<.05.

yielded significant role across total anxiety (F=167.30, p<.o5). The post hoc tests brought out that the mean difference between high and medium (5.72), high and low (8.99) and medium and low (3.27) on anxiety were significant. The mean values (Table 5.2) indicate that subjects with high EI had lower scores on total anxiety, which was followed by subjects with medium and high levels of EI respectively. The analysis of variance (ANOVA) on traits of anxiety revealed that EI levels yielded significant role across Low self control (Q3) (F=400.27, p<.05). The post hoc tests brought out the mean difference between high and medium (3.05), high and low (-6.46) and medium and low (3.49) on Low self control, these were significant. The mean values (Table 5.2) indicate that subjects with high EI had lower scores on Q3, which was followed by subjects with medium and low levels of EI respectively. Significant Emotional instability (C) displayed that EI levels yielded significant role across C (F=269.43, P<.05). The post hoc tests brought out the mean difference between high and medium (2.05), high and low (5.03) and medium and low (2.99), on Emotional instability, these were significant. The mean values (Table 5.2) indicate that subjects with high EI had lower scores on C, which was followed by subjects with medium and low levels of EI respectively. Significant

Suspicion (L) displayed that EI levels yielded non-significant role across L (F=.13, P<.05). The post hoc tests brought out that the mean difference between high and medium (.08), high and low (.07) and medium and low (.01) on L were non significant. The mean values (Table 5.2) indicate that subjects with 3 levels of EI scored approximately same on Suspicion trait. Significant Apprehension (O) showed that EI levels yielded significant role across O (F=14.93, P<.05). The post hoc tests brought out the mean difference between high and medium (.79), high and low (.92) and medium and low (1.72) on Apprehension and these were significant. The mean values (Table 5.2) indicate that subjects with medium EI had higher scores on L, which was followed by subjects with high and low levels of EI respectively. Significant Tension (Q4) displayed that EI levels yielded significant role across Q4 (F=18.62, p<.05). The post hoc tests brought out that the mean difference between high and medium (.03) and medium and low (1.63) were non-significant but on the high and low (1.66) was significant. The mean values (Table 5.2) indicate that subjects with high EI had higher scores on Q4, which was followed by subjects with medium and low levels of EI respectively. In the case of the medium level of EI it appears that people were engaged with all of the traits on an average but the Apprehension was increased in this group in comparison to the other traits.

Discussion

It would be recalled that the present work sought to examine the role of Emotional intelligence on traits of anxiety. The results revealed that there is a significant difference on EI levels across anxiety. Studies by Extremera and Berrocal (2006) supported these findings. Kloosterman *et al* (2005) also indicated that EI is highly related to social interaction anxiety. The mean values revealed that subjects with higher EI scored lower, on anxiety. On the other hand people with lower EI suffered more from anxiety. The study by Mikolajczak *et al* (2006) also supported these findings. In the traits of anxiety, the higher EI yielded lower score on 'Low self control' and 'Emotional instability'. The reason might be that according to Mayer and Salovey (1993), people with high level of EI have high Self control and Emotional stability and lack of Self-control and Emotional stability could be seen in lower EI individuals. Studies by Zee and Wabeke (2004) also supported these findings. They examined the usefulness of trait-Emotional Intelligence (TEI). Trait-EI was found to be substantially related to Extroversion, Agreeableness, Emotional Stability, and Autonomy. The other division 'Suspicious' was non significant among EI levels. The reason might be that there isn't any relationship between EI and Suspicion. The mean scores of 'Apprehension' and 'Tension' displayed that the people who scored higher on EI suffered more from Apprehension and Tension in comparison to the other traits. Of course this type of anxiety was general anxiety. From the results it clearly appears that the highest EI suffered less from total anxiety. Therefore this amount of Apprehension and tension could be general and related to the EI possessed. While anxiety could affect our lives on the other ways, our relative lack of knowledge about the principles of emotional intelligence and how stress affected it led to a disjunction. Stress also could change our interpersonal interactions in the workplace. Therefore we can learn or improve our emotional skills at any time in our life, even in the presence of stress. If individuals control and interpret their emotions and the emotions of others, then use that knowledge to cope better with stressful situations, they would have a better chance of experiencing daily life and workplace success.

Conclusion

The results of the present study suggest that emotional intelligence does have a significant effect on the traits of anxiety and indicate that emotional intelligence could help people to decrease their anxiety. On the other hand the chosen coping strategy could develop the level of emotional intelligence to manage the anxiety. Emotional intelligence can be taught and improved via training and development activities within the socaity. These programmes could help teachers, students and other people increase their emotional intelligence and thus have a positive effect on their performance also coping with anxiety. The ability to manage one's emotions and the emotions of others has been shown to be an important indicator of success in society. Universities, colleges and schools may want to examine their current educational teachers and students programmes and provide training during course offerings and internships to help aspiring teachers and students become aware of and develop their emotional intelligence. The findings of this research support the existing researches that postulate that emotional intelligence has a significant effect on individual performance in the business sector as well as in educational centers, even in homes.

REFERENCES

Adeyemo, D.A., Ogunyemi, B. (2003). Emotional Intelligence and Self-efficacy as Predictors of Occupational Stress Among Academic Staff in a Nigerian University, A Critical Review. *Applied Psychology: An International Review*, 53, 351-359.

Extremera, N., & Berrocal, P.F. (2006). Emotional Intelligence as Predictor of Mental Social, and Physical Health in University Students. *The Spanish Journal of Psychology*. 9, 45-51.

Gohm, K.L., Corser, G.C., Dalsky, D.J. (2005). Emotional Intelligence Under Stress: Useful, Unnecessary, or Irrelevant? *The Official Journal of the International Society for the Study of Individual Differences (ISSID)*. Retrieved May 28, 2006.

Hyde, A., Pethe, S., & Dhar, U. (2001). *Questionnaire and Manual of Emotional Intelligence Scale*. Lucknow: Vedant Publications.

Kloosterman, P.H., Antony, M.M., Parker, J.D.A. (2005). The Relationship between Social Anxiety and Emotional Intelligence (EI). *Journal of Psychology and Behavioral Assessmen*, Retrieved Joun 30, 2005.

Mayer, J.D. & Salovay, P.(1993). The Intelligence of Emotional Intelligence. *Intelligence.* 17, 433-442.

Mikolajczak, M., Luminet, O., Menil, C. (2007). Predicting Resistance to Stress: Incremental Validity of Trait Emotional Intelligence Over Alexithymia and Optimism. *Journal of Psicothem.* 18, 79-88.

Petrides, K.V., Furnham, A. (2004). Gender Differences in Measured and Self-estimated Trait Emotional Intelligence. *Sex Roles.* Retrieved October 25, 2004.

Salovey, P., Bedell, B., Detweiler, J.B., & Mayer, J. (1999). Coping Intelligently: Emotional Intelligence and the Coping Process. In C.R. Snyder (Ed.), Coping: *The Psychology of What Works* (pp.141-164). New York: Oxford University Press.

Slaki, M., Cartwright, S. (2002). Haelth, Performance and Emotional Intelligence: An Exploratory Study of Retail Managers. *Journal of Stress & Health.* 18, 63-68.

Zee, K., Wabeke, R. (2004). Is Trait-Emotional Intelligence Simply or More Than Just a Trait?. *Journal of Personality and Social Relations.* 18, 243-263.

6

Assessment of Religious Attitude Among Irani Population Influence of Gender, Occupation Marital Status and Income

Mojtaba Aghili[1]
Venkatesh Kumar G.[1]

ABSTRACT

In the present study an attempt is made to find out the influence of gender, occupation, marital status and income on religious attitudes of Iranian professional employees. The sample consists 1491 Professional employees of which 744 were males and remaining 747 were female employees. Religious attitude was measured by using Rajmanickam's Religious Attitude Scale (1988). Results revealed that Male respondents were found to have more religious attitude than female respondents in nature of God, formal religion, prayer and worship, spirits and spirit world and in total scores. Married respondents had higher religious attitude than unmarried once, and married men had more religious attitude than married women. Income and occupation did not have any influence over total religious attitude score of Iranian respondents.

Key words: Religious attitude, Iran, occupation, marital status.

Introduction

Many philosophical, spiritual, and psychological traditions emphasize the importance of the quality of consciousness for the maintenance and enhancement of well being (Wilber, 2000). Within the psychology of religion there has been increasing interest to furnish the different theoretical perspective with empirical support. One such approach is that based on the

1. **Professor, Department of Studies in Psychology, University of Mysore, Mysore, Karnataka (India).**

work about religious attitude and subjective well-being. Religion is a very widespread significant social and cultural force in the life of human beings. From the very beginning of human history, man is found himself submitting to some unknown powers. Rituals, sacrifices, ceremonies, singing and dancing were some of the expressions of his submission.

Religion may be defined as way of life revealed in emotional expressions and inspired by faith in God or in a Supernatural Power who controls and guides the actions of man an the destiny of the world. Psychologists have made attempts to study the human behaviour from different angles. Studies explain man's religious behaviour resulted in formulating different theories. Religion possesses all the characteristics of a sentiment. In it there are fear, distress, wonder, negative self-feeling. Each one of them originates from a corresponding instinct and all center on God. Allport (1951) has developed a concept of religious sentiment with special reference to behaviour. He says that a nature religious sentiment is a "disposition, built up through experience to respond favourably, and in certain habitual ways to conceptual objects and principles that the individuals regards as of ultimate importance to his own life, and as having to go with what he regards a permanent or central in the nature of things". Allport five factors, which create the religious sentiment, are bodily needs, temperament, viscerogenic and psychogenic needs, pursuit of meaning, and culture and conformity.

Among social scientists who pay attention to religion, it is commonly accepted that women are more religious than men. Numerous surveys going back at least a century have repeatedly found this to be the case (For reviews see Beit-Hallahmi and Argyle 1997; Francis 1997; Walter and Davies, 1998), evidence made plausible by the" traditional relegation of men to the public sphere and of both women and religion to the private sphere. Consequently Walter and Davie's observation (1998:640) that "women are more religious than men on every measure of religiosity" (which is the opening statement, not the conclusion, of their survey of research on women's religiosity) comes as close to a universally accepted truth as may be possible in the social sciences. Stark (2002), more recently, is surely correct when he states, "By now it is so taken for granted that women are more religious than men that every competent quantitative study of religiousness routinely includes sex as a control variable (p 496)".

Allport (1951) considers that culture plays an important part in the religious life of an individual in three ways. *Firstly*, every culture gives great importance to rites and myths and every culture try to retain religious beliefs and practices through some kind of organization. *Secondly*, wherever religious systems are shattered some alternative systems of belief are provided. *Thirdly*, religious systems are not independent parts of culture. They are intimately connected with it. Any attempt by one religion to take place of another would be impossible without making fundamental alternation in the culture itself. Religion in this context has Six related areas, Nature of God, prayer and worship, formal religion, Priests, Future Life, Spirits and Spirits world, functioning through the individual's attitude, whether one is highly religious or moderately religious or anti religious, he expresses it through his attitude and action. A religious attitude IS a positive or negative responsive tendency towards various aspects of religion, like Nature of God, prayer and Worship, Formal Religion, priest, Future life, spirits, and spirits world. An important factor implied in an attitude is response or reaction to the value. It may be favourable or unfavourable response involving some kind of action inherently or overtly towards God etc.

Method

Sample

The sample for the present research consisted of 1491 Professional Employees (Doctors, Lawyers, Engineers, and Educationists). The respondents were between 36 and 56 years of age. Seventy percent were women, 60 per cent were married. Ninety percent had a post graduate degree and 10 per cent had a graduate degree. All respondents were affiliated Islam religion. Respondents were randomly selected from different workplaces and universities in the North and south of Iran.

Tools Employed

1. Rajmanickam's Religious Attitude Scale (1988)

In the first step Rajmanickam' s Religious Attitude Scale (1988); (RRAS) was translated to Persian language and after that for checking of its validity, the translated form was sent to 3 psychometricians for review and their opinions about translation. Then translated form was sent to 2 English literatures for language correction, and again compared with original text to resolve possibly difficulties.

After translation and back translation, to ensure Cronbach (Cronbach, 1951) alpha reliability in the second step, questionnaire was tested on 300 people that get 0/915 for 56 questions. Only in No. 5 subscale, future life questions 5, 11, 17 and 59 were confused for subjects that caused validity of this subscale 0/194. Cronbach's alpha showed .901 values. Then these items were deleted in final form of questionnaire and RRAS with 56 questions administered to 1600 people. 109 questionnaires were rejected for incomplete response and 1491 questionnaire were considered for the analysis. Principal Component Analysis and Rotation Method, Varimax with Kaiser Normalization and screen plot show that this scale could be very well administered to Iranian sample. Responses to items are scored on a 5-point Likert-type scale: Strongly Disagree (1) to Strongly Agree (6). High scores on the scale indicates unfavorable attitude and low scores favorable attitude.

Result

Table 6.1: Mean scores of male and female subjects on different subscales of Rajmanickam's Religious Attitude scale with the results of Independent samples 't' test

Subscales	Gender	Mean	S.D	't' value	P value
Nature of God	Male	44.07	6.77	17.42	.000 (HS)
	Female	38.17	6.32		
Formal Religion	Male	43.38	6.89	36.16	.000 (HS)
	Female	29.76	7.64		
Future Life	Male	41.62	6.46	1.67	.096 (NS)
	Female	42.18	6.45		
Prayer and Worship	Male	42.07	6.77	7.44	.000 (HS)
	Female	39.61	5.98		
Priests	Male	25.01	3.86	0.9	.366 (NS)
	Female	25.19	3.63		
Spirits and Spirit world	Male	44.59	7.4	8.86	.000 (HS)
	Female	41.43	6.34		

Table 6.1 present results of Mean scores of male and female subjects on different subscales of Rajmanickam's Religious Attitude scale with the results of Independent samples 't' test. Table 6.3 presents mean and results of Results of two-way ANOVA for mean total religious attitude scores of male and female respondents with occupation, marital status and income levels.

In subscales like nature of God, formal religion, prayer and worship, spirits and spirit world and in total scores male and female respondents differed significantly as the obtained '1' values were found to be highly significant. From the mean values it is evident that male respondents scored significantly higher than female respondents in the above-mentioned areas. However, in subscales like future life and priests male and female respondents were found to have equal scores. On the whole male respondents were found to have more religious attitude than female respondents.

Table 6.2: Mean total religious attitude scores of male and female respondents with occupation, marital status and income levels

Variables		Gender				Total	
		Male		Female			
		Mean	SD	Mean	SD	Mean	SD
Occupation	Architects	240.20	31.31	216.08	26.63	226.91	31.20
	Medicine	241.35	31.59	218.05	26.84	231.36	31.77
	Clerical	240.48	32.04	214.22	28.03	227.06	32.76
	Teaching	239.82	29.15	215.20	25.93	227.24	30.13
	Others	243.26	30.87	223.15	24.07	235.08	29.88
Marital Status	Married	249.72	27.35	216.70	26.44	231.22	231.22
	Single	236.83	31.84	216.10	26.93	227.09	227.09
Income	Low	242.68	30.40	218.18	25.81	231.86	30.92
	High	240.19	31.30	215.94	26.92	227.68	31.54
Over all		240.75	31.10	216.33	228.52	228.52	31.4

Table 6.3: Results of two-way ANOVA for mean total religious attitude scores of male and female respondents with occupation, marital status and income levels

Parameters	Source of variation	F value	Df	P value
Occupation	Between Occupation (B)	1.079	5,1479	.366 (NS)
	Interaction (A x B)	0.260	5, 1479	.904 (S)
Marital Status	Between Marital status (C)	18.412	1,1487	.000 (HS)
	Interaction (A x C)	15.253	1,1487	.000 (HS)
Income	Between Income levels (D)	1.569	1,1487	.211 (NS)
	Interaction (A x D)	0.004	1,1487	.948 (NS)

Gender, Occupation and Total Attitude Scores

Occupation of the respondents did not have any impact on the religious attitude of the subjects as the obtained F value (1.079) was found to be non-significant. Even the interaction effect between' gender and occupation was found to be non-significant (F=0.260; P<. 904) indicating that the pattern of religious attitude of male and female respondents is same irrespective of their occupations.

Gender, Marital Status and Total Attitude Scores

Respondents with different marital status differed significantly (F=18.412; P<. 000) where married respondents (Mean 231.22) were found to have higher religious attitude than unmarried once (mean 227.09). Further, the interaction effect between gender and marital status was also found to be significant (F=15.253; P<. 000) where married men had highest religious attitude compared to any other groups.

Gender, Income and Total Attitude Scores

Income of the respondents did not have any impact on the religious attitude of the subjects, as the there was a non-significant F value (F= 1.569; P<. 211). Even the interaction effect between gender and income was found to be non-significant (F=0.260; P<. 904) indicating that the pattern of religious attitude of male and female respondents is same irrespective of their income level.

Discussion

Main findings of the present study are:

- Male respondents were found to have more religious attitude than female respondents in nature of God, formal religion, prayer and worship, spirits and spirit world and in total scores.
- Married respondents had higher religious attitude than unmarried once, and married men had more religious attitude than married women.
- Income and occupation did not have any influence over total religious attitude score of Iranian respondents.

The universality of higher female religiousness and insufficiency of any social explanation have led to proposals that it is a product of psychological or physiological differences. However, the female advantage in religiousness is not universal. Distinguishing Affective (personal piety) from Active (organizational participation) religiousness, in a third of nations (World Values Survey) women is no higher than men in active religiousness. Among Jews and Muslims worldwide, men are more religious than women. Combined, social factors actually explain much of the gender disparity in U.S. religiousness (General Social Survey); with personality, all of it in active religiousness (Sullins, 2003). The findings of the present study indicated that men are more religious than women, agrees with the findings earlier as the study sample was from Iran, typically Muslim.

In a study on British society it was found that males are significantly more likely to change their religious preferences than females. Furthermore, this relationship remains net of prior religious identification and background, as well as current socioeconomic attainments, marital status, parental status and age. This is not to suggest, however, that gender is the only factor in explaining religious movement. Other equally, if not more salient, determinants include parental religious background, religious activity in childhood, denomination of origin, as well as spousal religious homogamy.

In fact, more so than any other factor, it is religious socialization, or a respondent's religious experiences in childhood, which emerges as the key predictor or religious movement (Hayes, 1996).

Further, in the present study married respondents had higher religious attitude than unmarried ones, this is obvious as one's get married, the person will have more responsibilities towards the spouse and children, and the person will be more religious and even society expect the person to be more religious. However, income and occupation did not have significant influence over religious attitude, and religious attitude was found to be independent of income and occupation.

Francis (2002) discusses and evaluates empirical studies concerned with gender differences in religion. Within the psychology of religion two main groups of theories have been advanced to account for gender differences in religiosity. The first group of theories concentrates on social or contextual influences, which shape different responses to religion among men and women. This group may be divided into two categories: gender role socialization theories and structural location theories. The second group of theories concentrates on personal or individual psychological characteristics, which differentiate between men and women. This group may be divided into three categories: depth psychology theories, personality theories and gender orientation theories. It is concluded that gender orientation theories provide the most fruitful source for further research.

To conclude, gender may increasingly become a voluntary component of, rather than a prescribed constraint upon, personal identity. This is likely to strengthen, not weaken, the connection between religion and gender, but in a radically changed way. From religious identity being a choice constrained by gender, gender identity may increasingly become a choice informed by religion.

REFERENCES

Allport, W. Gordon. (1951) *The Individual and His Religion: A Psychological Interpretation.* London, Constable, 95.

Becker, R J (1958). Links Between Psychology and Religion, *American Psychologist*, 13, 566-568.

Beit-Hallahmi, Benjamin and Michael Argyle. 1997. The Psychology of Religious Behaviour, Belief and Experience. London: Routledge.

Cronbach, L.J. (1951). Coefficient Alpha and the Internal Structure of Tests. Psychomterika, 16, pp. 297-334.

Francis, LJ. 1997. The Psychology of Gender Differences in Religion: A Review of Empirical Research. Religion 27:81-96.

Francis, LJ. 2002. The Psychology of Gender Differences in Religion: A Review of Empirical Research. *Religion*, 27, 81-96.

Hayes. B.C. (1996). Gender Differences in Religious Mobility in Great Britain. The British Journal of Sociology, 47, 643-656.

Rajmanickam's Religious Attitude Scale (1988), Gujarat University.

Stark, Rodney. 2002. Physiology and Faith: Addressing the 'Universal' Gender Difference in Religious Commitment. *Journal for the Scientific Study of Religion* 41 (3):495-507.

Sullins, P. 2003. Gender and Religiousness: Deconstructing Universality, Constructing Complexity. Washington: The Catholoic University of America.

Walter, Tony and Grace Davie. 1998. The Religiosity of Women in the Modern West. *British Journal of Sociology* 49:640-660.

Wilber, Ken, 2000. Integral Psychology Consciousness, Spirit, Psychology, Therapy Shambhala Publications, 283.

7

Self-efficacy Among Employed Women Across Different Organisations

Srimathi N.L.[1]

ABSTRACT

The present study reports the level of self-efficacy among working women in different professions. A total of 325 women working in different organisations viz-industrial sectors, hospital setup, banking sectors, teaching profession and in call centers/BPO's were randomly selected for the present study. They were administered Carl Ryff's (1989) medium form of psychological well-being scale. Two-way ANOVA was employed to find out the significance of difference between women working in different professions. Results revealed that Women employees working in industrial sectors had least psychological well being scores in all the sub factors and total psychological well-being scores, followed by women working in health organisations. Women employees working in banking sector had medium level of psychological well-being scores. Implications of the present study and remedial measures to improve psychological well-being of working women have been discussed.

Introduction

The concept of self-efficacy has become one of the most studied topics between psychologist and educators. Self-efficacy can have impact on everything from psychological states to behaviour to motivation. An individual's self-efficacy plays a major role in how goals, tasks and challenges are approached. It is only in 1980s that self-efficacy pertaining to academic

1. **Department of Studies in Psychology, University of Mysore, Mysore, Karnataka (India).**

performance began to be investigated with great depth. Bandura (1986) defines the performance component of self-efficacy as people's judgment of their capabilities to organize and execute courses of action required to attain designated types of performances. According to Albert Bandura (1995) self-efficacy is the belief in one's capabilities to organize and to execute the course of action required to manage prospective situations. In other words, self-efficacy is a person's belief in his or her ability, to succeed in a particular situation. Bandura (1994) described these beliefs as determinants of how people think, behave and feel. It is concerned not with the skills one has, but with judgments of what one can do with whatever skills one possesses. Self-efficacy refers to and individual's conviction (or confidence) about his or her abilities to mobilize the motivation, cognitive resources and courses of action needed to successfully execute specific tasks within a given context (Luthans 2005). People with strong sense of self-efficacy.

- View challenging problems as tasks to be mastered.
- Develop deeper interest in the activities in which they participate.
- Form a stronger of commitment to their interest and activities.
- Recover quickly from setbacks and disappointments.

Albert Bandura (1997) suggested that those with high self-efficacy expectancies are healthier, more effective and generally more successful than those with low self-efficacy expectanicies. Hackett and Betz (1981) proposed the notion of self-efficacy expectations for the understanding of women's under representation in traditionally male dominated careers. Using the concept of career related self-efficacy expectation they contended that low career related self-efficacy expectations mediated the effects of traditional female sex role socialization on women's later career choices. More specifically they suggested that female socialization provides less access to the sources of information important to the development of strong expectations of efficacy with respect to career related behaviour.

In a recent study by Sahu and Sangeetha Rath (2003) 240 married women (120 working and 120 non-working) with their age range from 30-45 years with minimum qualification of graduation were chosen from Orissa. The study used:

1. A reduced version of 10 item scale of generalized self efficacy by Wagner *et.al* (1981).
2. A multi part questionnaire by Kanungo and Mishra as a measure of work and family involvement consisting of 8 items under each involvement.
3. Health behaviour questionnaire (HBQ) developed by Sahu (1990) comprising of 15 criteria relating to health.

Using a 2*2 factorial design the study reveals that the working women indicate greater self-efficacy than non-working women. The finding also shows the correlation between dimensions of well-being and self-efficacy to be positive and significant. Further the results show that involved women report greater self-efficacy than less involved women. Wolfe Sherel, Nordstrom-Cynthia R, Williams, Karen B (1999) examined the effects of enhancing self-efficacy perceptions in trainees prior to their participation in a training programme. The subjects were 90 individuals seeking telemarketing jobs. The authors explored whether enhancing self-efficacy perceptions affected trainees performance levels and turnover rates. Trainees assigned to the self-efficacy condition remained employed longer than did control group trainees. Results indicate no difference between the groups in terms of job performance levels.

Williams J.E. (1994) examined efficacy expectation and performance discrepancies of 131 employees who were designated as managers and supervisors. Findings indicated those managers and supervisors reporting greater efficacy expectation performed at higher levels.

Method

Sample

The simple stratified random sample consisting of 325 employed women working in 5 different organisations viz industrial sectors, hospital setup, banking sectors, teaching profession and in call centers/BPO's. This sample was drawn from Mysore city. Out of 325 employed women 68 women were in teaching profession, 67 were in hospital set up, 63 of them were working in industries, 67 were from Banking Sectors and 60 of them were working in call centers/BPO's. Age range of this sample was 25-50 years.

Tools used: Personal efficacy scale: By A P Singh and Dr Patiraj Kumar.

The questionnaire consists of 28 items to assess personal efficacy of the individual. A five point rating scale follows each item. There are two types of items in this scale positively worded items and negatively worded items. The total of both positive and negative worded items is the score of the subject on personal efficacy scale. The item's validity of the personal efficacy scale ranges from 2.1 to 0.54. The split half liability of the scale was determined by Spearman-Brown formula and it was found to be 0.72. The scores of social reaction inventory and Rosenberg self-esteem questionnaire were used as the validation criteria for this scale. The co efficient of correlation between the scores of social reaction inventory and personal efficacy scale was found to be +0.72 on a sample of 300 subjects. The co-efficient of correlation between the scores of Rosenberg self esteem and personal efficacy scale was found to be +0.81. Along with the above tool, demographic information on these working women was also elicited.

The obtained data were analyzed using two-way ANOVA to find out the effect of occupations on self-efficacy along with age, experience and marital status. SPSS for Windows (version 16.0) was employed for analysis.

Results

Table 7.1 presents mean self-efficacy scores of women working in different organisations. (*See on next page*)

Organisations, Age Groups and Self-efficacy Scores

In self-efficacy scores, women employees working in other professions (mean 120.61) had significantly (F=22.658; P=. 000) higher scores compared to women working in teaching professions and banking sector (means 105.97 and 114.20 respectively). However, women working industrial and health organisations had least self-efficacy scores (mean scores 82.98 and 85.60 respectively). Further, Scheffe's post hoc revealed that the mean scores of women in other professions and banking significantly differed from mean scores of women working in industry and health organisations, having mean scores of women teachers between these extremes. Age group comparisons revealed significant differences between employees in different age groups (F=2.576; P=.05), where women employees in younger age groups had higher self-efficacy compared to women in later age groups. The interaction between organisation and age groups was found be non-significant indicating that pattern of self-efficacy is same for women employees in different age groups irrespective of their professions.

Organisations, Experience and Self-efficacy Scores

Experience of the women employees did not have significant influence over self-efficacy (F=.242; P=.623). However, the interaction between organisation and experience was found to be significant (F=3.667; P=.006), where we find that women in health and industrial sector had low self-efficacy with lower experience, where as in other professions women with higher experience had low self-efficacy scores.

Organisations, Marital Status and Self-efficacy Scores

Marital status of the women employees did not have significant influence over self-efficacy (F= 3.073; P=.081). However, the interaction between organisation and marital status was found to be significant (F=3.873; P=. 004), where we find that married women in other professions had high self-efficacy scores, and in other professions unmarried women had higher self-efficacy scores.

Table 7.1: Mean self-efficacy scores of women working in different organisations with various demographic features and results of 2-way ANOVA

Variables	Organisations											
	Teachers		Banking Employees		Health Organisations		Industry		Others		Total	
Overall	Mean	S.D	Mean	S.D	Mean	S.D	Mean	S.D	Mean	S.D	Mean	S.D
	105.97	10.04	114.20	16.16	85.60	12.32	82.98	12.11	120.61	21.87	101.47	21.04
F=22.658; P=.000												
Age (In Years)												
Below 30	107.03	5.74	113.63	17.03	83.84	10.28	87.94	13.52	82.98	12.12	106.69	21.82
31-40	107.05	13.38	114.34	16.49	84.09	9.54	78.92	8.83	119.30	24.29	98.19	21.17
41-50	104.94	12.18	110.13	12.43	85.50	13.91	88.38	12.73	125.00	10.05	95.51	16.74
50+	98.60	5.55	133.50	6.36	108.67	10.02	99.00	26.87	125.00	–	107.00	16.46
F (age groups)=2.576; P=.050; F (Interaction-organisation x Age groups=1.719; P=.068)												
Experience												
Low	109.39	9.07	113.19	16.40	83.06	10.38	81.08	10.93	120.88	22.07	102.34	22.41
High	101.30	9.51	120.00	14.10	91.29	14.54	89.20	14.04	112.50	17.68	98.69	15.68
F (experience)=.242; P=.623; F (Interaction-organisation x experience=3.667; P=.006)												
Marital Status												
Married	105.16	11.22	113.88	16.24	84.56	12.17	81.25	9.29	124.94	22.89	99.15	21.49
Unmarried	107.90	6.188	115.64	16.45	96.33	8.76	93.56	20.67	115.50	19.79	109.23	17.49
F (marital status)=3.073; P=.081; F (Interaction-organisation x Age groups=3.873; P=.004)												

Discussion

Main findings of the present study are:

1. Women employees in other professions had significantly higher self-efficacy and women working in industrial and health organisations had least self-efficacy scores;
2. Age and marital status of the women employees did not have significant influence over their self-efficacy scores;
3. Women in health and industrial sector had low self-efficacy with lower experience, where as in other professions women with higher experience had low self-efficacy scores;
4. Married women in other professions had high self-efficacy scores, and in other professions unmarried women had higher self efficacy scores.

The results of the present study clearly reveal that women employees in industrial and health organisations had least self-efficacy scores. In industry women work for considerably longer hours (8 to 12 hours) compared to other sectors. In addition, such women are involved in risky and stress prone. This may lead to lower self-effiacy of women as they have to play multiple and risky jobs, this is more severe in medical professions where workings hours not rigidly defined. Where as in education sector, a teacher is one who helps students often in a school as well as in a family, religious or community settings. A teacher is an acknowledged guide or helper in the process of learning. In modern educational setting where scientific pedagogy is practiced, the teacher is defined as a specialized professional on the same level as many other professions. A 15 years review of stress (Whiston, 1993) among women revealed that in addition to pressures acting on all physicians, women physicians face specific stressors related to discrimination, lack of role models and support, role strain and overload. Though the depression rate does not vary from the general public, the rates of suicide and divorce are much higher. They often lack mentors to provide advice and guidance. They must cope with pressures of choosing when to have a child and conflicts between being wife and mother and having a career (Robinson, 2003). When 96 of 220 women in nontraditional occupations and 100 of 300 in traditional occupations completed self-efficacy scales, results showed employed women do have higher self-efficacy for working with people than with things. Among the differences between the two groups, traditional women had higher self-efficacy for serving and helping, nontraditional women for mentoring.

There are four major sources of self-efficacy according to Bandura (1994):

1. *Mastery experiences:* The most effective way of developing a strong sense of efficacy is through mastery experiences. Performing a task successfully strengthens our sense of self efficacy;

2. *Social modelling:* Witnessing other people successfully completing a task is another source of self efficacy. Seeing people similar to oneself succeed by sustained effort raises observer's belief that they too possess the capabilities, master comparable activities to succeed;
3. *Social persuasions:* People could be persuaded to belief that they have the skills and capabilities to succeed. Getting verbal encouragement from others helps people to focus on giving their best effort to the task at hand;
4. *Psychological responses:* Our own responses and emotional reactions to situations also play an important role in self-efficacy. Moods, emotional states, physical reactions and stress level can all impact on how a person feels about their personal feels about their personal abilities in a particular situation.

To conclude, promoting self-efficacy of employed women requires co-operation of people at individual, community level, government level and at the societal level at large.

REFERENCES

Bandura A (1977): Self-efficacy Toward a Unifying Theory of Behavioural Change. *Psychological Review*, 191-215.

Bandura A (1992): Exercise of Personal Agency Through Self-efficacy Mechanisms. In R Schwarzer (ed), *Self-efficacy — Thought Control Action*. Washington, DC: Hemisphere.

Bandura A (1994): Self-efficacy. In V.S. Ramachaudran (ed), *Encyclopedia of Human Behaviour*, 4, New York: Academic Press, pp. 71-81.

Bandura A., (1995): *Self-efficacy in Changing Societies*. Cambridge University Press.

Bandura A., (1986): *Social Foundations of Thought and Action*: A Social Cognitive Theory. USA-prentice-hall.

Bandura A., (1987): *Self-efficacy: The Exercise of Control*. New York. W.H Freeman.

Hackett, G. and Betz, N.E., (1981): A Self-efficacy Approach to the Career Development of Women. *Journal of Vocational Behaviour*. 18, 326-339.

Robinson, G., (2003): Depression and Anxiety. *Anxiety Disorders in Women*. 17, 180-189.

Sahu, F.M and Sangeetha Rath (2003): Self-efficiency and Well-being in Working and Non-working Women. *Psychology and Developing Societies*, 15, 187-098.

Wolfe Sherel, Nordstrom-Cynthia R, Williams, Karen B (1999): The Effect of Enhancing Self-efficacy Prior to Job Training. *Journal of Social Behaviour and Personality*. 13, 633-650.

Whiston, S.C. (1993) Employed Women; Helping Relationship; Interpersonal Relationship; Non-traditional Occupations; Self-efficacy. *Journal of Career Development*, 19, 175-86.

8

Self-efficacy, Self-confidence, Stress and Emotional Maturity of Science, Arts and Commerce Pre-university Degree Students

Geeta Pastey[1]
Vijaylaxmi A Aminabhavi[1]

ABSTRACT

This study is an attempt to see the influence of academic disciplines of adolescents on their self-efficacy, self-confidence, stress and emotional maturity. The sample of the study consists of 120 (66 Male +54 Female) students studying in 11th and 12th class at Karnataka College, Kittle College and Janata Shikshana Samithi College, situated at Dharwad, Karnataka State, India. The obtained data were subjected to one-way ANOVA and Scheffe's tests. Results revealed that academic discipline has significantly influenced the emotional maturity of adolescents ($F=3.094$; $P<0.05$) but not their self-efficacy, self-confidence and stress. More specifically, adolescents from science discipline have more emotional maturity compared to the adolescents from commerce discipline ($S= -4.66$; $p<0.001$). Further boys have shown significantly very high self-efficacy ($T=-4.85$; $p<0.05$), self-confidence ($T=-6.82$; $P<0.001$) and also tend to have better emotional maturity ($T=-5.25$; $P<0.001$) compared to girls. Lastly it is also found that birth order tend to influence significantly the emotional maturity of adolescents but not other variables.

Introduction

As the present days are highly competitive, the adolescents are expected to have all conducive abilities and characteristics. More specifically Pre university degree students are experiencing threat of competition and in

1. Department of Psychology, Karnataka University, Dharwad - 580 003, Karnataka (India).

dilemma with regard to their future. In such a condition, such students are expected to develop higher self-confidence, self-efficacy as well as emotional maturity to cope with the stress and beat the competition as well as to come out successfully in life. Thus the present investigation is an attempt to study the self-efficacy, self-confidence, stress and emotional maturity of pre university degree students studying in different faculties. Further, it is also intended to know the impact of the faculty in which they pursue their study on the above-mentioned variables.

Self-efficacy

Self-efficacy is "individual's assessment of his capabilities to organize and execute actions required to achieve successful levels of performance" (Bandura, 1980). Self-efficacy pertains to optimistic beliefs about being able to cope with a variety of stressors. People with low self-efficacy may believe that things are tougher than they really are a belief that may foster stress and narrow vision of how best to go about a problem (Pejars, 1996). Bandura (1977) introduces self-efficacy as a valid measure of one's psychosocial well-being. He suggested an individual's belief regarding their ability to perform an efficacious action comes from a variety of socially constructed elements: performance outcomes, vicarious learning, emotional arousal, and verbal persuasion. Self-efficacy beliefs help determine the outcomes one expects.

Pintrich and Schrauber (1992) states that besides the quantity of effort, the quality of effort in terms of the use of the deeper processing strategies and general cognitive engagement of learning has been strongly linked to self-efficacy perceptions, for example Pintrich and De Groot (1990) found that junior high school students high in efficacy were more likely to report using various cognitive and self-regulatory learning strategies.

Gian Vittorio Caprara *et al* (1998) tested the hypothesis that perceived self-efficacy to resist peer pressure for high-risk activities is related to transgressive conduct, both directly and through the mediation of open familial communication. Results of structural equation modeling confirmed that a higher sense of efficacy toward off negative peer influences was accompanied by open communication with parents about activities outside the home and by low engagement in delinquent conduct and substance abuse. Both the posited direct relationship between self-regulatory efficacy and transgressive conduct. The combined influence of self-regulatory efficacy and supportive parental communication and monitoring accounted for a substantial share of the variance in delinquent conduct and substance abuse.

In another study, Teresa E.Seeman *et al* (1993) hypothesized that stronger self-efficacy beliefs are associated with better cognitive performance at older ages. Thus was examined in a sample of men and women, age 70-79.Multiple domains of efficacy beliefs and cognitive abilities were examined. Analyses revealed considerable specificity in the observed associations. For men, multiple regression analyses revealed that instrumental efficacy beliefs were related to better performance on tests of memory and abstraction, independence socio demographic characteristics and physical and psychological health; there were no independent associations with individual tests of spatial ability naming, incidental recall, or delayed spatial recognition. For women, instrumental efficacy beliefs had no significant associations with the tests of cognitive ability. Interpersonal efficacy beliefs showed no significant associations for men or women.

Self-confidence

Self-confidence is also a very important personality trait. The self is a composite of a person's thoughts and feelings, strivings and hopes, fears and fantasies, his view of what he is what he has been, what he might become, and his attitudes pertaining to his worth. Self-confidence is a positive attitude of oneself towards one's self-concept. It is an attribute of perceived self. Self-confidence refers to a person's perceived ability to tackle situations successfully without leaning on others and to have a positive self-evaluation. In the words of Basavanna (1975), in general terms, self-confidence refers to "an individual's perceived ability to act effectively in a situation to overcome obstacles and to get things go alright". A self-confident person perceives himself to be socially competent person mature, intellectually adequate, successful, satisfied, decisive, optimistic, independent, self-reliant, self-assured, forward moving, and fairly assertive and having leadership qualities. Confident individuals anticipate successful outcomes. Students confident in their social skills anticipate successful social encounter. Those confident in their academic skills expect high marks on exams and expect the quality of their work to reap personal and professional benefits. The opposite is true of those who lack confidence. Agnihotri (1986) found significant positive relationship between the sense of alienation and lack of self-confidence. If the sense of alienation is high, the level of self-confidence is low.

A study on "Personality, peer relations, and self-confidence as predictors of happiness and loneliness" (2002) by Cheng, H. and Furnham A. aimed to examine to what extent peer relations, self-confidence and school performance correlated with self-rated happiness (OHI) and loneliness (UCLA L.S) in adolescents. Personality traits (EPQ), self-confidence (PEI), friendship and school grades were all significantly oppositely correlated with happiness and loneliness. Regression analysis revealed that extraversion and neuroticism were direct predictors of happiness and self-confidence, while psychoticism and extraversion was also a significant predictor of general confidence and social interactions, which directly influenced loneliness. Self-rated school performance was the only direct predictor of happiness whereas general confidence and social interactions were related to adolescent's self-reported loneliness.

Paliwal *et al* (2006) aimed to study school environment, school adjustment and self-confidence of 120 high school adolescents in the age group of 13 to 15 years. Results of the study revealed that larger number of girls scored in 'high' category in creative stimulation, cognitive environment, acceptance and permissiveness while average in rejection and control dimensions. Boys scored 'average' category in all the six dimensions. Majority of boys and girls scored 'average' category on school adjustment and self-confidence. Gender differences were non significant on all the aspects of school adjustment and self-confidence. Girls scored significantly higher on cognitive encouragement as compared to boys on school environment inventory. School environment indicated no correlation with self-confidence and school adjustment of students except on social adjustment, which was found negatively correlated with self-confidence.

Menu *et al.* (1996) conducted three separate experiments on a sample of 36 male and 36 female subjects belonging to the age group of 21±3 years, in order to investigate the effect of positive negative and no feedback upon the level of self-confidence. Results indicated a lower level of self-confidence in women than in men when feedback was not provided. A positive feedback enhanced while a negative one decreased self-confidence levels. It was also observed that continuous positive feedback affected the women more positively than men.

Stress

Stress is a psychological upset or disequilibrium (Kisker 1972). He explains that stress is a class of stimuli, which threatens a person in some manner and produces disturbance in behaviour and in inner experiences. Spielberger (1979) defined stress in two different ways. According to him, it is a dangerous potentially harmful or unpleasant external situation or conditions (stressors) that produce stress reaction and secondly to the internal thought, judgments, emotional states and physiological process that are evolved by stressful stimuli. The term stress means distress, oppressions hardships and adversity. The term stress often refers to a situation that causes people to react in a particular way. Some researchers have also used the term stress to describe the environmental characteristics that affect people adversely. Panchanathan and Shanmugaganesan (1992) carried out a study to find the relationship between Academic Achievement and Psychological Stress among 170 the University Post-Graduate Students. The results indicate that there is negative correlation between psychological stress and Academic Achievement. There is no difference in the academic achievement of the students on the basis of sex, nature of the type of family the students belong to.

Seema and Ravi aimed to assess the level of different stresses with regard to their frequency and amount among the adolescents studying Science and Commerce .The results revealed different levels of amount and frequency of stress among adolescents of both the streams.

Emotional-maturity

Emotional-maturity can be understood in terms of ability of self-control, which in turn is a result of thinking and learning (Jha, 2002). Emotional maturity is a process in which the personality is continuously striving for greater sense of emotional health, both intra-psychically and intra-personally. The emotionally mature is not one who necessarily has resolved all conditions that aroused anxiety and hostility but "it is a continuous process of seeing himself in clearer perspective, continually in a struggle to gain healthy integration of feeling, thinking and action".

Landau (1998) studied the relationship between emotional maturity and the developing self in the gifted individuals. In this, Emotional Maturity is seen to involve the integration of intrapersonal and interpersonal aspects of the personality. The developing self is thought to be more than the sum of its components and becomes a global factor in the development of a creative, actualizing gifted personality.

A study by Vithalrao (1992) revealed that as the family size increased, the degree of satisfactory adjustment decreased. The second born in general, in all the families was found well adjusted. The increase of family size with an addiction of lateral birth orders after the second born, had more negative effect on the first born, consequently the third and fourth born are better adjusted than the first born in the areas of home, health, social, emotional and in general adjustment.

The study by Rajamanickam and Merry (1992) on 300 adolescents from various socio-economic status and cultural groups brought to light certain important findings. There is a positive association between adjustment problems and psychosomatic disorders in the case of adolescent girls. The well adjust adolescent girls were emotionally stable and least prone to psychosomatic disorders and the maladjusted girls were emotionally unstable and more prone to psychosomatic disorders. Girls from affluent families were well adjusted and had the least psychosomatic disorders, whereas the girls from impoverished families had more adjustment problems and psychosomatic disorders. Girls from forward communities were well adjusted and free from backward and scheduled caste communities had more adjustment problems and prone to more psychosomatic disorders.

Vijayalaxmi and Sireesha (2008) studied the personality profiles of 200 students pursuing MBA course. The results showed that there were no significant differences among students in the personality profiles based on academic background except for measures of sensitivity and perfectionism. Another finding also indicated that there were significant gender based differences in some measures of personality like warmth, sensitivity, vigilance, abstractedness and openness to change.

Based on the above reviewed literature it is felt that there is need to go for a comparative study of students of different discipline for their self-efficacy, self-confidence, stress and emotional maturity.

Method

The present study has two objectives:

1. To study the influence of academic disciplines of Pre university students on their self-efficacy, self-confidence, stress and emotional maturity.
2. To examine the influence of some personal factors like sex and order of birth on the Self-efficacy, self-confidence, stress and emotional maturity of adolescents.

Sample

A quota sample of this study consists of 120 adolescent students (66 boys + 54 girls) studying at pre university level in three different disciplines such as Arts (40), Science (40) and Commerce (40). These students are selected from Karnataka College, Janata shikshan samithi college and Kittel college situated at harwad,Karnataka State. The age of the sample ranged from 16-18 years.

Tools Used

The Generalized Perceived Self-efficacy Scale

A scale developed by Jerusalem and Schwarzer (1981) was used .It consists of 10 items with four response options ranging from Not at all true to Exactly true. Cronbach's alpha reliability ranged from 0.76 to 0.90.Criterion-related validity is documented in numerous correlation studies where positive coefficients were found with favourable emotions, dispositional optimism, and work satisfaction. Negative coefficients were found with depression, anxiety, stress, burnout, and health complaints.

Agnihotri's Self-confidence Inventory (ASCI)

Scale developed by Rekha Agnihotri (1987) consists of 50 items with two-response alternatives viz., 'yes' or 'no'. Abbreviated name ASCI has been used so that the respondents may not decipher the real purpose of the test and fake good. For each item a score of one is assigned for a response indicative of lack of self-confidence. Hence lower the score, higher would be the level of self-confidence and vice-versa. Reliability coefficients are split-half 0.91, K-R Formula 0.89 and Test-Retest 0.78.As far as validity is concerned, item- analysis validity co-efficient biserial correlation with total scores yielded 0.25. The reported concurrent validity is 0.82.

Student's Stress Scale

A Students' Stress Scale by Deo (1997), which consists of 60 items related to stress creating situation, is used. Each item has *a, b, c* and *d* alternatives and are scored as 0, 1, 2 and 3 respectively. Higher the total score, higher the stress.

Emotional Maturity Scale

For measuring emotional maturity of adolescents, a scale developed by Singh and Bhargav (1984) was used. The scale has five components viz., unstability, emotional regression, social mal-adjustment, personality dis-integration and lack of independence. The scale consists of 10 items in each component except for the component i.e. lack of independence while has 8 items. The responses are scored according to weight age of 5 to 1(very much to never). Higher the score on the scale, lesser is the degree of emotional maturity and vice versa.

Procedure

The above-mentioned four scales were administered on the selected sample of adolescents. Some personal information was also collected. The obtained responses were scored and further transformed to standard (T) scores. These standard scores were further subjected to ANOVA and Scheffe's tests.

Results and Discussion

An inspection of Table 8.1 reveals that the academic discipline has significantly influenced Emotional maturity (F=2.28; P<0.05) whereas it has not significantly influenced self-efficacy, self-confidence and stress of adolescents.

Table 8.1: Sum of Squares, Mean Squares and 'F' Values showing the impact of Academic Disciplines (Science, Arts, and Commerce) on the Self-efficacy, Self-confidence, Stress and Emotional Maturity of Adolescents

Variables	Sources of Variance	Sum of Squares	Degree of Freedom	Mean Squares	'F' Values
Self-efficacy	SSA	202.81	2	101.40	1.61
	SSW	7366.18	117	62.96	
	SST	7568.99			
Self-confidence	SSA	64.87	2	32.42	0.42
	SSW	9141.33	117	78.13	
	SST	9206.17			
Stress	SSA	273.21	2	136.60	0.23
	SSW	70076.38	117	598.9	
	SST	70349.59			
Emotional Maturity	SSA	2687.14	2	1343.57	2.28*
	SSW	68797.32	117	588.01	
	SST	70484.32			

* P<0.05 Significant.

An inspection of Table 8.2 reveals that the order of birth of adolescents has not influenced their either self-efficacy (F=0.18 ;> 0.05), self-confidence (F=0.64; p>0.05), stress (F=0.06; P>000.005) nor emotional maturity (F=1.82; P>0.05).

Table 8.2: Sum of Squares, Mean Squares and 'F' values showing Impact of Order of Birth on the Self-efficacy, Self-confidence, Stress and Emotional maturity of Adolescents

Variables	Sources of Variance	Sum of Squares	Degrees of Freedom	Mean Squares	'F' Values
	SSA	5.80	2	2.9	
Self-efficacy	SSW	1828.20	114	16.04	0.18
	SST	1834.20			
	SSA	68.38	2	34.19	
Self-confidence	SSW	6086.51	114	53.39	0.64
	SST	6154.89			
	SSA	90.49	2	45.24	
Stress	SSW	82393.37	114	722.75	0.06
	SST	82483.86			
	SSA	6813.93	2	3406.96	
Emotional maturity	SSW	213010.55	114	1868.51	1.82
	SST	219824.48			

An inspection of Table 8.3 (*See on next page*) reveals that the difference between group comparisons is significant only for Emotional maturity but not for other variables. More specifically science and commerce students differ significantly from each other in their emotional maturity(S=-2.04; P<0.05). In other words, science students have significantly higher emotional maturity than the commerce students. It can be because the adolescents from science faculty have better cognition by which they will develop better understanding and are capable of managing their life situations.

A perusal of Table 8.4 (*See on page 58*) shows that the sex of adolescents has significantly very highly influenced their self-efficacy, self-confidence and emotional maturity (t=4.85; P<0.001), (t=-6.82; P<0.001) and (t=-5.25; p<0.001) respectively. Whereas the sex of adolescents has not influenced significantly their stress (t=1.17; P>0.05).

More precisely, boys have significantly higher self-efficacy, self-confidence and emotional maturity compared to girls. This fact reflects the impact of differential psycho cultural treat given to girls and boys during their development.

Table 8.3: Scheff's Test results revealing between group differenced with regard to Self-efficacy, Self-confidence, Stress and Emotional maturity of Adolescents based on the academic disciplines (Science, Arts and Commerce)

Variables	Groups	N	Means	Mean Difference	'S' Values
Self-efficacy	Science-	40	31.68	3.18	1.79
	Arts	40	28.50		
	Arts-	40	28.50	-1.8	-1.00
	Commerce	40	30.30		
	Science-	40	31.68	1.38	0.78
	Commerce	40	30.30		
Self-confidence	Science-	40	29.45	0.95	0.48
	Arts	40	28.50		
	Arts-	40	28.50	-1.8	0.91
	Commerce	40	30.30		
	Science-	40	29.45	-0.85	-0.43
	Commerce	40	30.30		
Stress	Science-	40	83.80	3.55	0.65
	Arts	40	80.28		
	Arts-	40	80.28	-2.72	0.5
	Commerce	40	83.00		
	Science-	40	83.80	-2.72	-0.5
	Commerce	40	83.00		
Emotional Maturity	Science-	40	95.80	-8.5	-1.56
	Arts	40	104.30		
	Arts-	40	104.30	-2.58	-0.47
	Commerce	40	106.88		
	Science-	40	95.80	-11.08	-2.04*
	Commerce	40	104.88		

* Significant; $P < 0.05$.

Conclusions

The analyzed and interpreted findings of the study have led to the following conclusions:

1. The academic disciplines of adolescents have influenced their emotional maturity of adolescents.

Table 8.4: Shows N, Means, SDs and 't' Values for Self-efficacy, Self-Confidence, Stress and Emotional Maturity Scores of Adolescent Boys and Girls

Variables	Groups	N	Means	SDs	'T' Values
Self-efficacy	Boys	66	32.61	22.61	4.85*
	Girls	54	30.67	18.1	
Self-confidence	Boys	66	28.5	22.46	-6.82*
	Girls	54	34.32	42.15	
Stress	Boys	66	80.28	58.89	-1.17
	Girls	54	84.00	51.73	
Emotional Maturity	Boys	66	102.25	39.2	-5.25*
	Girls	54	121.16	80.5	

* Very highly significant; $p<0.001$)

2. The academic disciplines of adolescents have influenced their self-efficacy, self-confidence and stress. More specifically, the adolescents from science discipline have higher emotional maturity compared to the adolescents from commerce discipline.
3. Male and female adolescents do doffer significantly very high in their self-efficacy, self-confidence and emotional maturity but not in their stress.
4. Order of Birth has not influenced the self-efficacy, self-confidence, stress and emotional maturity of adolescents.

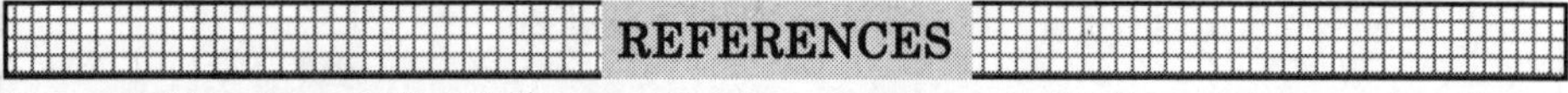

REFERENCES

Cheng, H.Furnham A. (2002) "Personality, Peer Relations and Self-confidence as Predictors of Happiness and Loneliness", *Journal of Adolescence*, 25, 327-339.

G, Paliwal, S.Dube & M.Mathur (2006) "A Study of School Environment, School Adjustment and Self-confidence of High school Adolescents of Both the Sexes", A.P.R.C., Agra, *Indian Psychological Review*, .66, 3-8.

Gian,Vittorio Caprara. Eugenia, Scabini. Claudio, Barbaravelli. Concetta, Pastorelli. Camillo, Regalia & Albert, Bandura (1998) "Impact of Adolescent's Perceived self-Regulatory Efficacy on Familial Communication and Antisocial Conduct", European Psychologist, Vol. 3, 1-2. file://jah.sagepub.com/cgi/content,abstract/5/4/455

Landau, E(1998) "The Self–The Global Factor of Emotional Maturity", *Roeper Review*, 20, 174-78.

Meenu, I.S. Muhar and Promila Batra (1996) "Effect of Feedback on Self-confidence", *Indian Journal of Psychology*.

N, Panchanatham and V, Shanmugaganesan (1992) "The Effective of Psychological Stress on Academic Achievement", *Journal of Community Guidance and Research*, 9, 139-149.

Neemi Avkiran (2000) "Interpersonal Skills and Maturity Influence Entrepreneurial Style of Bank Mangers", *Personnel Review,* Vol. 129(5), 654-75 http://www.emeraldinsight.com/insight/view Content Item.do: ise ssionid

Pintrich, P. and Schunk, D.(1996). *"Motivation in Education: Theory, Research and Application,* Ch. 3. Eaglewood Cliffs, NJ: Prentice-Hall http://www.ed.gov/parents/academic/help/adolescence/partx.html.www.

Seema, Kashyap and Ravi, Sidhu (2005). "Difference in Stress and Coping Mechjanism Used by Adolescents of Science and Commerce Streames", *Journal of Community Guidance and Research,*Vol. 22(1), 81-89.

Teresa E.Seeman, Judith, Rodln and Marilyn Albert (1993) "Self-efficacy and Cognitive Performance in High-functioning Older Individuals", *Journal of Aging and Health,* 1,455-74. http://jah.sagepub.com/cgi/content/abstract/5/4/455

Vijaya Lakshmi Nagarjuna and Sireesha Mamidenna (2008) "Personality Characteristics of Commerce and Engineering Graduates—A Comparative Study", *Journal of the Indian Academy of Applied Psychology,* 34, 303-08.

Vijay Pratap Singh (2004) *"Personality and Its Development"*, 157-195, New Delhi: Sarup and Sons.

9

Prevalence of Shyness Among Adolescents in Iran
Influence of Gender and Age

Kazem Sheriatnia[1]
Lancy D'Souza[2]

ABSTRACT

The present study reports the prevalence of shyness among adolescents in Iran, their age ranging from 12 to 18 years. A total of 469 male (n=234) and female adolescents (n=235) studying in classes from 6 to 12 from Iran were randomly selected for the study. They were further classified on the basis of age as early and late adolescents. They were administered. The Shyness Assessment Test (SAT) developed by D'Souza (2006) in one setting. Data on shyness was collected on three domains-cognitive/affective, action-oriented and physiological, including total shyness scores. Of the total sample studies, 16 per cent of them were found to have high levels of shyness, followed by 48.8 per cent low and remaining 35.2 per cent of them had medium level of shyness. Iranian adolescents had higher shyness in cognitive/affective and physiological domains compared to action-oriented domain Female subjects expressed more shyness than male adolescents in total shyness. Early adolescents were shyer than late adolescents. Further, the treatment aspects of shyness are also discussed.

Introduction

Shyness is a form of excessive self-focus, a preoccupation with one's thoughts, feelings and physical reactions. Shyness may vary from mild social awkwardness to totally inhibiting social phobia. Some inhibited children

1. **Department of Studies in Psychology, University of Mysore, Mysore, Karnataka (India).**
2. **Department of Psychology, Maharaja's College, University of Mysore Mysore-570 006, Karnataka (India).**

move from shy teenagers to adults and are often extremely self-conscious, so much so that they may painfully and ruthlessly analyze their behaviour after a social interaction, as unhappy incidents that lead them to avoid interactions with others in the future. The reactions for shyness can occur at any of the following levels: cognitive, affective, physiological and behavioural, and may be triggered by a wide variety of arousal cues. (Henderson and Zimbardo, 1996). Situational shyness involves experiencing the symptoms of shyness in specific social performance situations but not incorporating it into one's self-concept.

The percentage of adults in the United States reporting that they are chronically shy, so much so that it presents a problem in their lives, had been reported at 40 per cent + 3 per cent, since the early 1970's. Recent research indicates that the percentage of self-reported shyness has escalated gradually in the last decade to nearly 50 per cent (48.7% + 2%). The National Co-morbidity Survey in 1994 revealed a lifetime prevalence of social phobia of 13.3 per cent, making it the third most prevalent psychiatric disorder. Most referrals to shyness clinics meet criteria for generalized social phobia, and many meet criteria for avoidant personality disorder. Although it has been suggested that there is a greater heterogeneity of presentation among shy people than among those diagnosable with generalized social phobia, both shy and those with generalized social phobias demonstrate similar difficulties with meeting people, initiating and maintaining conversations, deepening intimacy, interacting in small groups in authoritative situations, and with self-assertion. Chronically shy individuals frequently have obsessive and/ or paranoid tendencies. Shy individuals would prefer to be with others but are over restrained by the experience of shyness (Brophy, 1996).

Research in the United States typically indicates that shyness is highest among Asian Americans and lowest among Jewish Americans. This difference prompted efforts to assess shyness across diverse cultures. Using culturally sensitive adaptations of the Stanford Shyness Inventory, colleagues in 8 countries administered the inventory to groups of 18 to 21 year olds, usually in college or work settings. The overall pattern of results indicates a universality of shyness since a large proportion of participants in all cultures reported experiencing shyness to a considerable degree — from a low of 31 per cent in Israel to a high of 57 per cent in Japan and 55 per cent in Taiwan. In Mexico, Germany and New Found land, shyness was more similar to the 40 per cent U.S. statistics. Other data from this cross-cultural research shows that the majority in each country perceive many more negative than positive consequences of being shy, and 60 per cent or more consider that shyness is a problem (except for Israel where the figure is 42%). There is no gender difference in reported shyness, but men have typically learned tactics for concealing their shyness because it is considered a feminine trait in most countries. In Mexico, males are less likely than females to report shyness (Henderson and Zimbardo, 1996).

A common observation in most of the shyness research is that the consequences of shyness are deeply troubling. Shyness leads to higher levels of anxiety (D'Souza, 2003), decreased levels of happiness (Sreeshakumar, D'Souza & Nagalakshmi, 2007), neurotic tendency and lower academic performance (D'Souza, Urs & James (2000), lowered performance in physical education students (D'Souza, Singh, Basavarajappa, 1999), lowered self-esteem and decreased self concept (D'Souza, 2005; D'Souza, Urs & Ramaswamy, 2003), increased fear reactions (D'Souza, Gowda & Gowda, 2006) and social and emotional maladjustment (D'Souza & Urs, 2001). Some other studies revealed that (Bell et al, 1994) young adults with high shyness may be at risk for Parkinson disease later in life.

The studies related to prevalence of shyness in Iran are not very well documented, especially among adolescents. A thorough search of literature did not yield fruitful results on the prevalence of shyness in Iran. In the present study an attempt is made to assess the prevalence of shyness in various domains like cognitive/affective, physiological and action-oriented and to see any influence of gender and age on shyness among adolescents in Iran.

Method

Sample: High school and pre university adolescents studying in classes 6 to 12 in Iran were selected for the present study. Of the total 469 students included in the study 234 of them were male students and remaining 235 were females. They were further classified into early and late adolescents (respective numbers 319 and 150). The sample was selected from Gonbad-e-kavoos city of Iran. Stratified Random sampling technique was used to select the sample.

Measures: Shyness Assessment Test (D'Souza, 2006).The shyness assessment test was developed by D'Souza (2006) of Maharaja's College, University of Mysore. It consists of 54 items and requires the subject to indicate his/her response by marking Yes, or No. The items in the test pertain to three domains of shyness — Cognitive/Affective, Physiological and Action oriented. Item analysis of the scale using SPSS programme resulted in Cronbach's alpha coefficient of 0.7119 for the Iranian population. Further, the scale had sufficiently high validity.

Procedure

The tests were administered to the subjects in groups of 6-10 subjects per group. Data collection was done in a single session the session lasted for about 25-30 minutes. First, the researcher, established rapport with the subjects and they were asked to introduce themselves. The purpose of the study was made clear to them. Then they were administered the Shyness questionnaire.

They were given appropriate instructions and the questions were read out to them. They were asked to indicate their responses in the respective sheets given to them. They were instructed to answer 'yes' or 'no' for each question. Whenever they had doubts in understanding questions, the test administrator made those questions clear to them in their local language.

Scoring and Analysis

For the shyness questionnaire, items worded in the direction of shyness, responses were scored 3 for 'high', 2 for 'moderate', 1 for 'low' and 0 for 'NO". High scores indicate high level of shyness and low scores indicate low level of shyness. Lastly, the scores were cumulated under 3 domains-cognitive/affective, action-oriented and physiological domain.

Once the scores were graded into low, medium and high levels, the frequencies under each level were subjected to chi-square test for various domains separately and to see the association between gender and age with shyness levels, contingency co-efficient test was applied. All the statistical calculations were done through SPSS for windows (version 15, Evaluation version).

Results

Table 9.1 presents analysis and test statistics of shyness levels for various domains by demographic variables of gender and age. (*See on next page*)

I. Shyness levels

(a) *Total shyness*

Of the 469 students studied in the present sample 16.0 per cent of them were found to have high levels of shyness, 35.2 per cent of them had medium levels of shyness and remaining 48.8 per cent of the sample had low levels of shyness. Chi-square test revealed a significant difference (χ^2=76.57; P<. 000) between frequencies of low, medium and high levels of shyness.

(b) *Cognitive/affective dimension*

In this dimension, 47.3 per cent of the sample had low levels of shyness, 35.2 per cent of them medium and remaining 17.5 per cent of them had high levels of shyness and chi-square test revealed a significant (χ^2=63.41; P<. 000) difference between these frequencies.

(c) *Physiological dimension*

As far as the physiological dimension is considered, a majority of the sample had low levels of shyness (55.4%), 24.5 per cent of them had medium levels of shyness and remaining 16.2 per cent of them had high levels of shyness and when chi-square test was applied to various frequencies a significant difference was observed (χ^2=108.49; P<.000).

Table 9.1: Frequency and per cent analysis and test statistics on various domains of shyness by demographic variables of gender and age

Variables/Domains		Levels of Shyness			Total	Statistical Inference
		Low	Medium	High		
Total shyness	Frequency	229	165	75	469	X^2=76.57; P<. 000 (HS)
	Per cent	48.8%	35.2%	16.0%	100.0%	
Cognitive/Affective	Frequency	222	165	82	469	X^2=63.41; P<. 000 (HS)
	Per cent	47.3%	35.2%	17.5%	100.0%	
Physiological	Frequency	260	125	84	469	X^2=108.49; P<. 000 (HS)
	Per cent	55.4%	26.7%	17.9%	100.0%	
Action-oriented	Frequency	278	115	76	469	X^2=146.90; P<. 000 (HS)
	Per cent	59.3%	24.5%	16.2%	100.0%	
Gender	Male Frequency	138	92	4	234	CC=0.159; P<. 008(HS)
	Per cent	59.0%	39.3%	1.7%	100.0%	
	Female Frequency	91	73	71	235	
	Per cent	38.7%	31.1%	30.2%	100.0%	
Adolescence	Early Frequency	164	94	61	319	CC=0.311; P<. 000 (HS)
	Per cent	51.4%	29.5%	19.1%	100.0%	
	Late Frequency	65	71	14	150	
	Per cent	43.3%	47.3%	9.3%	100.0%	

Note: X^2 = Chi-square; HS-Highly significant; CC-Contingency coefficient.

(d) Action-oriented dimension

In this dimension, 59.3 per cent of the sample had low levels of shyness, 35.25 of them medium and remaining 17.5 per cent of them had high levels of shyness and chi-square test revealed a significant (χ^2=63.41; P<.000) difference between these frequencies.

II. Gender and Shyness Levels

A significant association was observed between gender and levels of shyness as the obtained contingency coefficient value of 0.159 was found to be statistically significant (P<.008). From the frequencies and percentages it is clear that female adolescents had significantly higher levels of shyness (30.2%) as against male adolescents (1.7%).

III. Age groups and shyness levels

As far as the age groups and shyness levels are considered, a significant association was observed between age groups and shyness levels as the obtained contingency coefficient value of 0.311 was found to be significant at .000 level. From Table 9.1 it is clear that in high shyness levels, early adolescents showed higher levels of shyness (19.1%) than late adolescents (9.3%).

Discussion

The main findings of the present study are:

- On the whole 16.0 per cent of them were found to have high levels of shyness, 35.2 per cent of them had medium levels of shyness and remaining 48.8 per cent of the sample had low levels of shyness.
- Comparatively Iranian adolescents had higher shyness in cognitive/ affective and physiological domains compared to action-oriented domains.
- Female adolescents had higher levels of shyness compared to male adolescents.
- Early adolescents had higher levels of shyness than late adolescents.

Rubin, LeMare, and Lollis (1990) theorized that certain children, from infancy, are predisposed towards behavioural inhibition. Such wariness and inhibition results in a failure to establish normative peer relations, which leads to consequent failure to develop appropriate social skills. This lack of social skills then leads to further anxiety, insecurity, and withdrawal that is likely to result in the child receiving a negative reputation among his or her peers, eventually culminating in peer rejection. Many pre-school, school going children and adolescents, show initial wariness on meeting a stranger, have doubts about one's ability to contribute effectively to social encounters and the belief that others will negatively evaluate one's action/behaviour may contribute to the withdrawal behaviour and social anxieties that characterize shyness or social phobia (Crozier, 1995). As explained by Bruch, Hamer and Heimberg (1995), inhibition and withdrawal is often perceived as deviant by the peer group and responded to by rejection, isolation, or bullying.

In the present study almost 51 per cent of the adolescents showed either high or medium levels of shyness. This is more or less in agreement with the prevalence of shyness rates in Asian countries like Taiwan, Japan and India. However, the prevalence of shyness in Iran is high when compared to countries like US, UK and the western countries. The reason could be, Iran is being a conventional society compared to other countries like US, UK and others. It should be mentioned here that the culture of Gonbad-e-Kavoos city is different from Tehran as it is the biggest city in the Middle East. Whatever the situation may be, the culture of the Asian continent has different effects on human behaviour including shyness when compared to other continents, which follow exclusively western culture.

Further, as age increased, shyness decreased linearly. In early adolescence age, immediately after puberty, the individual would undergo a rapid physical and psychological transformation, which is not very pleasant for the pre-pubescent, and may increase the level of shyness in that particular age group. As expected, female adolescents showed more shyness than male adolescents, since they are more restricted. The changes, which they undergo both physically and psychologically, are more prominent than male adolescents, and could be the reasons for higher levels of shyness. Several studies are in agreement with these findings (D'Souza & Urs, 2007).

The treatment for shyness is multi-fold ranging from medication to simple behavioural therapies. Psychotherapies apply to any difficulty in the mental or psychological arena, but some therapists dedicate themselves more to some of them, as is the case of shyness and the anxiety disorders. Cognitive behaviour therapies aimed at treating shyness were found to be very effective than traditional therapies (Shariatnia and D'Souza, communicated). Equally effective was the cognitive behaviour group therapy (Shariatnia and D'Souza, 2007). There are dozens of approaches, but few of them are based on theoretical models and/or consistent experiments. In addition, to help shy individuals in their efforts to make conversation with others, teachers should consider including in the general curriculum information on such topics as the basic elements and protocol for approaching and engaging others in social conversation. Shy individuals tend to use alcohol and drugs to deal with their shyness. Parents, teachers, and mental health professionals should also be sensitive to the possibility of substance abuse issues.

REFERENCES

Bell, I. R., Schwartz, G.E., Amend, D., Peterson J.M., Kaszniak, A.W., & Miller, C.S. (1994). Psychological Characteristics and Subjective Intolerance for Xenobiotic Agents for Normal Young Adults with Trait Shyness and Defensiveness, a Parkinsonian Like Personality Type?. *Journal of Nervous and Mental Diseases*, 182, 367-374.

Brophy, J. (1996). *Teaching Problem Students*. New York: Guilford.

Bruch, M.A., Hamer, R.J., & Heimberg, R.G. (1995). Shyness and Public Self-consciousness: Additive or Interactive Relation with Social Interaction. *Journal of Personality*, 63, 1, 47-63.

Crozier, W.R. (1995). Shyness and Self-Esteem. *British Journal of Educational Psychology*. 65, 85-95.

D'Souza, L. (2003). Influence of Shyness on Anxiety and Academic Achievement in High School Students *Pakistan Journal of Psychological Research*, 18, 3-4, 109-118.

D'Souza, L. (2005). Shyness/Social Phobia: Influence on Self-concept and Academic Achievement in High School Students. Suggested Remedial Measures. *Artha — A Journal of Social Sciences*. 4 (1), 23-29.

D'Souza, L. (2006). *Shyness Assessment Test*. Mysore: University of Mysore.

D'Souza, L., & Urs. G.B. (2001). Effect of Shyness on the Adjustment of High School Students. *Pakistan Journal of Psychological Research*, 16, 3-4, 85-94.

D'Souza, L. & Urs, G.B. (2007). Assessment of Shyness Among Adolescent Students Studying in Rural and Urban Areas. *Asia Pacific Review of Rural and Tribal Issues*, 1, 10-14.

D'Souza, L., Singh, M. & Basavarajappa. (1999). Influence of Shyness on Performance, Personality and Intelligence of Students of Physical Education. *Psychological Studies*, 44, 92-94.

D'Souza, L., Urs, G.B., & James.M.S. (2000). Assessment of Shyness: Its Influence on the Personality and Academic Achievement of High School Students. *Indian Journal of Clinical Psychology*, 27, 286-289.

D'Souza, L., Urs. G.B., & Ramaswamy C. (2003). Relationship of Self-esteem with Shyness, Personality and Academic Achievement in High-school Students. *Artha — A Journal of Social Sciences*, 1, 228-234.

D'Souza, L., Gowda, H.M. R & Gowda, D.K.S. (2006). Relationship Between Shyness and Fear Among High School Students. *Pakistan Journal of Psychological Research*, 21, 3-4, 53-60.

Henderson, L & Zimbardo, P.(1996). *Encyclopedia of Mental Health*. San Diego: Academic Press.

Natesha, N. & D'Souza, L. (2007). Prevalence of Shyness Among Children: A Developemental Perspective of Age and Gender, *Asian Journal of Development Matters*, 1, 55-60.

Rubin, K.H., LeMare, L.J., Lollis, S. (1990) "Social Withdrawal in Childhood: Developmental Pathways to Peer Rejection" In: Asher, S.R., Coie, J.D. eds., Peer Rejection in Childhood. Cambridge Studies in Social and Emotional Development, Cambridge University Press, New York, pp. 217-249.

Shariatnia, K.& D'Souza, L. (2007). Effectiveness of Cognitive Behaviour Group Therapy on Shyness Among Adolescent in Iran. *Psychological Studies*, 52, 372-376.

Sreeshakumar, H Y., D'Souza, L & Nagalakshmi, K, 2007. Relationship Between Shyness and Happiness Among High School Students. *Psychological Studies*, 52, 121-123.

10

The Role of Life Skills Counselling in Reducing Anxiety Depression Among Alcoholics

Manjunatha P.[1]
Venkateshkumar G.[1]

ABSTRACT

The aim of the study is to determine the effectiveness of Life skills counselling as intervention for reducing the symptoms of anxious depression among alcoholics. An experimental design, with treatment and control group is used. The sample is selected by using convenience basis, from K.R. Govt. Hospital, Mysore. Qualified medical officials diagnose alcoholics. The sample of 120, both urban and rural adult males with high score on anxious depression is selected. Catttell's Clinical Analysis Questionnaire Part-II (CAQ) was used to assess the participants' symptoms. General Linear Model Repeated Measures of ANOVA is applied to the know effect of intervention programme. A significant 'F' was observed indicating differential decrease for experimental and control groups in the symptoms of anxious depression.

Introduction

In the Asian sub continent, per capita alcohol consumption increased by over 50 per cent between 1980 and 2000 (WHO, 2002), while India has experienced a 115 per cent increase in per capita alcohol consumption by adults since 1980 (Rahman, L., 2002). In India alcohol addiction has adverse health and social consequences, ranging from shifting the use of resources away from basic necessities such as food and shelter, to acquit consequences for the welfare of other members of the household especially children and

1. **Department of Studies in Psychology, University of Mysore, Mysore, Karnataka (India).**

women (Bonu, S., 2004). India is likely to face a heavy burden of medical and social problems due to increased alcohol consumption (Mohan, D., *et.al.*, 2001).

The World Health Organisation (2004) estimates that there are about 2 billion people worldwide who consume alcoholic beverages and 76.3 million with diagnosable alcohol use disorders. From a public health perspective, the global burden related to alcohol consumption, both in terms of morbidity and mortality, is considerable in most parts of the world. Alcohol consumption has health and social consequences via intoxication (drunkenness), alcohol dependence, and other biochemical effects of alcohol. In addition to chronic diseases that may affect alcoholics after many years of heavy use, alcohol contributes to traumatic outcomes that kill or disable at a relatively young age, resulting in the loss of many years of life due to death or disability. Alcohol causes 1.8 million deaths (3.2% of total) and a loss of 58.3 million (4% of total) of Disability-Adjusted Life Years (DALY). Unintentional injuries alone account for about one third of the 1.8 million deaths, while neuro-psychiatric conditions account for close to 40 per cent of the 58.3 million DALYs (WHO, 2002). The estimates suggest that alcohol-related problems to the society are of great magnitude and need urgent attention of social scientists.

Alcohol is implicated in a variety of mental disorders, which are not alcohol-specific. However, before the GBD 2000 study no major overview on alcohol-attributable burden of disease has included these conditions (English *et al.*, 1995; Gutjahr, Gmel & Rehm, 2001; Single *et al.*, 1999). While the causality of the relation is hard to define, sufficient evidence now exists to assume alcohol's causal role in depression, a common mental disorder. Adityanjee, M.D. and Wig, N.N. (1989) report that alcohol-related problems made up 17.6 per cent of the case load of psychiatric emergencies in an Indian General Hospital.

In the general population, alcohol dependence and major depression co-occur over proportionally, on both a 12-month and a lifetime basis (Kessler *et al.*, 1997; Lynskey, 1998). Among alcohol consumers in the general population, higher volume of consumption is associated with more symptoms of depression (Graham & Schmidt, 1999; Mehrabian, 2001; Rodgers *et al.*, 2000). Among patients in treatment for alcohol abuse and dependence, the prevalence of major depression is higher than in the general population (Lynskey, 1998; Schuckit *et al.*, 1997). Higher prevalence of alcohol use disorders has been documented for patients in treatment for depression (Blixen, McDougall & Suen, 1997). This suggests that alcohol use disorders are linked to depressive symptoms, and that alcohol dependence and depressive disorders co-occur to a larger degree than expected by chance.

In male alcoholics, major depression has a five per cent lifetime prevalence rate, compared to three per cent for the total male population. In the DSM-IV (APA, 1994), mood disorders must be of sufficient duration and intensity that they cause significant subjective distress or dysfunction in one or more of life's roles (relationships, work, and school). The Epidemiologic Catchment Area (ECA) data (1989), as cited in Frances & Miller (1991) indicate that major depression and dysthymia occur at least one and half times more often in alcoholics than in the general population. Many clinical investigators have observed high levels of anxiety and depressive symptoms among various groups of alcohol dependents (Davidson, 1995; Kishore, *et. al.*, 1994). In patients receiving treatment for alcohol problem, estimate of proportion that have anxiety problems have ranged from 22.6 per cent to as high as 68.6 per cent (Mullaney & Trippett, 1979). Cattell, R.B. (1973) states that in the factor anxious depression individuals describe themselves as clumsy and shaky in handling things. They dream a lot about frightening events, lack self-confidence and seldom speak out and say what they think. They are confused and unable to cope with sudden demands and are subject to disturbing dreams. It represents an aspect of depression, which can be incapacitating and profoundly disturbing. Cattell further says that this factor is common among people with alcohol dependence.

People with alcohol dependency need psycho-social interventions for a variety of psychiatric and personality problems in general and anxious depression in particular. So far, most interventions have focused on stress management training, exercise and cognitive therapy to promote adaptation, reduce depression, anxiety and psychological stress to enhance quality of life. A more intensive and focused intervention may be necessary to meet the specialized needs of alcoholics with multiple medical, social, and economic challenges. Life skills counselling is more suitable and an intensive intervention that combines individual psychological care to provide intensive on-going support in many factors of depression. Richard Nelson-Jones (2000), considered that with the knowledge of life skills an individual would possess awareness in each of these areas; responsiveness, realism, relating, rewarding activity, and right-and-wrong. He advocated life skills counselling as a "people-centred approach for assisting clients and others to develop self-helping skills". He designed a five-stage life skills counselling model DASIE, for helping clients to manage problems. DASIE is not only for managing or solving problems but also for addressing underlying problematic skills. The model provides a framework or set of guidelines for counsellor choices.

In the present study it is aimed to determine the effectiveness of Life skills counselling as intervention for reducing anxious depression in the people with alcohol dependence. The study utilized the dependent variable of anxious depression to assess the effectiveness of Life skills counselling as intervention and gain insight and understanding of people with alcohol dependence.

Method

Design

An experimental pre and post test design, with a treatment and control group, is used. The independent variables varied in the two treatments conditions; experimental and control groups. The dependent variable is the participant's symptoms of anxious depression. There are two groups of participants:

(*a*) experimental group for which the Life skills counselling is given.

(*b*) control group for which no Life skills counselling is given.

Sample

The sample is selected by using convenience basis, from K.R. Govt. Hospital, Mysore city alcoholic dependents as diagnosed by qualified medical officials. They are under treatment for de-addiction. The sample consists of 120, both urban and rural adult males with high score on anxious depression. The age ranges from 25-53; with the mean age 38.12 years.

Measures

Cattell's Clinical Analysis Questionnaire Part-II (CAQ) was used to assess the participants' symptoms of anxious depression. The CAQ part-II (1973), Questionnaire consists of 144 multiple-choice items representing either a symptom or attitude related to clinical factors of personality. It contains 12 factors for which multiple choice responses are given. The participants were asked to select a single answer in each question that corresponds most clearly with his actual condition at that particular time. Each factor describes a specific manifestation of clinical factors of personality. Only one factor is utilized in this paper.

Procedure

The CAQ part-II is administered to a large number of alcoholics. Those scored above the median level on the questionnaire, are selected for further study. The selected 120 participants were equally divided into two groups experimental and control group, randomly. The experimental group was given treatment with the five stages of Life skills counselling model (DASIE)[1] developed by Richard Nelson Jones. No treatment was given to control group but was kept under observation including the self-introduction. The time schedule for intervention is one-hour duration per session and two sessions per week. Total of 20 sessions are given spreading through two and a half

---

1 *D* =Develop relationship and clarify the problem, *A*=Assess and restate the problem in skills terms, *S*=State goals and plan Interventions, *I*=Intervene to develop life skills and *E*=Emphasize, take away and end.

month approximately. After the intervention, the experimental and control groups are measured again on the dependent variable and obtained post test scores.

Results and Discussion

To assure the randomization of the sample the data are subjected to independent samples 't' test in the pre-test. The experimental and control group's mean score and S.D. for anxious depression are 09.62, 0.49 and 09.60, 0.49 respectively. The 't' values are 0.185 and 'p' is 0.853 indicating a non-significant difference between experimental and control groups. Thus the equating as well as randomization of the groups was taken care of during the pre-test situation. General Linear Model Repeated Measures of ANOVA is applied to the know effect of intervention programme.

Repeated Measures of ANOVA revealed a significant decrease from pre to post test situation irrespective of the groups. 'F' value is 2649.834, found to be highly significant (p< 0.000). Irrespective of the groups in pre-test the mean anxious depression score 9.61 is reduced to 6.01 with the reduction of 3.6 scores which found to be significant. When reduction in the anxious depression scores with reference to groups are concerned again a significant 'F' is observed (F=2625.355; p< 0.000) indicating differential decrease for experimental and control groups. From mean values it is evident that experimental group had a reduction of 7.19 scores (from 9.62 to 2.43), where as control group had reduction of only 0.02 scores (from 9.60 to 9.52). So the decrease in the anxious depression has been basically in the experimental group, which can be attributed to the effectiveness of Life skills Counselling. However, the interaction effect between domicile groups with respect to change in the scores and domicile groups with respect to groups and change in scores are found to be non-significant. Between-subjects effects between groups (irrespective of conditions) together significant difference are observed (F = 2699.554; p<0.000). However, domicile groups wise and interaction between groups and domicile groups is found to be non-significant.

Summary

The life skills counselling intervention has reduced symptoms of anxious depression in alcoholic dependents. The major implication of this study is that it indicates a need for a possible shift in the thinking of the health policy makers of our country. The study has implications for the public health approach to the care and prevention. The study can also be useful for psychological counsellors, social workers and policy makers. These specialists to design intervention programmes aimed at sustaining people with alcohol dependence in good health can use findings.

Table 10.1: Mean and S.D. of pre-test and post-test scores on anxiety- depression of alcoholics of both experimental and control groups

Group	Domicile	Pre-test		Post-test		Change
		Mean	S.D.	Mean	S.D.	
Experimental	Urban	9.63	0.49	2.33	0.61	7.3
	Rural	9.60	0.50	2.53	0.63	7.07
	Total	9.62	0.49	2.43	0.62	7.19
Control	Urban	9.73	0.45	9.63	0.56	0.1
	Rural	9.47	0.51	9.53	0.57	- 0.06
	Total	9.60	0.49	9.58	0.56	0.02
Total	Urban	9.68	0.47	5.98	3.73	3.7
	Rural	9.53	0.50	6.03	3.58	3.5
	Total	9.61	0.49	6.01	3.64	3.6

Table 10.2: Summary results of GLM - Repeated Measures of ANOVA within and between subjects for anxiety-depression of Experimental and Control groups in pre-test and post-test situations

Within-subjects effects					
Source of Variance	Sum of Squares	df	Mean square	F	P
Pre-Post test	777.600	1	777.600	2649.834	0.000*
Group (A)	770.417	1	770.417	2625.355	0.000*
Domicile (B)	0.600	1	0.600	2.045	0.156**
A * B	1.667	1	1.667	2.783	0.812**
Error (Change)	32.867	112	0.293		
Between-subjects effects					
Intercept	14632.817	1	14632.817	51753.962	0.000*
Group (A)	763.267	1	763.267	2699.554	0.000*
Domicile (B)	0.150	1	0.150	0.531	0.468**
A * B	1.067	1	1.067	3.773	0.55**
Error		11			
	31.667		0.283		
(Change)		2			

HS = Highly Significant

** NS = Not Significant

REFERENCES

Adityanjee, M.D., Wig, N.N. (1989). Alcohol-related Problems in the Emergency Room of An Indian General Hospital. *Australian and New Zealand Journal of Psychiatry*, 23, 274-278.

American Psychiatric Association (1994). *Diagnostic and Statistical Manual of Mental Disorders* (4th ed.). Washington, DC: American Psychiatric Association.

Blixen, C.E., McDougall, G.J., & Suen, L. J. (1997). Dual Diagnosis in Elders Discharged from a Psychiatric Hospital. *International Journal of Geriatric Psychiatry*, 12, 307-313.

Bonu, S. (2004). Household Tobacco and Alcohol Use and Child Health: An Exploratory Study from India. *Health Policy*, 70, 67-83.

Cattell, R.B. (1973). A Check on the 28 Factor Clinical Analysis Questionnaire Structure on Normal and Pathological Subjects. In, Samuel, E. Krug (1980). *Clinical Analysis Questionnaire Manual*. Illinois: Institute for Personality and Ability Testing.

Davidson, K.M. (1995). Diagnosis of Depression in Alcohol Dependence: Changes in Prevalence with Drinking Status. *British Journal of Psychiatry*, 166, 199-204.

English, D.R., *et.al.* (1995). *The Quantification of Drug-caused Morbidity and Mortality in Australia-1992*. Canberra: Commonwealth Department of Human Services and Health.

Frances, R.J. & Miller, S. I. (1991). *Clinical Textbook of Addiction Disorders* (2nd ed.). New York, NY: Guilford Publications.

Graham, K., & Schmidt, G. (1999). Alcohol Use and Psychosocial Well-being Among Older Adults. *Journal of Studies on Alcohol*, 60, 345-351.

Gutjahr, E., Gmel, G. & Rehm, J. (2001). Relation Between Average Alcohol Consumption and Disease: An Overview. *European Addiction Research*, 7, 117-127.

Kessler, R.C., *et al.* (1997). Lifetime Co-occurrence of DSM-III-R Alcohol Abuse and Dependence with Other Psychiatric Disorders in the National Comorbidity Survey. *Archives of General Psychiatry*, 54, 313-321.

Kishore, P., Lal, N., Trivedi, J.K., & Dalal, P.K. (1994). A Study of Co-morbidity in Psychoactive Substance Dependence Patients. *Indian Journal Psychiatry*, 36, 133-137.

Lynskey, M.T. (1998). The Co-morbidity of Alcohol Dependence and Affective Disorders: Treatment Implications. *Drug and Alcohol Dependence*, 52, 201-209.

Mehrabian, A. (2001). General Relations Among Drug Use, Alcohol Use, and Major Indexes of Psychopathology. *Journal of Psychology*, 135, 71-86.

Mohan, D., Chopra, A., Ray, R., & Sethi, H. (2001). *Alcohol Consumption in India: A Cross-sectional Study*. In, Demers, A., Room, R. & Bourgault, C. Surveys of Drinking Patterns and Problems in Seven Developing Countries. Geneva: World Health Organisation.

Mullaney, J.A., & Trippett, C. J. (1979). Alcohol Dependence and Phobias: Clinical Description and Relevance. *British Journal of Psychiatry*, 135, 565-573.

Nelson-Jones, R. (2000). Lifeskills Counselling. In, Stephen Palmer (edr.). *Introduction to Counselling and Psychotherapy*. New Delhi: Sage.

Rahman, L. (2002). Alcohol Prohibition and Addictive Consumption in India. London: London school of Economics.

Rodgers, B., *et. al.* (2000). Non-linear Relationships in Associations of Depression and Anxiety with Alcohol Use. *Psychological Medicine*, 30, 421-432.

Schuckit, M.A., *et.al.* (1997). The Life-time Rates of Three Major Mood Disorders and Four Major Anxiety Disorders in Alcoholics and Controls. *Addiction*, 92, 1289-1304.

Single, E., *et.al.* (1999). Morbidity and Mortality Attributable to Alcohol, Tobacco, and Illicit Drug Use in Canada. *American Journal of Public Health*, 89, 385-390.

World Health Organisation (2004). *Global Status Report on Alcohol-2004*. Geneva.

World Health Organisation 2002. *The World Health Report 2002 — Reducing Risks, Promoting Healthy Life*. Geneva.

11

Occupational Stress in Employees of Different Occupational Status

Shashirekha T.[1]
Shivakumar Chengti[1]

ABSTRACT

In the present study an attempt is made to know the occupational stress of employees selected randomly from different sectors of occupations from Gulbarga city. A sample of 200 (both male and female) was selected and occupational stress scale was administered. Subsequently the data were subjected to statistical analysis. Results clearly indicated a variation in the occupational stress in different occupational status groups of employees of Gulbarga. The female employees exhibited higher occupational stress than the male sample. Manager has higher occupational stress than the engineer, supervisor, and clerk.

Introduction

Stress is usually thought of in negative terms. It is thought to be caused by something bad, although there are numerous definitions and much debate about the meaning of job stress. Ivancewich and Mattson (1987) define stress simply as the interaction of individual with the environment, but there they go on to give a more detailed working definitions as "an adaptive response, mediated by individual difference and/or Psychological processes, that is a consequence of any external (environment) action, situation or event that places excessive psychological or physical demands upon a person.

1. **Department of Psychology, Gulbarga University, Gulbarga, Karnataka (India).**

Beehr and Newman (I986) define job stress as "a condition arising from the interaction of people with their jobs and characterized by changes within people that face them to deviate from their normal functioning. Taking these two definitions.

'Stress' is defined as an adaptive response to an external situation that results in physical, Psychological and or behavioural deviations for organization participants. Job stress in generally defined in terms of relationship between person and environment. McGrath (I976) has noted that a "stress involves an interaction of person and environment". To define stress he said "there is potential for stress when an environment-situation is perceived expressing demand which threatens to exceed the person capabilities and resources for meeting it.

Margolis and Koroes (1974) defined job stress as a condition of work interacting with worker characteristics to psychological or physiological homeostasis. The casual situation/conditions are" job stresses and the disturbed homeostasis is job related strain. In addition to the short terms and chornic outcomes, response to stresses can be very short term and almost instantaneously surprisingly unlike the long term outcomes, these immediate-stress responses are always highly similar regardless of the stresses that provoked them. The intricate chain of physiological events that occurs when an organism encounters a stress was first investigated early in the twentieth by a former American Physiologist, Walter Cannon (1929). In his Harvard laboratory cannon exposed dogs and cats to a variety of stressors. But found that their responses regardless of the source of the stress always followed the same pattern. There are several factors which lead stress, especially occupational stress in the workers. The nature and complexity of job differs from one occupational position to another. It is the job characteristic inherent in an occupation, which generates lot of stress in the employees. Thus occupational status or position itself is a contributing factor to occupational stress. Therefore, an attempt is made in the present study to assess the occupational stress of employees of Gulbarga. The study also uncovers attempts to the gender differences in occupational stress of the sample.

Methodology

Sample

The sample of the study consists of 200 employees drawn randomly from Gulbarga. There was an equal number of sample categorization in the form of four levels of occupational status and gender. The respondents were administered occupational stress scale to determine the extent of their stress.

Tools

(a) Bio data schedule to collect demographic factors.

(*b*) Occupational stress scale developed by Sirvastav and Singh (1981); which consists of 46 items with 5 alternatives each. The scoring was done with 5 points scale to assess the stress of the sample.

Discussion

The data were subjected to statistical analysis. The 't' test was applied. The results are discussed in the two tables.

Table 11.1 gives the mean, SD and 't' values of occupational stress of employees belonging to four occupational status-supervisor, clerk, engineer and manager. It can be observed that the mean score of managers (151.25) is higher than engineers (145.2), clerks (139.5) and supervisors (132.32). This indicates that the occupational status with higher workload produces higher occupational stress in employees. All the 't' values are significant at 0.01 level. It is true that the position of manager involves overload, task complexity, time management, role conflict, and role stress etc. and hence the manger experiences significantly higher conflict than the employees of other occupational status. The position of engineers also involves various stressors followed by the ministerial staff i.e., clerks and supervisors. However supervisor experiences less conflict than the employees of other groups. Therefore, it can be concluded that occupational status leads occupational stress. Higher occupational status involves more occupational stress. Thus occupational status produces significant differences in the stress of employees.

Table 11.1: Mean, SD and 't' values of Occupational Stress of Employees in Different Occupational Status (N = 200)

Occupational Stress	Mean	SD
Supervisor[A]	132.32	7.5
Clerk[B]	139.5	6.9
Engineer[C]	145.2	7.3
Manager[D]	151.25	6.82

$T_{A\&B}$ = 5.12*, $T_{A\&C}$ = 8.82*, $T_{A\&D}$ = 13.3*, $T_{B\&C}$ = 5.27*, $T_{B\&D}$ = 8.5* and $T_{C\&D}$ = 4.32*

* Significant at 0.01 level.

Table 11.2 shows mean, SD and '1' values of occupational stress of male and female employees. The mean score of female employees is 173.28 and of male employees is 169.65. This shows that the mean score of the female is higher than the males. The higher score reveals higher stress. Thus the female workers are found to experience more occupational stress than the male workers. The '1' value of 2.46 is significant which tells that there are significant differences between male and female workers in the level of occupational stress. Bhatnagar and Bose (1985) found that branch managers scored differently on areas of stress.

Table 11.2: Mean, SD and 't' values of Occupational Stress of Male and Female Employees (N = 200)

Gender	Mean	SD	T value
Male	169.65	7.6	2.46*
Female	173.28	7.1	

* Significant at 0.01 level.

Kedar Nath (1986) studied the effect of organizational climates, stress and locus of control of job involvement among banking professionals. He observed that several behavioural scientists in the west as well in India have recognized that these varieties are crucial casual factors for job involvement among the Bank profession. Sen (1981) in his study investigated the main stress experienced by employees in banks at different levels. The study was conducted on a sample of employees at four levels of three banks.

Vijayalaxmi Aminabhavi and Triveni (1995) in their research of Occupational stress found differences in occupational stress of Bank Managers of different status. Thus these studies have lent support to the findings of present study.

Conclusion

- There is significant difference in the occupational stress among employees of different occupational status.
- Managers have higher occupational stress than engineers, Clerks and supervisors.
- There are significant gender differences in occupational stress: females have higher occupational stress than males.

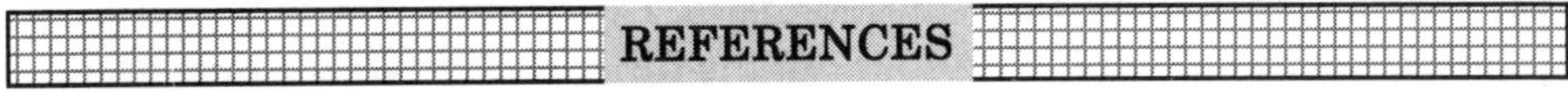

REFERENCES

Terry, A. Beer, Joseph, E., McGrath, (1992), Social Support, Occupational Stress and Anxiety. Published in Anxiety, *Stress and Coping*, 5, 7-19.

McGrath, J.E., (1976), Stress and Behaviour in Organizations. *Handbook of Industrial and Organizational Psychology*, Rand McNally.

Inancewich, J.M. and Mattson, M.T. (1987). Organizational Level Stress Management inter'-ersion: A Review and Recommendations. *Journal of Occupational Behaviour*.

Beehr and Newman (1986). "The Current Debate About the Meaning of Job Stress". Journal of Organization Behaviour Management Fall/Winter, p. 5-18.

Walter Cannon (1929). *Bodily Changes in Pain, Hunger, Fear and Rage*, New York Application.

Bhatnagar and Bose (1985). Organization Role Stress and Branch Manager *Prajnan*, 14(4), p. 349-360.

Kedar Nath (1986). *Organizational Climate; Role Stress and Locus of Control of Job Involvement Among Bank Persons*. Unpublished Ph.D. Thesis Banaras Hindu University, Varanasi.

Sen, P.C. (1981). *A Study of Personal and Organizational Correlates of Role Stress and Coping Strategies in Some Public Sector Banks*. Unpublished Ph.D. Thesis, Gujarat University, Ahmedabad.

12

Promotion of Reading Habits Between Professional and Non-professional College Students

Sudha S.T.[1]
Harinarayana N.S.[2]

ABSTRACT

The present study an attempt is made to examine the issues related to Reading promotion of professional and non-professional students. The issues studied are factors inspire them to study more; items that they read, other factors that help and encourage them to develop reading habits are discussed. A total of 1757 professional and non-professionals students from 52 colleges served as the sample for the present study. The data was collected by questionnaire. Descriptive statistics and Chi square tests were applied to find out the difference between course type and gender on various issues. Some of the important aspects to improve reading habits are reading more newspapers and journals (93.1%), reading more general books other than text books (92.5%), watching media programmes (83.3%), attending group discussions (82.3%) and so on. Chi-square tests revealed significant differences for all the options to improve reading habits of the students. This kind of trend was found to be same for students from professional and non-professional background, male and female students rom Kannada and English background and students studying in rural and urban areas. Some of the important aspects, which inspire reading habits, are appreciation by parents and teachers

1. Chief Librarian, St. Agnes Autonomous College, Mangalore, Karnataka (India).
2. Reader, Department of Studies in Library Science and Information, University of Mysore, Mysore, Karnataka (India).

(88.9%), curricular and co-curricular activities (85.1%), debates and quizzes (85.8%), library orientation and so on. Chi-square tests revealed significant differences for all the options to improve reading habits of the students.

Introduction

Reading is important for everybody in order to cope with new knowledge in the changing world of the technological age. The importance and necessity will hopefully continue to increase in the years to come. Reading is utmost important for all human beings in the complex and fast changing world to find his way in which he lives. Reading should surpass simply passing examinations. Reading is a vital tool for achieving emotional steadiness, benefit from free time hours, sharing the intricate experiences encountered in books and other reading materials and for keeping abreast of happenings in this global world at large. For this reason, teachers, parents, librarians and all concerned with shaping the emotional, cultural and educational growth and development of children must inculcate and nurture in them a good reading habit which, in turn, will arouse their interest in reading. Whereas interests signify relentless tendencies, habit can be described as a learned stimulus-response sequence. It is after forming the reading habit that students can be expected to develop interest and preferences. In many developing countries extensive literacy campaigns, have been launched in teaching people to write and to read. But knowledge of characters and reading techniques alone are not sufficient to develop real reading societies. Students should be motivated to read and informed how to utilize reading materials to improve their own personality and their social surroundings. 'Reading habit promotion' in the paper means behaviour which express the likeness of reading of individual, which occur regularly of leisure reading approach, types of reading, tastes of reading, items they read viewing on what they have read fixing on objectives of reading.

Objectives of the Study

- To identify the factors that helps in promoting the reading habits of the professional and non-professional college students.
- To assess the factors that helps and influences to develop reading habits of the professional and non-professional college students.
- To identify the factors that inspires the professional and non-professional college students to develop the reading habits.

Method

Sampling of Data Sources

The investigator field survey during by visiting 52 colleges (24+28) including professional and non-professional colleges of Dakshina Kannada

District, regarding the nature of the problem with the help of various tools of scales related to dependent and independent variables. The survey was done on the basis of gathering mass data to indicate the present trend of Reading Habits and the role of library. The study covered graduate students of professional courses such as B.E., B.Ed, MBBS, LLB and BDS as well as non-professional courses such as B.A, B.Sc, B.Com, BBM, and BCA. The total number of questionnaires distributed was 2200, out of which the base population figure of students of all those colleges is 1757. Forty-three questionnaires were rejected.

Tools Employed

Data was collected from the respondents through questionnaire. Issues related to role of libraries to improve the reading habits of professional and non-professional students of Dakshina Kannada District. The tools in the form of questionnaires and personal observation were employed in the present study.

Procedure

Initially, principals of the selected institutions were approached and permission was obtained to collect data from the respective institutions. The students were then approached and questionnaire on the role of library was administered to them, where at a time 2 to 3 students were involved. Whenever they had any doubt in understanding the questions/statements, the authors clarified them. Investigator clarified those questions. Later, the questionnaires were scrutinized and incomplete 43 questionnaires were rejected. Finally data from only 1757 students were included in the analysis. The data was analyzed through software SPSS for Windows (version 15.0).

Result

(i) Reading Promotion improving the reading habits

Whatever the options given for improving the reading habits, the majority of the students approved with those options. The agreement ranged from 71.8 per cent to 93.1 per cent. Some of the important aspects to improve reading habits are — reading more newspapers and journals (93.1%), reading more general books other than text books (92.5%), watching media programmes (83.3%), attending group discussions (82.3%) and so on. Chi-square tests revealed significant differences for all the options to improve reading habits of the students. This kind of trend was found to be same for students from professional and non-professional background (chi-square=3.8; P<. 924), male and female students (chi-square=1.621; P<.996), students from Kannada and English background (chi-square=6.307; P<.709) and students studying in rural and urban areas (chi-square= (14.073; P<.120) (Table 12.1).

Table 12.1 Responses for intending to improve the reading habits

Statements	Type of Education		Gender		Medium		Area		Total
	Non-prof	Prof	Male	Female	Kannada	English	Rural	Urban	
By reading more general books other than text book	864 94.2%	762 90.7%	760 92.9%	866 92.2%	124 96.1%	1502 92.3%	818 94.5%	808 90.7%	1626 92.5%
By reading more newspapers and journals	864 94.2%	772 91.9%	757 92.5%	879 93.6%	125 96.9%	1511 92.8%	818 94.5%	818 91.8%	1636 93.1%
By watching media programmes	773 84.3%	690 82.1%	675 82.5%	788 83.9%	102 79.1%	1361 83.6%	727 83.9%	736 82.6%	1463 83.3%
By using internet CDs and other e Sources	674 73.5%	609 72.5%	604 73.8%	679 72.3%	76 58.9%	1207 74.1%	616 71.1%	667 74.9%	1283 73.0%
By attending book talks	699 76.2%	562 66.9%	601 73.5%	660 70.3%	91 70.5%	1170 71.9%	569 65.7%	692 77.7%	1261 71.8%
By reading book reviews	727 79.3%	652 77.6%	653 79.8%	726 77.3%	108 83.7%	1271 78.1%	654 75.5%	725 81.4%	1379 78.5%
Meeting celebrities and authors	647 70.6%	549 65.4%	569 69.6%	627 66.8%	98 76.0%	1098 67.4%	567 65.5%	629 70.6%	1196 68.1%
By attending group discussions	771 84.1%	675 80.4%	678 82.9%	768 81.8%	106 82.2%	1340 82.3%	711 82.1%	735 82.5%	1446 82.3%
By attending reader's forum	669 73.0%	603 71.8%	606 74.1%	666 70.9%	95 73.6%	1177 72.3%	590 68.1%	682 76.5%	1272 72.4%
Earn while you learn	704 76.8%	633 75.4%	635 77.6%	702 74.8%	100 77.5%	1237 76.0%	654 75.5%	683 76.7%	1337 76.1%
CC P Value	3.800 .924 (NS)		1.621 .996 (NS)		6.307 .709 (NS)		14.073 .120 (NS)		

Note: CC— Contingency Co-efficient; HS— Highly Significant; NS— Non-significant.

S: Significant.

(ii) Inspiration to read

Whatever the options given for inspirations to read, the majority of the students approved those options. The agreement ranged from 68.4 per cent to 88.9 per cent. Some of the important aspects, which inspire reading habits, are — appreciation by parents and teachers (88.9%), curricular and co-curricular activities (85.1%), debates and quizzes (85.8%), library orientation and so on. Chi-square tests revealed significant differences for all the options to improve reading habits of the students. This kind of trend was found to be the same for students from professional and non-professional background (chi-square = 7.767; P<.803), male and female students (chi-square=3.653; P<.989), students from Kannada and English background (chi-square=3.923; P<.985) and students studying in rural and urban areas (chi-square= (5.951; P<.919). This study has linked with reading promotion by Clark (2005) (*See Table 12.2 on next page*).

(iii) Kinds of books read

This is lined by earlier studies confronted by Clark (2005). The Majority of the students liked to read books on the subjects like general knowledge (82.5%), health and medicine (81.6%), fun loving (79.7%), adventurous books (78.9%), science (76.6%), sports (76.2%), detectives (75.3%), and romantic contents (71.8%). From The Table 12.3, it is also evident that students were not in favour of reading astrology (54.3%) and biographies (56.4%). The Chi-square tests revealed significant differences for all the types of books liked by the students. This kind of trend was found to be the same for students from professional and non-professional background (chi-square=8.195; P<.897), students from Kannada and English background (chi-square=8.862; P<.851) and students studying in rural and urban areas (chi-square=6.423; P<.955). However, gender-wise comparison revealed that male students like to read more of general knowledge books, sports and literature, where as female students were more interested in reading humor and astrology (Chi-square=26.543; P<.022). (*See Table 12.3 on pages 88-89*)

Some of the important aspects to improve reading habits are — reading more newspapers and journals (93.1%), reading more general books other than text books (92.5%), watching media programmes (83.3%), attending group discussions (82.3%) and so on. Chi-square tests revealed significant differences for all the options to improve reading habits of the students. This kind of trend was found to be same for students from professional and non-professional background in all aspects.

Some of the important aspects, which inspire reading habits, are — appreciation by parents and teachers (88.9%), curricular and co-curricular activities (85.1%), debates and quizzes (85.8%), library orientation and so on. Chi-square tests revealed significant differences for all the options to improve reading habits of the students. This kind of trend was found to be the same for students from professional and non-professional background.

Table 12.2: Responses for inspiration to read more

Statements	Type of Education		Gender		Medium		Area		Total
	Non-prof	Prof	Male	Female	Kannada	English	Rural	Urban	
Appreciation by parents and teachers	819 89.3%	743 88.5%	728 89.0%	834 88.8%	114 88.4%	1448 88.9%	762 88.0%	800 89.8%	1562 88.9%
Creative and innovative class room teaching by using audio-visual aids	700 76.3%	677 80.6%	630 77.0%	747 79.6%	108 83.7%	1269 77.9%	697 80.5%	680 76.3%	1377 78.4%
Library orientation	776 84.6%	672 80.0%	681 83.3%	767 81.7%	111 86.0%	1337 82.1%	704 81.3%	744 83.5%	1448 82.4%
Book exhibition	766 83.5%	650 77.4%	661 80.8%	755 80.4%	117 90.7%	1299 79.8%	686 79.2%	730 81.9%	1416 80.6%
Curricular co-curricular, extra curricular activities	781 85.2%	715 85.1%	687 84.0%	809 86.2%	108 83.7%	1388 85.3%	733 84.6%	763 85.6%	1496 85.1%
Extension programmes like seminar, colloquiums, workshops etc.	781 85.2%	688 81.9%	679 83.0%	790 84.1%	106 82.2%	1363 83.7%	712 82.2%	757 85.0%	1469 83.6%
Earn while you learn	720 78.5%	647 77.0%	636 77.8%	731 77.8%	108 83.7%	1259 77.3%	658 76.0%	709 79.6%	1367 77.8%
Organizing different competitions	760 82.9%	657 78.2%	654 80.0%	763 81.3%	110 85.3%	1307 80.3%	687 79.3%	730 81.9%	1417 80.6%
Debates and quizzes	808 88.1%	700 83.3%	683 83.5%	825 87.9%	109 84.5%	1399 85.9%	736 85.0%	772 86.6%	1508 85.8%
Organizing lectures on various disciplines by eminent personalities	765 83.4%	662 78.8%	665 81.3%	762 81.2%	110 85.3%	1317 80.9%	694 80.1%	733 82.3%	1427 81.2%
Visiting different types of libraries and other information centers	739 80.6%	647 77.0%	645 78.9%	741 78.9%	94 72.9%	1292 79.4%	649 74.9%	737 82.7%	1386 78.9%

(Contd…)

Statements	Type of Education		Gender		Medium		Area		Total
	Non-prof	Prof	Male	Female	Kannada	English	Rural	Urban	
Mobile library services	608 66.3%	594 70.7%	574 70.2%	628 66.9%	87 67.4%	1115 68.5%	570 65.8%	632 70.9%	1202 68.4%
Instituting a prize for the best user of library	699 76.2%	605 72.0%	626 76.5%	678 72.2%	102 79.1%	1202 73.8%	614 70.9%	690 77.4%	1304 74.2%
CC P Value	7.767 .803 (NS)		3.653 .989 (NS)		3.923 .985 (NS)		5.951 .919 (NS)		

Note: CC— Contingency Co-efficient; HS— Highly Significant; NS— Non-significant

S: Significant

Table 12.3 Responses for different kinds of books you like to read at leisure time

Different Kinds of Books	Type of Education		Gender		Medium		Area		Total
	Non-prof	Prof	Male	Female	Kannada	English	Rural	Urban	
Adventurous	710 77.4%	676 80.5%	635 77.6%	751 80.0%	107 82.9%	1279 78.6%	690 79.7%	696 78.1%	1386 78.9%
Astrology	500 54.5%	454 54.0%	391 47.8%	563 60.0%	63 48.8%	891 54.7%	457 52.8%	497 55.8%	954 54.3%
Biography	516 56.3%	475 56.5%	471 57.6%	520 55.4%	73 56.6%	918 56.4%	456 52.7%	535 60.0%	991 56.4%
Classics	583 63.6%	517 61.5%	507 62.0%	593 63.2%	95 73.6%	1005 61.7%	520 60.0%	580 65.1%	1100 62.6%
Crime	635 69.2%	582 69.3%	577 70.5%	640 68.2%	88 68.2%	1129 69.3%	598 69.1%	619 69.5%	1217 69.3%
Detectives	681 74.3%	642 76.4%	597 73.0%	726 77.3%	96 74.4%	1227 75.4%	643 74.2%	680 76.3%	1323 75.3%
Fun loving	739 80.6%	662 78.8%	649 79.3%	752 80.1%	99 76.7%	1302 80.0%	690 79.7%	711 79.8%	1401 79.7%
General Knowledge	780 85.1%	669 79.6%	697 85.2%	752 80.1%	119 92.2%	1330 81.7%	702 81.1%	747 83.8%	1449 82.5%
Health and Medicine	738 80.5%	695 82.7%	667 81.5%	766 81.6%	106 82.2%	1327 81.5%	700 80.8%	733 82.3%	1433 81.6%
Humour	651 71.0%	650 77.4%	578 70.7%	723 77.0%	88 68.2%	1213 74.5%	632 73.0%	669 75.1%	1301 74.0%
Literature	656 71.5%	563 67.0%	586 71.6%	633 67.4%	104 80.6%	1115 68.5%	581 67.1%	638 71.6%	1219 69.4%

(Contd…)

Different Kinds of Books	Type of Education		Gender		Medium		Area		Total
	Non-prof	Prof	Male	Female	Kannada	English	Rural	Urban	
Philosophy and religion	592 64.6%	546 65.0%	530 64.8%	608 64.7%	94 72.9%	1044 64.1%	558 64.4%	580 65.1%	1138 64.8%
Romantic	671 73.2%	591 70.4%	591 72.2%	671 71.5%	97 75.2%	1165 71.6%	623 71.9%	639 71.7%	1262 71.8%
Science	690 75.2%	655 78.0%	635 77.6%	710 75.6%	105 81.4%	1240 76.2%	639 73.8%	706 79.2%	1345 76.6%
Sports	711 77.5%	627 74.6%	672 82.2%	666 70.9%	105 81.4%	1233 75.7%	638 73.7%	700 78.6%	1338 76.2%
CC P Value	8.195 .879 (NS)		26.543 .022 (S)		8.682 .851 (NS)		6.423 .955 (NS)		

Note: CC— Contingency Co-efficient; HS— Highly Significant; NS— Non-significant

S: Significant.

Gender-wise comparison revealed that male students like to read more of general knowledge books, sports and literature, where as female students were more interested in reading humor and astrology.

Discussion

The authors during their investigation interacted with many students, regarding the reading habits of the student community. The research experience of the authors arrived at the following discussions regarding the reading habits and its promotion. The true purpose of education is to enable the students to become capable of facing any situation arising in their own life. Learning broadly depends on the self-education that one acquires through reading. Reading is the major contributing factor to acquire the capabilities to face the challenges in the competitive world. This needs to be identified in various colleges imparting education in different disciplines. While considering the economic, social, geographic, psychological and technological conditions of the students in Dakshina Kannada district, a few means and modes are suggested for implementation. These suggestions would help them not only to improve their reading skills but also enhance their inclination towards reading.

To conclude, the overall analysis stresses the need for lot of changes and development in non-professional colleges of Dakshina Kannada District. Libraries have to make special effort in consultation with the college authorities, administrators, policy makers and educationists to promote the reading habits of the students. Libraries have to put in strenuous efforts to provide effective services both in accessing the information resources and also to impart the same to the student community, to involve them in serious reading the government and UGC should also take proper initiatives to release adequate grants to provide quality education and promote intensive reading based on innovative teaching techniques. The syllabus should be framed in such a way that enables the students to go for intensive learning, to fulfill their academic pursuits, but also to think objectively, act rationally, and be prepared to face life with all the uncertainties. In this context roles of non governmental organizations, government sectors, libraries, school and family are very important for mutual cooperation to promote reading habits of students especially, the role of libraries are very important as libraries are very important institutions as information centers and life long educational agencies

REFERENCES

Bonfadelli, H. (1989). Libraries Contribution to the Promotion of Reading. *Schulbibliothek Aktuell*, 2, 83-91.

Ogunrombi S.A and Gboyega Adio.(1995). Factors Affecting the Reading Habits of Secondary School Students. *Library Review*, 44(4), 50-57.

Carter, C.J. (1986).Young People and Books: A Review of Research into Young Peoples' Reading Habits. *Journal of Librarianship*, 18(1), 1-22.

Clark, C., & Foster, A. (2005). Children's and Young People's Reading Habits and Preferences: The Who, What, Why, Where and When. Retrieved June 7, 2007, http://www.literacytrust.org.uk/Research/Reading_Connects_survey.pdf

Clark, C. (2005). Young People and Reading—A School Study. Retrieved June 7, 2007, http://www.literacytrust.org.uk.

Elkin J., Train B., & D Benham D, (2003). *Reading and Reader Development: The Pleasure of Reading*. London: Facet Publishing.

Kanade, Y.G., & Chudamani, K.S. (2006). A Discourse on Promotion of Reading Habits in India. *The International Information and Library Review*, 38(3), 102-109.

Morrisette, H. (1984). *Christian Perspective of Education*. Bombay: Xavier Board of Higher Education.

Surekha, P. (2005). Promoting Children's Reading Habits Future Perspective, New Challenges and Development of Book Culture. *Herald of Library Science*, 41, (n.p.).

Zwarenstein, M. (1986). Motivating Children to Read. *Canadian Library Journal*, 43(6). 402-406.

13

The Impact of Event, Depression and Coping Strategy of People Affected by Flood *A Qualitative Study*

Shanmukh V. Kamble[1]
Vijayalaxmi A Aminabhavi[1]

ABSTRACT

This study is focussing on the post traumatic stress, depression and coping strategies employed by the flood victims. To achieve this objective Focused Group Discussion (FGD) was conducted on the affected sample of Manjari village, which is on the bank of river Krishna, Belguam district, Northern part of Karnataka state. FGD was conducted for two groups Group A consisted of 9 members (Male= 2, Female 7). Group B consisted of 10 members (Male=2, Female=8). The age ranged from 30-50 years. The qualitative analysis of their responses revealed that they were higher hyper aroused and the impact intruded their thoughts and feelings as well as they could not get rid of that bitter experience. They experienced high depression. It was also found that the victims used basically escape-avoidance, social support, planful problem solving, positive reappraisal and distancing as coping strategies. More interestingly it was observed that group B members showed post traumatic growth. Further social implications are discussed.

Keywords: Post traumatic stress, Depression, Coping strategies, Flood victims.

1. **Professor, Department of Psychology, Karnataka University, Dharwad - 580 003, Karnataka (India).**

Introduction

Nature provides the natural environment for human existence, but nature also can be the cause of many natural disasters like earthquake, famine, land sliding, fires, hurricanes, volcanic eruption and nuclear power plan explosions. Traumas related to psychological disturbances have been documented in victims of environmental disasters (Lindemann 1944), concentration camp survivors (Davidson 1967), combat veterans (Grinker and Spielgel, 1945, Sonneberg, Blank & Talbott 1985) and rape survivors (Burnam *et al* 1988). Typical symptoms experienced by these victims include guilt, impaired concentration; sleep disturbances, ahnedonia, anxiety and depression.

When a person has been the victim of a highly stressful event symptoms of stress experience may persist long after the event is over. As we have seen, the aftereffects of stress can include physiological arousal, distractibility and other negative side effects that last for hours after a stressful event has occurred. Such long-term reactions have been documented in the wake of violent wars, such as occurred in Vietnam and Gulf war (Ford *et al* 2001; D.W. King, Gudanowski & Vreven 1995). But they may also occur in response to assault, rape, domestic abuse, a violent encounter with nature such as earthquake or flood (Ironson et al, 1997) a disaster 9/11 (Fagan *et al* 2003) and being a hostage (Vila *et al* 1999) increase the risk of traumatic stress exposure and resulting posttraumatic stress syndrome.

The person suffering from posttraumatic stress syndrome has typically undergone a stressor of extreme magnitude (Lamprecht & Scak, 2003) One of the reactions to this stressful event is a psychic numbing, such as reduced interest in once enjoyable activities, detachment from friends or constrictions of emotions, excessive vigilance, sleep disturbances, feelings of guilt impaired memory or concentration, avoidance of the experience, an exaggerated startle response to loud noise (Carlier, Voerman & Gersons, 2000).

Although most of the research on disaster has focused on posttraumatic stress disorder as the outcome of interest (Rubonis & Bickman, 1991) some studies have focussed on successful adaptation and the positive outcomes that may ensure following successful coping with disaster and its aftermath.

Nolen-Hoeksema & Morrow (1991) in their study of natural disaster earthquake (1989) did a follow up study on measures of emotional health and styles of responding to negative moods, results revealed that subject (students) who, before the earthquake, already had elevated levels of depression, had stress symptoms and a ruminative style of responding to their symptoms had more depression and stress symptoms for both follow-ups.

Frederickson, Tugade, Waugh & Larkin (2003) did a study on the September 11 2001, terrorists attack on the world trade center event, finding suggested that positive emotion in the aftermath of crisis buffer resilient people against depression and fuelled thriving, shoed a paradoxical increase in psychological resources a pattern of post crisis growth.

Ibanez, Buck, Khatchikian &Norris (2004) used an unstructured interview method to study the various coping strategies used by survivors after a disaster, 16 women, 11 men were asked to recount how they coped with a specific disaster and its aftermath interviews were carried out in three cities, Guadalajra , Jalisco (n=10), Homestead, Florida (n=6) and Puerto Angel Oaxaca experienced hurricane "Andrew" and hurricane 'Paulina' respectively. Analysis of common themes revealed seeking support, seeking meaning, problem solving and avoidance as primary coping strategies in all three cities. Seeking support was the most commonly cited coping strategies, seeking support maybe an universal coping strategy for disaster survivors, whereas other coping strategies varied by context specific factors such as type of disaster, resource availability and stage of disaster recovery.

All the above reviewed studies reveal that the victims of hurricane, earthquake and many other natural disasters have developed many psycho-physical problems. However, such studies in the Indian context are almost nil. Thus the present study is taken up with the objective of investigating the impact of event, depression, and coping strategies employed by people affected by flood. The flood in North Karnataka, especially in Belgaum district was unexpected and unprecedented. There was a massive destruction of property of people. Hence there was felt need to go for some psychological studies with respect to them.

Location

Belgaum district is located in the north-western part of Karnataka state India. The district is located at an elevation varying from 900 to 4,500 metres above MSL. It extends over an area of 13,415 sq.kms, from which is 6.99 per cent of the total geographical area of the state. The district received 177.5 mm rainfall against an average of 103.7 mm in the month of June 2005. The same trend continued in July too with the district receiving 534.73 mm as against 417.78 mm. Thus, an excess of 127.99 mm rain had been received. Particularly heavy downpour on 16th and 26th of July almost equaled the average monthly volumes expected for the month of July. As a result, there was huge overflow in all seven rivers especially in 'Markandeya' and 'Hiranyakeshi' rivers. The district received heavy inflow into the river Krishna, Vedganga and Doodaganga from northern riparian state Maharashtra.

Out of the ten taluks in the district, 5 taluks namely Athani, Chikkodi, Raibag, Hukkeri and Gokak were heavily affected on the account of heavy rainfall and river overflow, on 3rd August 2005, two helicopters were used for rescuing 10 people in Manewadi (Manjri) village of Chikkodi taluk, which was totally marooned.

Method

This exploratory investigation was conducted to study the post traumatic stress, depression and coping strategies employed by the flood victims of Manjari village dwelling on the banks of Krishna river in Chikkodi taluk, of Belgaum district. Qualitative method was employed for several reasons. Most of the respondents of the study are illiterate and such studies can obtain more in depth information only with qualitative research. Given the limited research in this area, it was important to consider several possible contextual variables that could affect posttraumatic stress, depression and coping strategies following a disaster.

The present study sought to address the following basic research questions with the flood victims:

1. How Post traumatic stress and flood victims had experienced depression?
2. What strategies did the flood affected people use most frequently in coping with the disaster situation?

Variables

Impact of event: Recalling of the event, experiencing of nightmares, intense emotional upset produced by stimuli that symbolized the event, loss of concentration, staying asleep, hyper vigilance or exaggerated startled responses.

1. *Depression:* Sad most of the day, loss of interest and pleasure in usual activities insomnia, poor appetite, fatigue, feelings of worthlessness.
2. *Coping strategies:* Respondents' efforts to try to manage the demands produced by the disaster.

Sample

Two groups were involved for obtaining the data namely group A consisted of 9 members, 2 males and 7 females and the age ranged from 32-50 years. Second group B consisted of 10 members, 2 males and 8 females' age ranging form 38-58 years. All respondents were illiterate and come from lower SES group. These respondents were contacted for the purpose of collecting information relation to stress, depression and stress coping, after 6 weeks after flood problem.

Procedure

Focussed group discussion method was employed to collect the information about post traumatic stress, depression and stress coping behaviour of those flood affected men and women whose range ranges from 30 years to 50 as the number was more they were divided into 2 groups and the focussed group discussion was conducted in the local language that is Kannada.

The whole focussed group discussion was designed in such a way to gain the responses based upon their experiences relating to post traumatic stress, depression and coping strategies.

Interviewers constituted of one researcher, coordinator and a native member of that village. The researcher briefed the coordinator and the native member about how communities may respond in the aftermath of a natural disaster, the purpose of briefing them was to inform them on what they might find in the field. The specific variable under study was introduced to them, namely post-traumatic stress, depression and coping strategies.

The focussed group discussion for each group lasted 3-5 hours. The members (researcher, coordinator and native member) went to the village and met the inhabitants staying on the banks of river Krishna. All the members came out to meet; the native introduced the researchers and told them the purpose of visit there and some of the willing members agreed to participate in the focussed group discussion. The focussed group discussion was conducted in one of the victims' house. Interviewers established rapport through lengthy informal conversation about the event and showed genuine interest in their narrations. Further researchers monitored the discussion by asking questions in their native understandable languages. The researcher, coordinator and the native member started writing down the information as the group members started their discussion, the session started by asking them "how the disaster affected you, please give us your responses".

Data Analysis

A qualitative analysis was carried out to have overall picture about their post-traumatic stress, depression and coping strategies.

Analysis of results of Group A

Post-traumatic stress: Most of them experienced insomnia, little noise was enough to make them startle, and the sight of water especially bringing them bank of the bitter experiences.

"I was trying hard to sleep, although I slept after sometimes, I felt that I was wading through the river and the water raised to my chest level and I was about to b drowned, I instantly got up to realize I had a dream, but I was really feeling as if it was so real not a dream".

Depression: All the informants showed and experienced loss of interest, insomnia, fatigue, poor appetite, lack of concentration, and feeling of worthlessness. "I find things confusing, there is unhappiness, I feel so sleepy, yet I cannot sleep, I feel nobody like me not even God, why he did this to me?"

Coping strategies: Social support: 25 per cent of all coping strategies mentioned by informants of group A related to interacting with others. "We all console ourselves, but government helped us greatly, the professional groups (NGOs) provided us with good food, even now good people do come to see and help us".

Positive reappraisal: 25 per cent of all coping strategies involved positive reappraisal. "Yes I found new faith, faith and trust in humanity, I came to know that good people are there to help us during crisis like this".

Distancing: 20 per cent of all coping strategies involved distancing. "I at least felt that it's my fate, I always have bad luck".

Painful problem solving: 20 per cent of all coping strategies mentioned involved planful problem solving. "I have lost, I have made up my plans, this experience has given me motivation to start new life, I have made plans and will follow it".

Escape Avoidance: 10 per cent of all the coping strategies involved escape avoidance. "I still remember those good old days when the sugar cane harvest was best, we got good yield, good pay, I wish something would happen like that again".

Analysis of Results of Group B

The numbers of informants in this group were 10 members.

Post traumatic stress: It was observed that all the members have had the symptoms of Post traumatic stress since, it is defined by a cluster of symptoms, since most of the flood victims had directly experienced the flood, the event must have created intense fear, horror or a sense of helplessness. They have had been experiencing nightmare, intense emotion, upset by the signs of rain, or a cry of child, had trouble sleeping, hyper vigilant, difficulty concentrating. "I was inside, my child cried out loud, my heart started beating fast, my hands were trembling I thought maybe the river has started rising again".

Depression: all the 10 informants showed and experienced loss of interest in things, insomnia, fatigue, had feelings of worthlessness, helplessness and lack of concentration. 'I am crying, everyday; I am left with nothing oh No' (breaks down into tears).

Coping strategies: Social support: 35 per cent of all the coping strategies mentioned by informants related to interacting with others in the community. "We all have a strong feeling that ... our community members will support us, every evening, we all sit around in the temple, and the elder person *'ajja'* gives us advice about how to go on with our life. All of us one by one, talk about ourselves and end up feeling, that there are members in our community who experienced the same pain, which we underwent and so the bonding is more for us, talking with other members of our community is really relieving experience for us".

Planful problem solving: 23 per cent of all the coping strategies mentioned by informants involved in planful problem solving. 'I need to restart my life again, I will take a loan, the place where I had been to stay along with my wife at her place, I came across one person, who promised me loan. I shall invest in the shop business, my wife will also go to farm to work as a labour, I will double my effort work at night time as a Guard at farm if possible".

Positive reappraisal: 23 per cent of all the coping strategies involved in positive reappraisal. "I never knew how much strength I had, I pulled so many of my community people helped them to climb into the truck, I got the strength from where? I myself did not know it maybe God helped me".

Escape-avoidance: 17 per cent of all the coping strategies involved escape avoidance. "Earlier, I used to smoke 4 beedies, but now I have even started to enjoy drinks, that packet you get".

An interesting development was observed while discussing with the second group B more specifically this group members came out with more positive feelings by expressing that "what ever happened is happened. It is not a curse, we take it as a life lesson, to meet and overcome challenge" in other words, in research language this can be identified as post-traumatic growth.

Discussion

Analysis of the data gathered by focused group discussion revealed that Group A used social support, positive reappraisal, distancing, planful problem-solving and escape avoidance as coping strategies. Group B used social support, positive reappraisal, planful problem solving and escape avoidance as coping strategies.

The findings of this study support the earlier findings. Most of the members' experienced posttraumatic stress, according to Carlson and Dalenberg (2000) exposure to sudden and highly stressful traumas such as disasters, activates core traumatic stress responses that include cognitive, affective, behavioural and physiological avoidance. The more intense the experience, the more likely it is that one will have traumatic stress reaction involving. These avoidance responses are thought to keep the traumatic information in the unconscious an can result in a period of numbing an denial (Horowitz, 1986). Almost all the members experienced high level of depression. Nolen-Hoeksema & Morrow (1991) reported in their study of earthquake, where most of the subjects had depression. The coping strategies employed were social support, positive reappraisal, planful problem-solving and escape-avoidance. This study falls in line with the study reported by Ibanez, Buck, Khatchikian &Norris (2004) most respondents used social support, avoidance, problem solving and avoidance as coping strategies.

The observed Post-traumatic growth is supported by most of the earlier studies. Reports of post-traumatic growth have been found in people who have experienced bereavement, rheumatoid arthritis, HIV infection, cancer, bone marrow transplantation, heart attacks, coping with the medical problems of children, transportation accidents, housefires, sexual assault and sexual abuse, combat, refugee experiences, and being taken hostage (Tedeschi and Calhoun, 2000). These changes include improved relationships, new possibilities for one's life, a greater appreciation for life, a greater sense of personal strength and spiritual development. There appears to be a basic paradox apprehended by trauma survivors who report these aspects of post-traumatic growth: Their losses have produced valuable gains. In this study too, the members of group B, who showed the post-traumatic growth, observed it. Miles, Demi & Mostyn-ake (1984) found that Kansas city Hyatt hotel collapsed killing over 1000 people and injuring nearly 200, the experience left some workers with an increased understanding of the fragility of life, and other become more altruistic and compassionate.

Strengths

1. The use of qualitative methods and analysis allowed the 'voice of people' to be heard and to guide future research that maybe conducted when natural disaster strikes.
2. It was first psychological research conducted on flood victims in the northern Karnataka region (Belgaum district).

Limitations

Although male and female informants were used, gender differences could not be analyzed due to the size of sample. In addition, the small sample size and the exploratory nature of the study strongly limit the extent to which the findings can be generalized to other populations.

Social Implication

Apart from the material and medical relief for the natural disaster victims; efforts should be made to provide psychological and mental support, in terms of counselling and helping the victims to develop the skills to manage their crisis in an effective way.

The immediate aftermath of tragedy is a time during which clinicians must be particularly sensitive to the psychological needs of the patient. Never engage in the insensitive introduction of didactic information or trite comments about growth coming from suffering. This is not to say that systematic treatment programmes designed for trauma survivors should not include growth-related components, because these may indeed be helpful (Antoni *et al.*, 2001). A posttraumatic growth perspective can be used even in critical incident stress management (Calhoun and Tedeschi, 2000). However, even as part of a systematic intervention programme, matters related to growth are best addressed after the individual has had a sufficient amount of time to adapt to the aftermath of the trauma.

REFERENCES

Antoni MH, Lehman JM, Kilbourn KM *et al.* (2001), Cognitive-behavioural Stress Management Intervention Decreases the Prevalence of Depression and Enhances Benefit Finding Among Women Under Treatment for Early-stage Breast Cancer. *Health Psychology*, 20(1): 20-32.

Burnam, M.A., Stein, J.A., Golding, J.M., Siegel, J.M., Sorenson, . B., Forsythe, A.B., & Telles, C.A. (1988). Sexual Assault and Mental Disorders in a Community Population. *Journal of Consulting and Clinical Psychology*, 56, 843-850.

Calhoun LG, Tedeschi RG (1999), Facilitating Post-traumatic Growth: A Clinician's Guide. Mahwah, N.J.: Lawrence Erlbaum Associates Publishers.

Calhoun LG, Tedeschi RG (2000), Early Post-traumatic Interventions: Facilitating Possibilities for Growth. In: Posttraumatic Stress Intervention: Challenges, Issues, and Perspectives, Violanti JM, Paton D, Dunning C, eds. Springfield, Ill.: Charles C. Thomas Publishers, pp. 135-152.

Carlier I.V.E.; Voerman A.E.; Gersons B.P.R. (2000) The Influence of Occupational Debriefing on Post-traumatic Stress Symptomatology in Traumatized Police Officers: British Journal of Medical Psychology Volume 73, Number 1, March 2000, pp. 87-98(12).

Carlson, E.B. & Dalenberg, C.J (2000). A Conceptual Framework for the Impact of Traumatic Experiences. Trauma, Violence and Abuse, 1, 4 28.

Coffman, S. (1994). Children Describe Life After Hurricane Andrew. *Paediatric Nursing*, 20, 363-375.

Davidson, S. (1967). A Clinical Classification of Psychiatric Disturbances of Holocaust Survivors and Their Treatment. *The Israel Annals of Psychiatry and Related Disciplines*, 5, 96-98.

Grinker, R.R., & Spiegel, J. E (1945). *Men Under Stress.* New York: Blakiston.

Horowitz, M., J (1986). Stress Response Syndrome. Second Edition. J. Ironson, Northvale,NJ.

Ibanez, G., Buck, C. A , Katchikian, N. & Norris, F.N(2004) Qualitative Analysis of Coping Strategies Among Mexican Disaster Survivors, *Anxiety, Stress, and Coping,* March 2004, Vol. 17, No. 1, pp. 69-85.

Ironson. G., Benight. C.C., Klebe. K., Carver. C., S (1999) Conservation of Resources and Coping Self-efficacy Predicting Distress Following a Natural Disaster: A Causal Model Analysis where the Environment Meets the Mind Anxiety, *Stress and Coping,* Vol. 12 Issue 2 pp. 107-126.

King, D.W., King, L.A., Gudanowski, D.M., & Vreven, D.L. (1995). Alternative Representations of War Zone Stressors: Relationships to Post-traumatic Stress Disorder in Male and Female Vietnam Veterans. *Journal of Abnormal Psychology*, 104, 184-196.

Lamprecht, F & Sack, M. (2002) Post-traumatic Stress Disorder Revisited, *Psycho-somatic Medicine*, 64: 222-237.

Lindemann, E. (1944). Symptomatology and Management of Acute Grief. *American Journal of Psychiatry*, 101, 141-148.

Miles, M.S., Demi, A.S., & Mostyn-Aker, P. (1984). Rescue Workers' Reactions following the Hyatt Hotel Disaster. *Death Education*, 8, 315-331.

Nolen-Hoeksema, S., & Morrow. J.(1991) A Prospective Study of Depression and Post-traumatic Stress Symptoms After a Natural Disaster: The 1989 Loma Prieta Earthquake. *Journal of Personality and Social Psychology* 1991, Vol. 61, No. 1, 115-121.

Rubonis, A. V., & Bickman, L. (1991). Psychological Impairment in the Wake of Disaster: The Disaster-psychopathology Relationship. *Psychological Bulletin*, 109, 384-399.

Saylor, C.F., Swenson, C.C., & Powell, P.(1992). Hurricane Hugo Blows Down the Broccoli: Pre-schoolers' Post-disaster Play and Adjustment. *Child Psychiatry and Human Development*.

Sonnenberg, S.M., Blank, A. S., Jr., & Talbott, J. A. (Eds.). (1985). *The Trauma of War: Stress and Recovery in Vietnam Veterans.* Washington, DC: American Psychiatric Press.

Vila, G., Porche, L, M., Mouren-Simeoni, M.,(1999) *An 18-Month Longitudinal Study of Post-traumatic Disorders in Children Who Were Taken Hostage in Their School Psycho-somatic Medicine*, 61: 746-754.

14

Assessment of Shyness and Anxiety and Their Relationship Among Women Athletes

Lancy D'Souza[1]

ABSTRACT

In the present study an attempt is made to assess the levels of shyness and anxiety among women athletes and to establish relationship between shyness and anxiety. A total of 140 women athletes were selected from the University of Mysore. The sample selected randomly from intercollegiate level sports held at Mysore. They were classified into five groups based on their involvement in the games—Ball games, Racket games, Human Powered games, Cognitive skills and multiple games. They were administered shyness scale and Taylors manifest anxiety scale. The assessment of shyness was done in 3 levels—Low, moderate, and high. Results revealed that 34.3 per cent of the total sample had low shyness, 61.4 per cent moderate and 4.3 per cent of the sample had high shyness. In anxiety measurement, 7.1 per cent of the sample had high anxiety, 91.4 per cent of the sample had normal anxiety and 1.4 per cent of the sample had low anxiety. In total shyness athletes with cognitive skills had highest shyness and athletes with human powered games had least shyness. Anxiety correlated positively and significantly more with psychological domain of shyness, followed by social domain. Significant positive relationship was found between physical domain of shyness and anxiety to a lesser extent. Remedial measures for reducing shyness and anxiety are highlighted in the discussion.

1. **Department of Psychology, Maharaja's College, University of Mysore, Mysore-570 006, Karnataka (India).**

Introduction

The ability to cope with pressure and anxiety is an integral part of sports, particularly among elite athletes (Hardy *et al*, 1996; Orlick *et al*, 1988). Researchers have reported that over 50 of consultations among athletes at an Olympic festival were related to stress or anxiety related problems (Murphy, 1988). According to Endler as cited in Cox (1994) there are five different aspects associated with anxiety that are closely related to fear. These are:

1. Threat to self-esteem as a result of failure;
2. Threat to personal harm;
3. Unpredictability or fear of the unknown;
4. Fear of disruption of daily habits; and
5. Fear of being negatively evaluated by others.

Thus the situation the athlete is placed in (objective demand), the evaluation of the situation (perceived threat) and the influence of anxiety on personality (the response) will affect anxiety. Therefore, if an athlete's perception of ability to respond is not equal to the demand perceived, anxiety will occur anxiety levels measured on the basis of norms given-high anxiety, normal anxiety and low anxiety results when the individual doubts his or her ability to cope with the situation that causes him or her stress (Hardy *et al.*, 1996). Another important point that needs to be clarified is the difference between state and trait anxiety (Spielberger, 1966). While state anxiety can be considered to be more situational in nature and is often associated with arousal of the autonomic nervous system, trait anxiety can be thought of as a world view that an individual uses when coping with situations in his or her environment (Spielberger, 1966). Trait anxiety influences performances in that individuals with high trait anxiety will attend more`to information related to state anxiety (Hardy *et al.*, 1996). Previous research outside of sport and exercise psychology has indicated that individuals with high trait· anxiety who are state anxious attend to threat related information, while individuals with low trait anxiety who are state anxious will attend away from threat related information (MacLeod, 1990). Within the context of sports, those individuals who are low trait anxious and experience high state anxiety would find it facilitative to a peak performance; but, those individuals with who are high trait anxious and experience state anxiety will find it debilitative to athletic performance (Hardy *et.al.*, 1996).

Doubts about one's ability to contribute effectively to social encounters and the belief that others will negatively evaluate one may contribute to the withdrawal behaviour and social anxieties that characterize shyness (Crozier, 1995). In general, significant relationships are established between shyness and anxiety (D'Souza, 2003), where high shyness evokes high anxiety in the persons. Much of the empirical research correlating shyness with other variables has been carried out with adolescents, college students or adults (Chen, 1995; Kemple, 1995). However, not many studies have been conducted on athletes (D'Souza *et al*, 1999). In the present study an attempt is made to assess the levels of shyness and anxiety among women athletes and establish the relationship between shyness and anxiety.

Method

Objectives

1. To assess the levels of shyness and anxiety among women athletes.
2. To find out whether athletes with different sports background differ in shyness and anxiety.
3. To find out the relationship between different domains of shyness and anxiety.

Hypotheses

1. Athletes with different games background differ significantly in their shyness scores.
2. Athletes with different games background differ significantly in their anxiety scores.
3. There will be significant correlation between shyness and anxiety scores.

Sample

Table 14.1: Distribution of the sample according to groups

Groups	Games Involved	N
Ball games (BG)	Handball, Football, Volleyball and Basket Ball	30
Racket games (RG)	Ball badminton, Shuttle badminton Lawn tennis and Table tennis	52
Human Powered games (HPG)	Athletics and Kho-Kho	22
Cognitive skills (CS)	Chess	20
Multiple games (MG)	Combinations of games	16
Total		140

A total of 140 women athletes sewed as subjects for the present study. The sample was selected during Inter-collegiate competitions held annually for women athletes at Mysore. These women athletes were selected from each college of University of Mysore, and further sent for selections for

Inter-varsity competitions in various sports and games. Further, the women athletes were classified into groups on basis of games/sports they involved, and the following table gives brief summary of the sample selected.

Tools Employed

(a) Shyness Questionnaire

This questionnaire was developed by Crozier (1995) of University College of Cardiff. It consists of 26 items and requires the subject to indicate his/her response by ticking "YES/NO" OR 'DON'T KNOW". The items of the questionnaire are based on situations or interactions like performing in front of the class, being made fun of, being told off, having one's photograph taken, novel situations involving teachers, school-friends interaction and so on. The items pertain to three domains-Physical, Psychological and Social. Of the 26 items, shyness is indicated by a 'YES response for 21 items and a NO" response for 5 items. Item analysis of the scale using SPSS programme resulted in Cronbach's alpha coefficient of 0.817.

(b) Taylor's Manifest Anxiety scale

This scale measures the individual's level of anxiety. Taylor originally developed this scale in 1951, which consisted of 200 items. Later, in 1953, it was reduced to 50 items. The test retest reliability of the scale was found to be 0.89. In 1993, Nataraj and Nataraj of Mysore University examined the original form of the scale and reduced it to 40 items. In the present study, 40-statement version was used. The response alternatives are 'True' or 'False'. In this form, there are 30 items related to 'anxiety' and remaining 10 items are lie items. The validity is high, and the test-retest reliability is at 0.96.

Procedure

Initially the athletes were briefed about the study and consent was taken from them for inclusion in the study. The information on type of games/ sports involved and other details were recorded and later they were given Shyness questionnaire developed by Crozier (1995). Whenever they had doubts in understanding particular statement or question, researcher clarified such statement/questions. Next day they were given Taylor's manifest anxiety scale (Nataraj & Nataraj, 1993). Once both the questionnaires completed, they were scored according to the manual provided by the respective authors. Later a master chart was prepared and all the data were fed into computer for further analysis.

Statistical Analysis

Chi-square test was applied to find out the difference between frequencies of various levels of shyness and anxiety. To find out the difference between athletes in different groups of games in mean shyness and anxiety scores, One-way ANOVA followed by Duncan's Multiple Range Test (DMRT-post hoc test) was employed. Lastly to find out the mutual relationship between different domains of shyness and anxiety, Pearson's product moment correlation was applied. All the statistical methods were carried out through SPSS (2006) for Windows (Version 15, Evaluation Version).

Results

(a) Assessment of shyness and anxiety levels

From the Table 14.2, it is clear that 34.3 per cent of the total sample had low shyness, 61.4 per cent moderate and 4.3 per cent of the sample had high shyness. When chi-square test was applied to those frequencies, a significant chi-square value was observed (chi-square-68.629; P<.000) indicating that majority of the sample had moderate shyness and very few of them had high shyness. In anxiety measurement, 7.1 per cent of the sample had high anxiety, 91.4 per cent of the sample had normal anxiety and 1.4 per cent of the sample had low anxiety. Chi-square test revealed a significant difference between the frequencies of various levels of anxiety (chi-square 13.314; P<.000) where more than 9/10 of the sample had normal anxiety.

Table 14.2 Presents frequencies under various levels of shyness and anxiety along with results of chi-square tests.

Table 14.2:

Factors					
Shyness			Anxiety		
Levels	**Frequency**	**Per Cent**	**Levels**	**Frequency**	**Per Cent**
Low	48	34.3	Low	2	1.4
Moderate	86	61.4	Normal	128	91.4
High	6	4.3	High	10	7.1
Total	**140**	**100.0**	**Total**	**140**	**100.0**
Chi-square	68.629	213.314			
Significance	.000 (Highly Significant)		.000 (Highly Significant)		

(b) Shyness, anxiety and groups

Table 14.3 presents mean scores on shyness and anxiety of athletes in different groups with results of One-Way ANOVA and DMRT.

Table 14.3:

Variable	Games/Sports	Mean	S.D	F Value	P Value
Shyness	Ball games (BG)	22.00h	8.502	3.847	.005 (HS)
	Racket games (RG)	21.73 b	11.721		
	Human Powered games (HPG)	16.09a	7.702		
	Cognitive skills (CS)	27.20 h	6.879		
	Multiple games (MG)	18.13a	10.726		
	Total	**21.27**	**10.197**		
Anxiety	Ball games	13,87a	3.126	2.826	.027 (S)
	Racket games	15.54b	3.340		
	Human Powered games	14.363	2.735		
	Cognitive skills	16.40b	3.500		
	Multiple games	13.88″	3.704		
	Total	**14.93**	**3.360**		

Note: Means with different superscripts are significantly different from each other as indicated by DMRT. HS—Highly Significant; S—Significant.

In total shyness athletes with cognitive skills had highest shyness (mean 27.20) and athletes with human powered games (mean 16.09) had least shyness. One-way ANOVA revealed a significant difference between these 5 groups (F^3.847; P<.005). In anxiety, again a significant difference was observed between athletes playing different sports/games (F=2.826; P<.027) where athletes with cognitive skills (mean 16.40) and racket games (mean 15.54) had high anxiety, where as athletes with ball games (mean 13.87) and multiple games (mean 13.88) had least anxiety.

(c) Relationship between shyness and anxiety

From the Table 14.4, it is clear that anxiety correlated positively and significantly with total shyness to a maximum extent (r =. 525; P<. 000). In other words higher shyness resulted in higher anxiety and vice-versa. Further, domain-wise correlations with anxiety revealed that higher correlation coefficients were found between anxiety psychological domain of shyness (r =.477; P<.000), followed by social domain (r =.469; P<.000). Significant positive relationship was found between physical domain of shyness and anxiety (r =.268; P<.001) to a lesser extent.

Table 14.4 presents results of product-moment correlation between domains of shyness and anxiety with significance levels.

Table 14.4:

Variable 1	Correlation	
	Coefficient	P value
Shyness-Physical	.268	.001 (HS)
Shyness-Social	.469	.000 (HS)
Shyness-Psychological	.477	.000 (HS)
Shyness-Total	.525	.000 (HS)

Note: df=138; HS— Highly Significant.

Discussion

Main findings of the present study are:

1. 61.4 per cent of the sample selected had moderate shyness, and 91.4 per cent of the sample had normal anxiety.
2. In shyness factor, athletes with cognitive skills had highest shyness and athletes with human powered games had least shyness.
3. Athletes with cognitive skills and racket games had high anxiety, where as athletes with ball games and multiple games had least anxiety.
4. Anxiety correlated positively and significantly more with psychological domain of shyness, followed by social domain.

The athletes who were involved in games related to cognitive skills like chess and so on had high shyness and anxiety. The reason could be these athletes are not exposed outward much, and the nature of the game is such that they have to think a lot, where muscle power, physical endurance do not matter much. In games like chess, multiple strategies have to be planned, each move has to be calculated cautiously and this game being individual one, the ego involvement is much against the opponent, hence more anxiety. Even the status attached to cognitive games like chess is high compared to other games as it is considered 'intellectuals game'. In human powered games like Kho-Kho, which do not involve much of cognitive capacity as like in chess, and these athletes are exposed much outside, we would expect them to have less shyness and anxiety.

Several studies have explored the relationship between shyness and anxiety. Shyness has been associated with depression, loneliness, fearfulness, social anxiety, neuhticism, and lowered self-esteem (Schmidt *et al*, 1995). Schroeder (1995) explored the cognitive aspect of shyness and social anxiety with regard to interpersonal perception skills and found that socially anxious subjects had difficulty in social information processing tasks. Shyness evokes negative effect, which leads to sadness, unhappiness and fearfulness, and tendency to describe oneself as 'shy natured' is associated with low global self esteem and with feelings of low self worth in several domains of the self (Crozier, 1995), Shy adolescents tended to be lower in self-esteem, more introverted, and more anxious than their non-shy counterparts (Lawrence *et al*, 1992). A study by Van-Ameringen *et al* (1998) after studying 225 patients concluded that both shyness and behavioural inhibition are associated with anxiety disorders in children and adults. So, we can definitely say that there is a direct link between shyness and anxiety, where higher levels of shyness lead to increased anxiety, which ultimately affects the performance.

To conclude, the study of shyness and anxiety reaction in the field of sports has become an important part in the field of sports psychology. The problem of understanding the reasons for shyness and anxiety is not impossible or difficult. But once the causes in an athlete are understood by the coach himself or with the help of sports psychologists or professional clinician, various kinds of remedial techniques may be applied and help may be rendered to overcome excessive shyness and anxiety, which may affect the performance (Singh, 2004). Although anxiety can have a considerable impact on performance, it is important to consider other components of an athlete's functioning as well. The mental health model of Performance (Morgan, 1985) does this by using the Profile of Mood States (McNair *et al*, 1971). According to the model, peak performances are achieved by individuals who pose psychological states with high levels of vigor and low levels of tension, depression, anger, fatigue, and confusion. Some of the suggested remedial measures to reduce anxiety and shyness are Yoga/Meditation, Jacobson's Progressive Muscular Relaxation (JPMR) or Jacobson's Advanced Progressive Muscular Relaxation (JAPMR), Social skills training, Cognitive restructuring, Drug therapy for extreme shyness and so on.

REFERENCES

Chen, X (1995). Social Functioning and Adjustment in Chinese Children—A Longitudinal Study. *Developmental Psychology*, 31, 31-39.

Cox, R. (1994). *Sport Psychology, Concepts and Applications* (3rd ed.) USA: WCB Brown & Benchmark Publishers.

Crozier, W.R. (1995). Shyness and Self-esteem. *British Journal of Educational Psychology*. 65, 85-95.

D'Souza, L, 2003. Influence of Shyness on Anxiety and Academic Achievement in High School Students. *Pakistan Journal of Psychological Research* (Pakistan), 18, 3-4, 109-118.

D'Souza, L., Singh, M. & Basavarajappa. (1999). Influence of Shyness on Performance, Personality and Intelligence of Students of Physical Education. *Psychological Studies*, 44, 92-94.

Hardy, L. (1996) A Test of Catastrophe Models of Anxiety and Sports Performance Against Multidimensional Anxiety Theory Models Using the Method of Dynamic Differences. *Anxiety, Stress and Coping: An International Journal*, 9, 69-86.

Hardy, L., Jones, G., & Gould, D. (1996). *Understanding Psychological Preparation for Sport: Theory and Practice of Elite Performers.* Chichester: Wiley Publications.

Kemple, K M. (1995). Shyness and Self-esteem in Early Childhood. *Journal of Humanistic Education and Development*, 33, 173-182.

Lawrence, B., & Bennett.S. (1992). Shyness and Education: The Relationship Between Shyness, Social Class and Personality Variables in Adolescents. *British Journal of Educational Psychology*, 62, 257-263.

MacLeod, C. (1990). Mood Disorders and Cognition. In M. W. Eysenck (Ed.), *Cognitive Psychology: An International Review*. Wiley, Chichester.

McNair, D.M., Lorr, M., & Droppelman, L. F. (1971). *Profile of Mood States Manual*, Educational and Industrial Testing Services, San Diego, CA.

Morgan, W.P. (1985). Affective Beneficence of Vigorous Physical Activity. *Medicine and Science in Sport and Exercise*, 17, 94-100.

Murphy, S.M. (1988). The On-site Provision of Sport Psychology Services at the 1987 U.S. Olympic Festival. *The Sport Psychologist*, 2a 337-351.

Nataraj, V & Nataraj N. (1993). *Manual of Experiments in Psychology*. Mysore: Srinivasa Publications.

Orlick, T., & Partington, J. (1988). Mental Links to Excellence. *The Sport Psychologist*, 2, 105-130.

Singh, A. (2004). *Psychology of Coaching*. New Delhi: Friends Publications.

Schmidt, L.A., &, Nathan, F.A. (1995). Individual Differences in Young Adults' Shyness and Sociability: Personality and Health Correlates. *Personality and Individual Differences*, 19,455-462.

Schroeder, J.E. (1995). Self-concept, Social Anxiety, and Interpersonal Perception Skills. *Personality and Individual-Differences*, 19, 955-958.

Spielberger, C.S. (1966). Theory and Research on Anxiety. In C.S. Spielberger (Ed.), *Anxiety and Behaviour*, Academic Press, New York, 3-20.

Van-Ameringen,M, Mancini, C., & Oakman, J.M. (1998). The Relationship of Behavioural Inhibition and Shyness to Anxiety Disorder. *Journal of Nervous and Mental Disease*, 186, 425-431.

15

Impact of Study Method on Educational Aspiration of Mountain, Valley, Hill and Plain Sectors High School Students

Ram Chandra Aryal[1]
G. Venkatesh Kumar[2]

ABSTRACT

Purpose of the study was to find the effectiveness of study method intervention for increasing the adjustment score of high school students. Students were divided into two groups e.g. experimental and control. The PQRST study method intervention was used for experimental groups after taking pretest. The sample was selected by using average basis (exam score of previous year) rrom mountain, valley, hill and plain sectors' schools of Nepal. The sample size was B+G = 240 of grade nine. Educational aspiration scale (EAS), developed by Sharma and Gupta was used to measure educational aspiration scores of the students. General linear Model Repeated Measure of ANOVA was applied to measure the effect of study method intervention on educational aspiration increase. A significant "F" observed indicating differential increased in experimental groups. However the interaction between sectors and groups within subjects' effects found non-significant.

Introduction

Nepal a land locked country between two big countries India and China has 1904 private and 3135 government high schools. About 268390 girls and 31886 boys are studying at high schools (ministry of education, 2005). Area of the country: 147,181 esq, population of the country male 11563921 and

1. **Lecturer, Department of Psychology, Tribhvan University. (T.U) Katmandu, (Nepal).**
2. **Professor, Department of Studies in Psychology, University of Mysore, Mysore, Karkataka (India).**

female 11587502, birth rate 30: 62 per 1000 population and life expectancy at birth 62: 8. The enrollment of high school students is growing every year. They are in need to know effective study method to continue their academic life.

Level of educational aspiration is as psychological construct, which reflects a cognitive type of motivation of the individual (Sharma & Gupta, 1980). The term level of aspiration involves the estimation of ones ability (whether over, under or realistic) for his/her future performance on the strenbrth of his/her past experience (goal discrepancy) his/her ability and capacity, the efforts that one can make toward attaining the goal thus set by him.

All aspirations are strivings for something beyond the person's present status. Aspirations can be divided into three major categories, positive and negative, immediate and remote, and realistic and unrealistic. Realistic aspirations lead to success, satisfaction and self-esteem. Unrealistic aspirations lead to failure accompanied by feelings of guilt, embarrassment, shame and unworthiness. The person who is unrealistic about what he wants to be and what he does usually finds it "burdensome" (Jersild, 1963). The more unrealistic the person is in his thinking, the greater will be the gap between his aspirations and achievement. This is where unreal has its most damaging effect on personality.

Educational aspiration is a strong desire to achieve higher education. Educational aspirations mainly depend upon academic performance. The prevailing trend among the students is that: when they know a better method to study and to achieve good score in the exams they are more inspired in their studies. Thus aspiration is altered by performance. Whatever task a student does are performed by a definite method. The same method does not apply to all tasks. Even the same task requires alternative methods as the time and situation changes. The same lesson applies to the students in their studies. They have to use different study techniques according to the nature of the subject matter for better performance, which will in turn yield more educational aspirations, Staton (1982).

The effects of achievement have greater impact on the person's personality because the person expects more from himself then from others. Educational aspiration shapes the personality of a person. According to the educational aspirations the students evaluate themselves and their self-concept, Gibson & Mtchell (2005).

A person's aspirations are determined by a feeling of inferiority in some physical or social relationship. In well adjusted people, the driving force behind the need for achievement or the "will to power", is adjusted to reality. In poorly adjusted people it is unrealistic and unrelated to social drives, thus leading to failure and maladjusted behaviour. While the well adjusted person generally tries to compensate for failure or weakness by excelling in activities in which his ability is greatest, the poorly adjusted overcompensates or tries to excel where he is the weakest in an attempt to deny his weakness, (Adler, 1925).

Students who are bright have more realistic aspiration at all ages than those of average or below average intelligence. They are better able to recognize their own weakness and environmental limitations. But the less bright students overestimate their abilities and they set unrealistic goals. Boys and men usually set a greater aspiration in school work, athletics and vocational advancement than girls and women. As a result they set aspirations above their capacities in these areas. In adulthood, sex differences in aspirations are even more marked than in childhood and adolescence. Men's aspirations concentrate on achievement whereas women's concentrate on personal attractiveness and social acceptance (Turner, 1964).

If the schools' system and government authorities are dictators, people are discouraged from developing higher aspirations. In democratic system people are encouraged to aspire high and are lauded for having higher aspirations. From the child hood they are told that everyone can be successful and they get equal opportunity for the success.

This is sad that often in democratic societies people are encouraged to have unrealistic aspirations. Most people discover that competition with those who are superior rarely leads to success. As a result they lower their aspirations. By adulthood, the pattern of aspiring to what others aspire to has become a well-established habit. Thus aspirations are more often influenced by competition with others than by individual's interests, abilities and needs.

According to Hurlock adolescence period is as follows: early adolescence 10-12 initial adolescence 13-16 late adolescence 17-21. According to Encyclopedia of educational psychology the period of adolescence of girls is generally 13-21 years and in the boys from 15 to 21 years.

Future success of an adolescent depends upon the norm of group. Cooperation education aspiration forms the group they belong. Adolescent learn the value of education from the teachers and the family members. They are too conscious about their own personality. This is thinking, logical power and decision-making age. The heart of adolescence is full of aspiration. They want to achieve some thing great. They want to follow the model of their heroes of great ideal person. If they are properly guided to give an outlet their energy for better education, they will utilize their abilities at optimum level, Kochhar (1989).

An investigation conducted by researchers Holland, *et. al.* (1990), found that classified vocational aspirations—singly or in combination—of Navy recruits (467 men and 250 women) were superior to the Vocational Preference Inventory. Predictions for persons with coherent vocational aspirations (aspirations all in the same occupational category) were very predictive over a short time interval.

To ensure academic success, the careful planning of class schedule is important. Study schedule should be realistic including other responsibilities. One of the worst habits students can develop are waste their time and money. The ability to retain and recall large amounts of information is essential for becoming an effective student; a good memory alone is not enough. In other words, being a good student requires more than the simple regurgitation of facts in an exam. One must also be able to take factual information and use it as a critical thinking to address key questions and solve problems, Brophy & Good (1986).

Schraw, *et.al.* (2007), conducted a grounded theory study of academic procrastination to explore adaptive and maladaptive aspects of procrastination and to help guide future empirical research. The authors describe in detail informants' perceptions of procrastination, which were used to construct a 5-component paradigm model that includes adaptive (i.e., cognitive efficiency, peak experience) and maladaptive (i.e., fear of failure, postponement) dimensions of procrastination. These dimensions, in turn, are related to conditions that affect the amount and type of procrastination, as' well as cognitive (i.e., prioritizing, optimization) and affective (i.e., reframing, self handicapping) coping mechanisms.

Different authors like Grouzet, *et.al.* (2005), investigated the structure of goal contents in a group of 1,854 undergraduates from 15 cultures around the world. Results suggested that the 11 types of goals the authors assessed were consistently organized in a circumplex fashion across the 15 cultures. The circumplex was well described by positing 2 primary dimensions underlying the goals: intrinsic (e.g., self-acceptance, affiliation) versus extrinsic (e.g., financial success, image) and self-transcendent (e.g., spirituality) *versus* physical (e.g., hedonism). The circumplex model of goal contents was also quite similar in both wealthier and poorer nations, although there were some slight cross-cultural variations.

A study by O'Brien, *et.al.* (2000), tested a proposed model investigating the relations among attachment to and separation from parents, career self-efficacy, and career aspiration over a 5-year period with a sample of 207 young women. Results suggested that being attached to parents may lead to the development of confidence in pursuing career-related tasks, which in turn influences career aspiration. Separation from parents did not have direct effects on career self-efficacy.

O'Malley, *et. al.* (1979), did an investigation where the self-esteem of 3,183 male and female seniors in a nationwide sample of the high school class of 1977. Comparisons were drawn with 1,715 males from the class of 1969. thus the study showed that educational accomplishments underwent a reduction in centrality--became less important-for self-esteem during the late teens and early twenties.

Korman, Abraham K. (1971) reports five studies which support the general proposition that high expectancies of competence by others are positively related to performance. Rosenfeld, Howard; Zander, Alvin (1961), conducted an investigation and the data were obtained from a questionnaire given to 400 boys in the 10th grade. Students tend to accept the teacher's suggestions for aspirations when they are rewarded, bu~ tend to ignore or oppose what teachers desire when indiscriminate coercion is perceived. These tendencies affect the degree to which students set their aspired grades congruent with their perceived capacities. Disapproval of inadequate performance appears to have no effect on aspiration, but disapproval of a good performance seems to have a negative effect. Tendencies to accept teacher influence are lowered under indiscriminate reward but increased by reward for adequate performance.

Method

A pre and posttest design with an intervention programme for experimental group is used. The independent variables were same in experimental and control groups. The dependent variable is the educational aspiration score of the students. There are two groups of participants:

(a) experimental group for which study method intervention is given; and

(b) control groups for which no study method intervention is given.

Sample

The sample is selected by using average basis (performance score of previous exam), from mountain, vaHey, hill and plain sectors' schools of Nepal. The sample consists 240 (boys and girls) who were average performer in their classes. The age ranges from 13 -18, mean age is 15.5 years. Then randomly assigned them in to two groups equally as experimental and control groups.

Measures

1. Personal information sheet used to know the following information:

   (i) Gender

   (ii) Age

   (iii) Grade

(iv) Name of school

(vi) District

(vii) Date

2. Educational Aspiration scale (EAS) for high Scholl students, developed by Sharma & Gupta (1980) was used to obtain the educational aspiration score of participating students. The EAS, consists 45 items alternative response either 'a' or 'b'. The participants have to response only one alternative for all 45 items.

The total educational aspiration score was obtained by adding the scores according to the following manner:

1. Alternate 'A' for question no: 2, 3, 5, 6, 10, 22, 23, 24, 25, 28, 29, 33, 35, 37 and 41 will count score 1.
2. Alternate 'B' for question no 1, 4, 7, 8, 9, 11, 12, 13, 14, 15, 16, 17, 18, 19, 20, 21, 26, 27, 30, 31, 32, 34, 36, 38, 39, 40, 42, 43, 44 and 45 will count score 1. The total score determines the standing on the scale of the individual.

Procedure

The selected 240 (boys and girls) participants were 'equally divided into two experimental groups and control groups randomly. The experimental groups were given PQRST study method intervention programme developed by Staton, Thomas F (1982). No intervention was given to control groups.

The intervention programme continued for 8 months and end of the every month one session (20 minutes motivating lecture and 80 minutes PQRST study method is taught to practice) by the investigator. After the intervention, the experimental and control groups were measured again on the dependent variable and obtained post test scores.

Result and Discussion

To assure the randomization data of the sample is tested using independent sample 't' test in the pre-test. The experimental and control groups mean score and S.D. are 28.62-4.54 and 29.60-3.73 respectively. The 't' values for the EAS is -1.833 and "P" is .068 Indicating a non-significant difference between experimental and control groups. General linear Model Repeated Measure of NAOVA is applied to know the effect of intervention programme on adjustment.

Between pre-test to post test scores there is no significant difference. But in compare to pre and post with group a significant difference was observed (F= 12.902; P< .000).Mean score of experimental group increased by 1.76 (pre-28.62 -Post 30.38) where control group has reduction by -.0.93

(Pre 29.60 - Post 28.67). However between subjects effect between experimental vis control and sector was found non significant. Subject's effects were found significant (F=1351.998; P < .000). Thus experimental group has better educational aspiration. From the mean aspirations score it is evident that schools of plain sector improved mean aspiration by 3.8 (pre 26.85- post 30.65) through the PQRST study method intervention.

Table 15.1: Mean and S.D of pre-test and post test score on educational aspiration of mountain, valley, hill and plain sectors' schools of both experimental and control groups on educational aspiration

Group	Sectors	Pre-test		Post-test		Change
		Mean	S.D	Mean	S.D	
Experimental	Mountain	29.70	5.32	30.75	43.25	1.05
	Valley	29.25	3.83	30.65	5.10	1.04
	Hill	28.33	4.96	29.78	5.21	1.45
	Plain	26.85	3.82	30.65	4.25	3.8
	Total	**28.62**	**4.54**	**30.38**	**4.84**	**1.76**
Control	Mountain	30.65	3.13	29.95	4.47	0.7
	Valley	29.55	3.62	28.83	4.63	0.72
	Hill	29.60	3.38	27.75	5.52	1.85
	Plain	28.65	5.00	28.90	5.78	0.22
	Total	**29.60**	**3.73**	**28.67**	**5.11**	**0.93**
Total	Mountain	30.17	4.22	30.35	4.36	0.18
	Valley	29.4	3.72	29.74	4.38	0.34
	Hill	28.96	4.17	28.76	5.36	0.2
	Plain	27.75	4.41	29.77	5.01	2.22
	Total	**29.07**	**4.13**	**29.65**	**4.89**	**0.58**

Table 15.2: Result of Repeated Measure ANOVA - Within and between subjects' effects for mean pre and post test scores of mountain, valley, hill and plain in experimental and control group on educational aspiration

Within-Subjects Effects					
Source of Variances	Sum of Squares	df	Mean Square	F	P
Pre-post test	36.426	1	36.426	2.451	.119 **
Exp-Con	191.709	1	191.709	12.902	.000*
Sectors	68.362	3	22.787	1.534	.207**
Exp-Con Sectors	15.029	3	5.010	.337	.798 **
Error (change)	3447.338	232	14.859		

* = Significant

** = No Significant

(Contd...)

Between- Subjects Effects					
Exp-Cont	7.176	1	7.176	.264	.608 **
Sectors	139.304	3	46.435	1.705	.167 **
Exp-Cont	13.238	3	4.413	.162	.922 **
Sectors					
Error	6316.688	232	27.227		

* = Significant

** = No significant.

Summary

The PQRST study method intervention increased educational aspiration of the students of experimental groups. This study method is useful to promote academic performance. The study also has significance for school teachers, parents, counselors and government policy maker. Finding can be use by these specialists to design intervention programme, for better educational aspiration of high school students.

REFERENCES

Adler, A. (1925). *Individual Psychology*, New York: Harcourt Brace.

Brophy, J, E., & Good, T. (1986). *Teacher Behaviour and Student Achievement: Handbook of Research on Teaching*. In M. Wittrock (Ed.), New York: Macmillan, 328-375.

Fry, Ron. (2005). *How to Study Programme*. Thomson Delmar Learning.

Gibson, Robert L., & Mtchell, Marianne H. (2005). *Introduction to Counselling and Guidance* (6th Ed.). Delhi: Pearson Education.

Grouzet, Frederick M.E., Kasser, Tim., Ahuvia, Aaron., Dols, Jose Miguel Fernandez., Kim, Youngmee., Lau, Sing., Ryan, Richard M., Saunders, Shaun., Schmuck, Peter., Sheldon, Kennon M (2005). *Journal of Personality and Social Psychology*, 89(5), 800816.

Holland, John L., Gottfredson, Gary D., Baker, Herbert G. (1990). Validity of Vocational Aspirations and Interest Inventories: Extended, Replicated, and Reinterpreted. *Journal (if Counselling Psychology*, 37(3), July 1990, 337-342.

Kochhar, S.K. (1989). *Guidance & Counselling*. New Delhi: Sterling Pub. Pvt. Ltd. L-10 Green Park.

Korman, Abraham K (1971). Expectancies As Determinants of Performance. *Journal of Applied Psychology*, 55(3), 218-222.

Kuhlen, R. G. (1963). Needs, Perceived Need Satisfaction, Opportunities, and Satisfaction with Occupation. *Journal of Applied Psychology*, 47, 56-64.

Ministry of Education, Nepal in Figure-2005. *Central Bureau of Statistics*. Retrieved January 4, 2007 from http://www.moe.gov.np

O' Brien, Karen M., Friendman, Suzanne Miller., Tipton, Linda c., Linn, Sonja Geschmay (2000). Attachment, Separation, and Women's Vocational Development: A Longitudinal Analysis. *Journal Counselling Psychology*, 47 (3), 301-31.

O' Malley, Patrick M., Bachman, Jerald G (1979). Self-esteem and Education: Sex and Cohort Comparisons Among High School Seniors. *Journal of Personality and Social Psychology,* 37(7), 1153-1159.

Rosenfeld, Howard., & Zander, Alvin (1961). The Influence of Teachers on Aspirations of Students. *Journal of Educational Psychology,* 52(1), 1-11.

Schraw, Gregory; Wadkins, Theresa; Olafson, Lori,(2007). *Journal of Educational Psychology.* Vol. 99(1) 12-25.

Shaffer, L.F., & EJ. Shoben. (1956). *The Psychology Adjustment,* (2nd Ed.), Boston: Houghton Mifflin.

Sharma V.P; Gupta Anuradha (1980). *Manual for Educational Aspiration Scale* (EAS) Agra: National Psychological Corporation.

Staton, Thomas F. (1982). *How to Study*? Nashville TA: Distributor: Post Box; 40273, 37204.

Turner, R.H. (1964). *Some Aspects of Women's Ambition.* Amer. J. Social. 70, 271-285.

16

Impact of Life Skills Counselling on Suicidal Depression Among Alcoholics

Manjunatha, P.[1]
Venkateshkumar G.[1]

ABSTRACT

The aim of the study is to determine the effectiveness of Lifeskills counselling as intervention for reducing the symptoms of suicidal depression among alcoholics. An experimental design, with treatment and control group is used. The sample is selected by using convenience basis, from K.R. Govt. Hospital and JSS General Hospital, Mysore. Alcoholics are diagnosed by qualified medical officials. The sample of 120, both urban and rural adult males with high score on suicidal depression is considered. Catttell's Clinical Analysis Questionnaire Part-II (CAQ) was used to assess the participants' symptoms. General Linear Model Repeated Measures of ANOVA is applied to the know effect of intervention programme. A significant 'F' was observed indicating differential decrease for experimental and control groups in the symptoms of suicidal depression.

Introduction

In the Asian sub continent, per capita alcohol consumption increased by over 50 per cent between 1980 and 2000 (WHO, 2002), while India has experienced a 115 per cent increase in per capita alcohol consumption by adults since 1980 (Rahman, L., 2002). In India alcohol addiction has adverse health and social consequences, ranging from shifting the use of resources

1. **Professor, Department of Studies in Psychology, University of Mysore, Mysore, Karnataka (India).**

away from basic necessities such as food and shelter, to acquit consequences for the welfare of other members of the household especially children and women (Bonu, S., 2004). India is likely to face a heavy burden of medical and social problems due to increased alcohol consumption (Mohan, D., *et.al.*, 2001).

The World Health Organization (2004) estimates that there are about 2 billion people worldwide who consume alcoholic beverages and 76.3 million with diagnosable alcohol use disorders. From a public health perspective, the global burden related to alcohol consumption, both in terms of morbidity and mortality, is considerable in most parts of the world. Alcohol consumption has health and social consequences via intoxication (drunkenness), alcohol dependence, and other biochemical effects of alcohol. In addition to chronic diseases that may affect alcohol after many years of heavy use, alcohol contributes to traumatic outcomes that kill or disable at a relatively young age, resulting in the loss of many years of life due to death or disability. Alcohol causes 1.8 million deaths (3.2% of total) and a loss of 58.3 million (4% of total) of Disability-Adjusted Life Years (DALY). Unintentional injuries alone account for about one third of the 1.8 million deaths, while neuro-psychiatric conditions account for close to 40 per cent of the 58.3 million DALYs (WHO, 2002). The estimates suggest that alcohol related problems to the society are of great magnitude and need urgent attention of social scientists. Alcohol has implicated in a variety of mental disorders which are not alcohol-specific. However, before the GBD 2000 study no major overview on alcohol-attributable burden of disease has included these conditions (English et al., 1995; Gutjahr, Gmel & Rehm, 2001; Single *et al.*, 1999). While the causality of the relation is hard to define, sufficient evidence now exists to assume alcohol's causal role in depression, a common mental disorder. Adityanjee, M. D. and Wig, N. N. (1989) report that alcohol-related problems made up 17.6 per cent of the case load of psychiatric emergencies in an Indian General Hospital.

In the general population, alcohol dependence and major depression co-occur over proportionally, on both a 12-month and a lifetime basis (Kessler *et al.*, 1997; Lynskey, 1998). Among alcohol consumers in the general population, higher volume of consumption is associated with more symptoms of depression (Graham & Schmidt, 1999; Mehrabian, 2001; Rodgers *et al.*, 2000). Among patients in treatment for alcohol abuse and dependence, the prevalence of major depression is higher than in the general population (Lynskey, 1998; Schuckit *et al.*, 1997). Higher prevalence of alcohol use disorders has been documented for patients in treatment for depression (Blixen, McDougall & Suen, 1997). This suggests that alcohol use disorders are linked to depressive symptoms, and that alcohol dependence and depressive disorders co-occur to a larger degree than expected by chance.

In male alcoholics, major depression has a five per cent lifetime prevalence rate, compared to three per cent for the total male population. In the DSM-IV (APA, 1994), mood disorders must be of sufficient duration and intensity that they cause significant subjective distress or dysfunction in one or more of life's roles (relationships, work, and school). The Epidemiologic Catchment Area (ECA) data (1989), as cited in Frances & Miller (1991) indicate that major depression and dysthymia occur at least one and half times more often in alcoholics than in the general population. In addition, depression is associated with an elevated risk of suicide (Bernheim, 1997). Cattell, R.B. (1973) states that suicidal depression factor centers on thoughts of self-destruction. Individuals report that they are disgusted with life, that life has become empty and meaningless. They entertain thoughts of death as a viable alternative to their present, hopeless situation. In short they have reached the end of their rope. Cattell further says that these factors are common to alcoholics.

People with alcohol dependency need psycho-social interventions for a variety of psychiatric and personality problems in general and suicidal depression in particular. So far, most of the interventions have focused on stress management training, exercise and cognitive therapy to promote adaptation, reduce depression, anxiety and psychological stress to enhance quality of life. A more intensive and focused intervention may be necessary to meet the specialized needs of alcoholics with multiple medical, social, and economic challenges. Lifeskills counseling is more suitable and an intensive intervention that combines individual psychological care to provide intensive on-going support in many factors of depression.

Richard Nelson-Jones (2000), considered that with the knowledge of lifeskills person would possess awareness in each of these areas; responsiveness, realism, relating, rewarding activity, and right-and-wrong. He advocated lifeskills counseling as a "people-centered approach for assisting clients and others to develop self-helping skills". He designed a five-stage lifeskills counseling model DASIE, for helping clients to manage problems. DASIE is not only for managing or solving problems but also for addressing underlying problematic skills. The model provides a framework or set of guidelines for counsellor choices.

In the present study it is aimed to determine the effectiveness of Lifeskills counseling as intervention for reducing suicidal depression in the people with alcohol dependence. The study utilized the dependent variable of suicidal depression to assess the effectiveness of Lifeskills counseling as intervention and gain insight and understanding of people with alcohol dependence.

Method

An experimental pre and post test design, with a treatment and control group, is used. The independent variables varied in the two treatment conditions; experimental and control groups. The dependent variable is the participant's symptoms of suicidal depression. There are two groups of participants:

(a) experimental group for which the Lifeskills counseling is given;

(b) control group for which no Lifeskills counseling is given.

Sample

The sample is selected by using convenience basis, from K.R. Govt. Hospital and JSS General Hospital, Mysore city - alcoholic dependents as diagnosed by qualified medical officials. They are under treatment for de-addiction. The sample consists of 120, both urban and rural adult males with high score on suicidal depression. The age ranges from 25-53; with the mean age 38.12 years.

Measures

(a) Personal Information Schedule (PIS) is used to know the following information:

1. Gender
2. Age
3. Marital Status
4. Domicile
5. Educational Level
6. Occupation

(b) Cattell's Clinical Analysis Questionnaire Part-II (CAQ) was used to assess the participants' symptoms of suicidal depression.

The CAQ part-II (1973), Questionnaire consists of 144 multiple choice items representing either a symptom or attitude related to clinical factors of personality. It contains 12 factors for which multiple choice responses are given. The participants were asked to select a single answer in each question that corresponds most clearly with his actual condition at that particular time. Each factor describes a specific manifestation of clinical factors of personality. Only one factor is utilized in this chapter.

Procedure

The CAQ part-II is administered to a large number of alcoholics. Those scored above the median level on the questionnaire, are selected for further study. The selected 120 participants were equally divided into two groups –

experimental and control group, randomly. The experimental group was given treatment with the five stages of Lifeskills counseling model (DASIE) developed by Richard Nelson Jones. No treatment was given to control group but was kept under observation including the self-introduction. The time schedule for intervention is one hour duration per session and two sessions per week. Total of 20 sessions are given spreading through two and a half month approximately. After the intervention, the experimental and control groups are measured again on the dependent variable and obtained post test scores.

Results and Discussion

To assure the randomization of the sample the data are subjected to independent samples 't' test in the pre-test. The experimental and control group's mean score and S.D. for suicidal depression are 09.60, 0.49 and 09.43, 0.56 respectively. The 't' values are 1.723 and 'p' is 0.088 indicating a non-significant difference between experimental and control groups. Thus the equating as well as randomization of the groups was taken care of during the pre-test situation. General Linear Model Repeated Measures of ANOVA is applied to the know effect of intervention programme.

Repeated Measures of ANOVA revealed a significant decrease from pre to post test situation irrespective of the groups. 'F' value is 2756.250, found to be highly significant ($p < 0.000$). Irrespective of the groups in pre-test the mean suicidal depression score 9.52 is reduced to 6.02 with the reduction of 3.5 scores which found to be significant. When reduction in the suicidal depression scores with reference to groups are concerned again a significant 'F' is observed ($F=2916.000$; $p < 0.000$) indicating differential decrease for experimental and control groups. From mean values it is evident that experimental group had a reduction of 7.1 scores (from 9.60 to 2.50), where as control group had reduction of only — 0.1 scores (from 9.43 to 9.53). So the decrease in the suicidal depression has basically in the experimental group which can be attributed to the effectiveness of Lifeskills Counselling. However, the interaction effect between domicile groups with respect to change in the scores and domicile groups with respect to groups and change in scores are found to be non-significant. Between-subjects effects between groups (irrespective of conditions) together significant difference are observed ($F = 2605.719$; $p<0.000$). However, domicile groups wise and interaction between groups and domicile groups is found to be non-significant.

Conclusion

The Lifeskills counseling intervention has reduced symptoms of suicidal depression in alcoholic dependents. The major implication of this study is that it indicates a need for a possible shift in the thinking of the health policy makers of our country. The study has implications for the public health approach to the care and prevention. The study also has significance for psychological counselors, social workers and policy makers. Findings can be used by these specialists to design intervention programmes aimed at sustaining people with alcohol dependence in good health.

Table 16.1: Mean and S.D. of pre-test and post-test scores on suicidal depression of alcoholics of both experimental and control groups

Group	Domicile	Pre-test		Post-test		Change
		Mean	S.D.	Mean	S.D.	
Experimental	Urban	9.40	.50	2.50	.51	6.9
	Rural	9.80	.41	2.50	.63	7.3
	Total	**9.60**	**.49**	**2.50**	**.57**	**7.1**
Control	Urban	9.47	.51	9.53	.57	- 0.06
	Rural	9.40	.62	9.53	.51	- 0.13
	Total	**9.43**	**.56**	**9.53**	**.54**	**- 0.1**
Total	Urban	9.43	.50	6.02	3.59	3.41
	Rural	9.60	.56	6.02	3.59	3.58
	Total	**9.52**	**.53**	**6.02**	**3.57**	**3.5**

Table 16.2: Summary results of GLM — Repeated Measures of ANOVA within and between subjects for suicidal depression of Experimental and Control groups in pre-test and post-test situations

Source of variance	Sum of Squares	df	Mean Squares	F	P
Within-subjects Effects					
Pre-Post test	735.000	1	735.000	2756.250	0.000*
Expt-Control	777.600	1	777.600	2916.000	0.000*
Urban-Rural	0.417	1	0.417	1.563	0.214**
Expt-Control Urban-Rural	0.817	1	0.817	3.063	0.083**
Error (Change)	29.867	112	0.267		
Between-subjects Effects					
Intercept	14477.067	1	14477.067	53336.567	0.000*
Expt-Control	707.267	1	707.267	2605.719	0.000*
Urban-Rural	0.417	1	0.417	1.535	0.218**
Expt-Control Urban-Rural	0.817	1	0.817	3.009	0.086**
Error	30.400	112	0.271		

* HS = Highly Significant

** NS = Not Significant

REFERENCES

Adityanjee, M.D., Wig, N.N. (1989). Alcohol Related Problems in the Emergency Room of an Indian General Hospital. *Australian and New Zealand Journal of Psychiatry*, 23, 274-278.

American Psychiatric Association (1994). *Diagnostic and Statistical Manual of Mental Disorders* (4th ed.). Washington, DC: American Psychiatric Association.

Bernheim, K.F. (1997). *The Lanahan Cases and Readings in Abnormal Behaviour*. New York: Lanahan Publishers, Inc.

Blixen, C.E., McDougall, G.J., & Suen, L. J. (1997). Dual Diagnosis in Elders Discharged from a Psychiatric Hospital. *International Journal of Geriatric Psychiatry*, 12, 307-313.

Bonu, S. (2004). *Household Tobacco and Alcohol Use and Child Health: An Exploratory Study from India*. Health Policy, 70, 67-83.

Cattell, R.B. (1973). A Check on the 28 Factor Clinical Analysis Questionnaire Structure on Normal and Pathological Subjects. In, Samuel, E. Krug (1980). *Clinical Analysis Questionnaire Manual*. Illinois: Institute for Personality and Ability Testing.

English, D.R., *et.al.* (1995). *The Quantification of Drug Caused Morbidity and Mortality in Australia-*1992. Canberra: Commonwealth Department of Human Services and Health.

Frances, R.J. & Miller, S.I. (1991). *Clinical Textbook of Addiction Disorders* (2nd ed.). New York, NY: Guilford Publications.

Graham, K., & Schmidt, G. (1999). Alcohol Use and Psycho-social Well-being Among Older Adults. *Journal of Studies on Alcohol*, 60, 345-351.

Gutjahr, E., Gmel, G. & Rehm, J. (2001). *Relation Between Average Alcohol Consumption and Disease*: An Overview. European Addiction Research, 7, 117-127.

Kessler, R.C., *et al.* (1997). Lifetime Co-occurrence of DSM-III-R Alcohol Abuse and Dependence with Other Psychiatric Disorders in the National Comorbidity Survey. *Archives of General Psychiatry*, 54, 313-321.

Lynskey, M.T. (1998). The Co-morbidity of Alcohol Dependence and Affective Disorders: Treatment Implications. *Drug and Alcohol Dependence*, 52, 201-209.

Mehrabian, A. (2001). General Relations Among Drug Use, Alcohol Use, and Major Indexes of Psychopathology. *Journal of Psychology*, 135, 71-86.

Mohan, D., Chopra, A., Ray, R., & Sethi, H. (2001). Alcohol Consumption in India: A Cross-sectional Study. In, Demers, A., Room, R. & Bourgault, C. Surveys of Drinking Patterns and Problems in Seven Developing Countries. Geneva: World Health Organization.

Nelson-Jones, R. (2000). Lifeskills Counselling. In, Stephen Palmer (edr.). *Introduction to Counselling and Psychotherapy*. New Delhi: Sage.

Rahman, L. (2002). *Alcohol Prohibition and Addictive Consumption in India*. London: London School of Economics.

Rodgers, B., *et. al.* (2000). Non-linear Relationships in Associations of Depression and Anxiety with Alcohol Use. *Psychological Medicine*, 30, 421-432.

Schuckit, M.A., et.al. (1997). *The Life-time Rates of Three Major Mood Disorders and Four Major Anxiety Disorders in Alcoholics and Controls*. Addiction, 92, 1289-1304.

Single, E., *et.al.* (1999). Morbidity and Mortality Attributable to Alcohol, Tobacco, and Illicit Drug Use in Canada. *American Journal of Public Health*, 89, 385-390.

World Health Organization (2004). *Global Status Report on Alcohol-2004*. Geneva.

World Health Organization 2002. *The World Health Report 2002 — Reducing Risks, Promoting Healthy Life*. Geneva.

17

Marginalization of Women
Its Influence on Mental Health Well-being and Productivity

Geetha Appachu[1]

ABSTRACT

From womb to grave, in times of peace as well as war; women face discrimination at the hands of the state, community and the family. Female infanticide deprives countless women of life itself. Every year partners, relatives, friends and strangers, by employers, colleagues and security officials, rape millions of women. 'Marginalized women' today are the focus of concern and, several of their issues are strongly debated to bring about positive changes. Relief's, improvements and facilities for various groups of marginalized women are remarkable achievements in the progress of our present society. Several professional bodies have highlighted their efforts to support different marginalized women sectors but have also mentioned their concern about its very existence and alarming increase in the size of these sectors. Current world scenario indicates the role of various organizations in working for the cause of different sectors of marginalized woman. Has the momentous of this work shadowed the issue of 'marginalization of women'?

Looking into the various definitions of the concept "Marginalization" we can have following:

- Margin is the line we draw to mark the difference between the main area, the line that marks corner area and the line that marks the non-used areas.

1. **Consultant Psychologist, Bangalore, Karnataka (India).**

- Marginal means insignificant/barely adequate
- Marginalize means, make or treat as insignificant
- Marginalized means, prevent from having attention or power

With an objective to highlight the influence of this marginalization on health, well-being and productivity, we need to view health as multi-dimensional, espousing a social model of health (WHO Ottawa charter for Health Promotion, 1986).

The definition of mental health used in 1981 WHO report on social dimensions of mental health states that:

> "Mental health is the capacity of the individual, the group and the environment to interact with one another in ways that promote subjective well being, the optimal development and the use of mental abilities (cognitive, affective and relational), the achievement of individual and collective goals consistent with justice and the attainment and preservation of conditions of fundamental equality".

The definition has several advantages in relation to women's mental health because it:

- Stresses the complex web of interrelationships that determine mental health and that the factors that determine health operate on multiple levels.
- Goes beyond the biological and the individual.
- Acknowledge the crucial role of the social context.
- Highlights the importance of justice and equality in determining mental well-being.

The definition does not mention gender, but gender can impact on the production of mental health at every level- the individual, the group and the environment and is critically implicated in the differential delivery of justice and equality. Gender configures both the material and symbolic position women occupy in social hierarchy as well as the experiences, which condition their lives.

Maximalists who believe that there are fundamental differences between men and women have viewed male behaviour as the norm, so women are always compared to men. Feminist theorists have recently argued, women's well-being is not solely determined by biological factors and reproduction, but also by the effects of workload, nutrition, stress, etc. It is also very important to sight psychological boundaries for every one in society when we consider health, both mental and physical. Although psychological boundaries are not so readily apparent as geographical borders or physical intrusions, they are just as real because psychological boundaries represent our unique inner territory.

Today, various sectors do convince our society of the marginalization. Unfolding our understanding of marginalization will aptly begin by looking into the ancient Indian society. By advocating separate expectations for the behaviour of men and women, the Ramayana successfully served to reinforce India's patriarchal structure. The sex appropriate ideals that are prominent throughout the Ramayana were a reflection of the values that structures ancient Indian society. The epic expresses that there are different expectations for the behaviour of women and that of their male counterparts.

The virtuous women of the story possess exaggerated feminine qualities while the immortal women's actions more closely resemble the behaviour of the men. In either case, the women are subordinate and are considered possessions rather than partners. Urmila, wife of Lakshmana — her life stands up to speak and indicate marginalization of women. Lakshmana accompanying Rama in his exile is said to have acted according to will without giving a thought to the sensitivity of women. No doubt, his cause was noble but we must also remember that he got married in fact, at the same time as Rama. His filial duty was so strong that he felt his wife's presence would be an obstruction in his performance, so he did not consider taking Urmila along to the forest even when she wanted to. Urmila spent those 14 years in front of an oil lamp, continuously feeding it with oil in order to keep the flame burning — always afraid and hoping that the flame indicated her husband's safety. In the story, women are subordinate to all men, even the evil ones. The pious women are portrayed as child like and na"ive, lacking intelligence to make decisions or to protect themselves.

One of the greatest works of our Indian Literature — Mahabharata also depicts women characters quite critically. On reading the Mahabharata, a reader realizes that women's behaviour is mainly criticized and condemned basically because they violated social norms and fail to contribute to the family unity as Ganga, Amba and in a way, Draupadi did. Mahabharatha incorporated philosophical, religious and social basic ideas of the traditional Indian society.

The marginalization of women is not culture specific as other texts from the west also had similar concepts. The birth of Helen of Troy was the consequence of an evening of notorious seduction or deception. Marginalization is the foundation of Helen's existence — deception, manipulation and rape, and the inability to know her origins. We can question the powers of this character, where it was found that, others determined her every move! The most obvious marginalization here is the object of the gaze- an object inherently passive, in the control of the subject.

Although controversial, the functioning of women in our society indicates marginalization. Women's development across her life span in our society today indicates that in the family, in the community, at work, there are unique issues and problems that they confront. Infancy issues like ear piercing, colour of cloths, colour and types of toys, childhood issues like work distribution told by parents to girls, sex appropriate dressing, sex appropriate behaviour and games is evident of marginalization. During adolescence and as young adults issues of falling in love always have a different perspective for girls, where most communities disown them. Issues of menopause have always explained that females are silent victims while male menopause has always got the necessary medical attention. At the workplace, popular sayings like, "Think Manager. ... think MALE; Think Secretary ... think female" have always existed.

Massachusetts Institute of Technology (MIT) — 2002 report on the status of women faculty explains specific manifestations of marginalization and the inequalities that can arise from it. Of the several points highlighted it speaks of marginalization having a cumulative and deleterious effects on faculty members productivity. It leads to professional exclusion and a sense of being undervalued. This report was an outcome of a study to provide support to women's career.

Marginalization can take many forms and can occur for complex reasons. Consider the mental health issues of women. Depression in women manifests in headaches, sleepless nights, constant tension, detachment, irritability, loss of appetite, fear, self-blame, lack of concentration, lack of interest in any kind of activity. Psycho-social stressors originate from the external social environment such as women's inferior social position, lack of power; homelessness, economic hardships and man-made and natural disasters. They create learned helplessness and reduce motivation to lead an active life.

Over the past century, the landscape of war has featured many intractable conflicts that have taken millions of lives. Both men and women suffer negatively and participate as aggressors, but women are more susceptible to harm and abuse in the environment racked by violent conflicts whether or not they are engaged in conflict. Even in the absence of war, women's lives are subject to neglect and exploitation. Commonly, female lives are valued less which is obvious in events like female infanticide, they have fewer opportunities for education and training, they do not have access to critical health information, their decision making capability is non-existent and they suffer as victims of domestic violence.

In today's society, women are routinely terrorized, raped, mutilated, abducted into slavery, murdered and exploited. This physical harm is likely to impact the victims psychologically. In addition, these women who are the victims are looked upon as bringing shame to the society. This might lead them to disguise or hide their injuries, leading to grievous mental or physical harm. For example, refusing counseling, concealing symptoms of sexually transmitted diseases and avoiding prenatal care.

Psychiatric labelling does not take cognizance of material reality faced by women on day-to-day experiential levels. The Universalist approach uses diagnostic categories of mental illnesses such as neurosis, psychosis, mania, phobia, paranoia so on and so forth. The philosophical basis of psychiatry as a bio-medical discipline prevents mental health professionals to take into consideration larger reality and macro issues resulting from socio-economic and other factors. Limitations of the bio-medical perspectives lie in their narrow focus on somatic and psychological factors in their diagnostic efforts, ignoring the impact of socio-cultural and socio-demographic factors. Marginalization of mental health concerns results from the understanding that mental distress is a manifestation of an individual problem, not directly related to social oppression and not common to all women. Focus is more on the treatment of the illness, not on preventive and promotive efforts.

Implications of such reading may evolve personal responsibility in generations to come, to address our roles in the issues of marginalization, and be the true contributors of world peace, well-being and productivity.

An Unknown Author wrote.

HERE'S TO THE WOMEN....

Who knows where she is going

And will keep on until she gets there;

Who knows not only what she wants from life But what she has to offer in return.

Here's to the woman

who is loyal to family and friends,

who expects no more from others'

than she is willing to give.

Here's to the woman

Who guides and inspires

Not by quoting others' philosophies

But by living her own good example.

Who accepts both victories and disappointments

with the same grace

And who can rise above life's challenges

and move on...

Here's to the woman
Who gives the gifts of her thoughtfulness,
who shows her caring with a word of support,
her understanding with a smile;
A woman who brings joy to others just by being herself.

REFERENCES

Ahuja N. (2004). *A Short Text Book of Psychiatry*, 5th Edition. Jaypee Brothers Medical Publishers Pvt. Ltd., New Delhi.

Behera J.R. (1998) *Political Socialization of Women*. Atlantic Publishers, New Delhi.

Bhatia A. (2000). *Women's Development and NGO's*. Rawat Publications, Jaipur.

Eade D. (2006). *Development with Women*. Rawat Publications, Jaipur.

Fellin P. (1996). *Mental Health and Mental Illness: Policies, Pragrammes and Services*, Peacock Publishers Inc, Illinois, U.S.A.

Gelder M., *et al* (2006). *Psychiatry*, 3.0 Edition. Oxford University Press, New Delhi.

Jefferson J.W., Griest JH, Ackerman OM (1983) *Lithium Encyclopedia for Clinical Practice*, American Psychiatric Press, Washington D.C.

John E Hary and Nair J (1998) *Question of Silence: The Sexual Economics of Modern India*. Paul's Press, Oakland.

Kapur R (1996) *Feminist Terrains in Legal Domains*. Rai Press, New Delhi.

Koss MP (1990). *The Women's Mental Health Research Agenda*. American Psychologist.

Loutfi MF (2001) *Women Gender and Work*, Rawat Publishers, New Delhi.

Malhotra M (2004) *Empowerment of Women*, Chawla Offset Press, New Delhi.

Miskaben SM (1996). *To Survive and to Prevail*. Chaman Offset Printers, New Delhi.

Mohanty B (2005). *Violence Against Women*, Kanishka Publishers, New Delhi.

Naber B (1995). *Caste As Women*, Penguin Books, India.

Rodden J (2004). *The Philosophy of Psychiatry*, Oxford University Press, New York

Rayaprol A (1997) *Women in the Indian Diaspora*, Oxford University Press, New Delhi.

Sharma SP (2005). *Fundamentals of Mental Health Education*, Kanishka Publishers, New Delhi.

Singh B (2004). *Working Women in India*. Anmol Publications Ltd. New Delhi.

18

Media's Role in Women's Assessment of Self Image

Manika Ghosh[1]
Murali Mohan N.[2]

ABSTRACT

Women are equal or near equal to men in as far as sheer number is concerned, constituting almost 50 per cent of the world population. However, it is common knowledge that this is where all comparisons end. Women's lives, the social pressures they are subjected to and the compulsions to comply with them are in great measure a contrast to that of men. Society holds certain beauty myths, and women are condemned for not taking care of themselves, "since it implies defying hierarchy of men in society" (Smolak & Moore, 2007). Media, which is a powerful tool influencing public opinion, has only been propagating these myths. As a result women's body image has undergone a significant change over the years. This has created another form of psychosocial control over women. This paper tries to examine the impact of mass media on women's lives in relation to their physical and psychological health.

From the earliest humans, women have been associated with sexuality (Salisbury, 2007). Although modem civilization has brought about socio-economic and political changes women's live and the way women are viewed

1. **Professor & HOD, Dept. of Psychology, Maharani's Science College, Bangalore, Karnataka (India).**

2. **CIIL, Mysore, Nanjunda Road Trust, Mysore, Karnataka (India).**

have changed little. Patriarchal society that we live in even today expects women to achieve certain standards of aesthetics, although it is physically, emotionally and financially costly (Travis & Payne, 2007).

Women's lives, the social pressures they are subjected to and the compulsions to comply with them are in great measure a contrast to that of men. Although they constitute nearly 50 per cent of the world population their social status is lower than that of men. Women, throughout times around the world have been viewed as an object of sexuality (Salisbury, 2001). Her role has been one of a procreator; therefore her life is seen as revolving around child bearing and child rearing. Archaeological excavations of societies that existed 4-6 thousand years ago have unearthed one of the earliest portrayals of women in petroglyphs, hieroglyphs and burial statuettes, representing women essentially with characteristics of fertility and nurturance and men with hunting or warring (Friedman & Schustack, 2004) although this did not necessarily mean a rigid difference in status. With time however, gender difference was formalized by identifying women not only as different but lesser. Plato described women as weaker and inferior. Aristotle very specifically depicted women as incomplete and incompetent. In the Christian Bible too men were described as possessing higher moral authority.

In later years psychologists too subscribed to this view of women's inferiority. Under Jarwin's influence the functional school of psychology (late 1800s — early 1900s) declared that behaviour and thought evolve as a result of their functionality for survival. According to functionalists (all males) women's energies was to be expended on pregnancy, childbirth and lactation with no resources remaining for developing her abilities (Lips & Colwill, 1978). The first modern comprehensive theory of personality that addressed the etiology of gender differences was that of Sigmund Freud who explained the sexual dimorphism or gender difference in terms of physical difference in genitals declaring that 'anatomy is destiny'. His theory further promoted concept of women being incomplete and inferior to man (Freud, 1979). Males and females look so different and have such different sex organs and hormones". It it is assumed they must think, act and feel differently too. Besides, there is a contribution of power to the social roles of males who is seen as protector and provider. These concepts were used to both explain and justify the dominant position:' men and submissive position of women in the contemporary society. Thus gender saying that is one of the most basic social categorizing gave way to gender stereotype, a pre-conceived notion of the traits supposedly possessed by males and females (Unger & Crawford, 1993). Gender stereotype that existed for long only conveniently explained by the theories of psychology.

In Indian scenario women's position has not been any better, rather worse in many cases. Paradoxically while on one hand women are worshipped as an embodiment of 'Shakti' or power on the other hand no efforts are spared to render her 'Nishakti' — a powerless, helpless object. Akin to this inferior status of women in society and her role as a procreator is the emphasis on her sexuality and a need to look desirable. Physical attributes of women have been described at great lengths in our mythology, literature, sculpture, paintings and even in temple arts. Patriarchal society that we live in expects women to achieve certain standards of aesthetics. Society holds certain beauty myths that have been handed down through ages. Following are some of the beauty myths:

(a) Beauty is inherent therefore certain women inherently occupy a privileged position;

(b) Beauty is the measure of feminity;

(c) One must continuously strive towards achieving beauty;

(d) Beauty comes from within therefore it is an indication of goodness or virtue;

(e) The most common myth is that there is only one perfect most beautiful woman;

(f) The fairest of fair. This implies that each woman should strive to become the chosen one in orderto avoid being considered inherently deficient.

These beauty myths are so strong that the whole social fabric revolves around these. Women strive hard to achieve them although it is physically, emotionally and financially costly (Travis & Payne, 2001). They are condemned for not taking care of themselves, "since it implies defying hierarchy of men in society" (Smolak & Moore, 2001). Women therefore are subjected to social pressures to comply with the socially constructed standards of beauty. These standards may be culturally determined, just as small feet of women in olden days China and long necks in some African tribes women were considered beautiful in their respective cultures. Inherent to these standards of beauty is a strong emphasis on youthfulness and condescension for ageing. In certain cultures menopause for example is viewed as a disorder (Griffen, 1977), for it is associated with feeling of loss of fertility and or feminity.

However, women's movement of the 1970s signalled a major shift in women's roles in society and a change in perspective on gender differences. It is interesting to note that these changes also coincided with women now for the first time being admitted to many prestigious colleges, and moving in larger numbers to higher status careers such as medicine, law and business. This made people less likely to assume women to be inferior. This trend of women's empowerment and enhancement of economic status soon spread to the rest of the world. India too was not far behind. Women moved on from traditionally female jobs like secretaries, nurses, teachers, bookkeepers to other high paying professions entering every male bastion. They joined the administrative services, technical field, police, military etc. The literacy rate and also women joining portals of higher education gradually but steadily improved throughout the world. The number of women in the different work force steadily expanded, in the last few decades, and the feminist movements have been far reaching, yet there has been little change in gender stereotypes (Fan & Marini, 2000, Spence & Buckner, 2000) gender stereotypes have proved to be remarkably enduring. A study by Helgeson (1994) found physical appearance comes more to mind when thinking of a woman than a man. This has been found true across cultures. A study of an ethnically diverse sample of students from the University of Houston were asked to list the first 10 adjectives that came to mind when they thought of members of a particular group. Each participant was asked to describe eight groups that varied in gender and ethnicity. In three out of the four ethnic groups only women were described as attractive, a clear physical trait. The results are shown in the Table 18.1.

Table 18.1: Table showing stereotypes toward men and women from different ethnic groups

Gender	African American	Asian American	Anglo American	Mexican American
Women	Speak loudly Dark skin Antagonistic Athletic Pleasant and Friendly	Intelligent Speak softly Pleasant and Friendly Short Attractive Intelligent	Attractive Intelligent Egotistical Pleasant and Friendly Blond or light hair	Black, Brown or dark hair Attractive Pleasant and Friendly Lower class Dark skin
Men	Athletic Antagonistic Dark skin Muscular Criminal activities	Short Achievement Upper class Oriented Speak softly Hardworking	Intelligent Egotistical Pleasant and Friendly Racist	Lower class Hard working Antagonistic Dark skin No college Education

Adapted from Niemann *et.al.* (1994), (as found in Taylor *et.al.* 2006, Helgeson 2006).

In job field too although women match men in education, skills and motivation gender bias continues to follow them. They are believed to be less employable and promtable and to have less ability to make decisions and to cope with stress (Rudman & Glick, 1999). A male employer may compliment a woman employee on her attractiveness rather than on her competence and offer her an easy job (Munson, *et. al.*, 2000).

Media's Portrayal of Women

Stereotypes by definition are "beliefs about the typical characteristics of group members" (Taylor *et.al*, 2006), which develop as a part of different forms of social learning. The mass media represents a very potential source of social learning and plays a crucial role in building and breaking several stereotypes. Gender stereotype is no exception. With the communication boom, mass media has a much wider reach today than ever before. Media reflecting the prevailing social norms continues to portray gender stereotypes — one of women's inferior status and the compulsive emphasis on her physical attributes. "One has to only pick up any newspaper to realize that one is living in a patriarchy", said Virginia Woolf. This description aptly fits the entire mass media not just the print, even today. Television, movies, popular music, and other mass media convey messages about the nature of masculinity and feminity (Martin, 2004). Following a set pattern the order of importance in news coverage is — events and issues, politics, economy, law religion, issues like women's health, position, work experiences, deprivation ~nd tyranny they are subjected to prompt far less coverage (Joseph & Sharma, 1994). Formal news business is not just the powerful talking to the less powerful but essentially 'men talking to men'; women's pages are a deliberate exception (Molotch, 1990, King & Scott, 1977). Women's coverage in the Indian press is mostly restricted to fashion, cookery and beauty care following the'patterns set by the Western media (Bath la, 1998).

Systematic research has shown that the most common commercials depict a male expert instructing a female consumer about a product, for example the Harpick ad shows a male star demonstrating the benefits of a toilet cleaner to a visibly gratified women customer or a male dentist instructing a mother on the benefits of a particular brand of toothpaste on her child's oral health. A study that was conducted in 1970s and replicated since, in 5 continents, found 70 per cent of men were shown as experts, whereas 86 per cent of women were product users (McArther & Resko, 1975). Commercials also depict women as anxious housewife piecing together delicious and nutritious meals, working tirelessly towards keeping the family healthy, clean and happy. Young women appear to be obsessed with grooming, looking fair (fair and lovely ad), wearing the right clothes or perfume competing for a man's attention either for marriage or employment.

Women are often depicted as sex objects (Schultz, 2004). Scantily clad women pose actively in ads selling, electronic gadgets, beer, soft drinks, and clothes to cars. Mallika Sherawat advertising for Pepsi and the anorexic model posing for a and of jeans are pointers here. Sexy ads are growing daring every year. Although any people enjoy looking at these ads it is not clear whether sex sells: research s evidence suggests a very low rate of recall for information that accompany sexy illustration (Schultz, 2004), yet advertisers continue to make them relying on their ecotourism and shock value.

Archer and his colleagues analyzed thousands of photographs from Newspapers and magazines in the U.S. to discover that photos of men tended to show their faces but that of women focussed on their bodies. The same tendencies, termed as face-ism by Archer were found in 11 different countries Hong Kong to Kenya (Taylor, 2006). Subsequent research corroborated these ads in magazines like Glamour, Vogue, Esquire were 4 times more likely show female anatomy than men's (Pious & Neptune, 1997).

Methods Women Adopt

Media portrayals of thin image messages have given rise to a misperception that being thin equals being healthy. Pursuing the elusive perfect physique numerous women chronically follow certain unhealthy weight loss practices. They fast or go on a strict diet, continually use laxatives or diet pills, engage in cigarette smoking or over exercise their bodies, all of which pose high health risks. In the past decade preoccupations with weight control among adolescents have reached epidemic proportions (Taylor, 2003). Many women also resort to surgical alteration of appearance or cosmetic surgeries. According to American society of plastic surgeons the number of cosmetic surgeries doubled from 1997 to 1999 (Smolak & Moore, 2001). The most common surgeries include liposuction, breast and or buttock implants, no scientific study is yet available on its medical effects though. In India exact figures are not available may be either because most of the procedures are done outside India or records are not revealed in orderto maintain confidentiality of the clients. But the body standards prevailing in the glamour world in the country leaves no doubt that these procedures are commonplace. Most of them strive for a Euro-American standard of height and weight, which makes unnatural interventions necessary.

Physical Consequences

The obsession with weight watch coupled with high rate of obesity has created a vicious circle of intermittent weight gain and weight loss. These cycles of weight loss and weight gain may have adverse health consequences. It results in lowered metabolic rate, which can lead to general propensity to gain weight. There may also be a change in fat distribution and have long-term effect on blood pressure, a risk factor for cardiovascular diseases. The low percentage of fat distribution may lead to amenorrhea (cessation of menstruation) and fertility problems (Taylor; 2003).

Obsessive concern with weight loss can give rise to excessive dieting. People who are dieting become irritable, lack concentration, experience fatigue, headaches, stomachaches, which may interfere with their performance. Dieting may eventually lead to eating disorders like anorexia nervosa and bulimia nervosa. Recent years have seen a dramatic increase in the incidence of eating disorders in the adolescent female population of Western countries (Taylor, 2003). A study at NIMHANS has found an increasing trend in India too, although it may not have yet reached the epidemic proportion of the West.

REFERENCES

Dennerstein Lorraine, Astbury, Jill & Morse Carol (1993). *Psycho-social and Mental Health Aspects of Women's Mental Health*, WHO, Geneva.

Joseph Ammu & Sharma Kalpana, (1994). Whose News? *The Media and Women's Issues*, Sage Publications.

King Josephine & Scott Mary, (1977). Is This Your Life? *Image of Women in Media*, VIRAGO, London.

Lips, H.M., & Colwill, N.L., (1978). *Psychology of Sex Differences*, Englewood Cliffs, NJ: Prentice-Hall.

Martin, CL., Ruble, D. (2004). Children's Search for Gender Cues: Cognitive Perspectives on Gender Development. Current Directions in Psychological Science, 13, 67-70.

Molotch B. (1990). *Women in the Media*, Sage Publications.

Munson, L.J., Hulin C, & Drasgow F. (2000). *Longitudinal Analysis of Dispositional Influences and Several Harrasments: Effects on the Job and Psychological Outcomes*, Personnel Psychology, 53.

Pious, S. & Neptune, D. (1994). *Racial and Gender Biases*.

19

Adolescent Reproductive Health
Choice or Chance?

N.Sucharita[1]

ABSTRACT

Reproductive health in general and adolescent reproductive health in. particular has not received concerted attention in our country so far. The traditional view of marriage as 'protection' to girls in puberty from premarital sexual exploitation thrusts them into conjugality even before physical maturity is attained. This paper presents hospital-based data of 51 married adolescent girls in their antenatal phase, consulting a local hospital in the city of Visakhapatnam. This qualitative study included a personal data sheet and a semi structured interview schedule to assess sexual and reproductive health knowledge of the respondents. Findings from the study revealed that two-thirds of the adolescents were married before the legal age of marriage, one-fourth of the sample were un demourished and 98 per cent were anaemic. Themes from content analysis revealed knowledge of sexual and reproductive health to be minimal. Contraceptive knowledge, HIV awareness, negotiating reproductive decision-making and fertility issues were found to be low.

Introduction

Reproductive health is relatively a new phenomenon for gendered concerns in the area of reproductive behaviour. Reproductive choice can be

1. **Research Scholar, Department of Psychology, Andhra University, Visakhapatnam, Andhra Pradesh (India).**

defined as "one that requires as a precondition the existence of a feasible set of acceptable options on matters relating to reproduction and sexuality that is available to the individual woman. It also assumes as a prerequisite, a certain capability and access over the resources and information, as well as decision making power of the individual for making informed choices" (Mukhopadhyay & Savithri, 1998). In this context, reproductive choice in India is synonymous with fertility regulation. In other words it has been centered on issues such as number of children a woman would want to have, when she wants them and her need to access to contraceptive devices in order to operationalize that want.

Fertility control measures concerned with population momentum left women with no rights and very little control in the domain of reproduction; reinforcing the secondary status of women in the family and society (Hussain, 2003; Datta, 2003). As Petchesky (1980) remarks, "Women's reproductive situation is never the result of biology, but mediated by social and cultural organization". Gender inequalities evident through structural factors constrict women's well being, social power and ability to set the terms of sexual relations and childbearing (Datta, 2003).

In a rapidly changing world, confronted by HIV/AIDS, 'adolescence' — a period of critical capability building (Sen, 1997) — is now recognized as central to the social and economic development. Within the age and gender stratified patriarchal family system in India (Karve, 1965), women are less empowered to exercise their sexual and reproductive choices, but young and newly married women are powerless, invisible and voiceless. In India adolescent brides comprise one of the largest groups of vulnerable women, whose special needs have gone unnoticed (Jejeebhoy, 1998). With the onset of puberty, the gender role differentials existing in childhood become widened for girls as restrictions are placed on education, social and physical mobility. While marriage is observed as a social and cultural event, reproductive behaviour and reproductive choices are segregated into the private domain mostly controlled by men. According to the National Family Health Survey-2(NFHS-2, 1998), the median age of marriage among women in India is 16 years for the country as a whole (less than legal age of 18 years), while in states like Andhra Pradesh the median age is 15 years or less. It is reported that 36 per cent between 13-16 years of age and 61 per cent of girls below 19 years have already begun childbearing (Jejeebhoy, 1998).

The consequences of early marriage and childbearing include acute health risks such as maternal mortality, complications during labour, spontaneous abortions (United Nations Population Fund, 1998L low birth weights in infants and neonatal mortality (Population Reference Bureau, 2006; Jejeebhoy, 1998); and contracting reproductive and sexually transmitted diseases. In addition, factors such as limited opportunities for education (Llyod, Mensch & Clark, 1998; Mensch & Llyod, 1998) and skill development further compromised their economic standards of living leading to lack of empowerment including inability to exercise decision-making power (George & Jaswal 1995).

There is a dearth of information about the sexual and reproductive knowledge among married adolescents (Jejeebhoy, 1998; Mensch, Bruce & Greene, 2003). There is therefore a need for better understanding of the factors that constrain married adolescents in making sexual and reproductive choices as they form one of the most vulnerable sections of the population.

This paper examines issues relating to reproductive choice among married adolescent girls in their antenatal phase and the coping mechanism adopted by them in the context of their transition from childhood to childbearing. It seeks to understand and explore the relationship of gender inequity in making reproductive choices.

Method

Setting and Sample

The study was conducted in the outpatient clinic of the Department of Gynecology in the Government Victoria Hospital in the city of Visakhapatnam in Andhra Pradesh. This hospital was chosen for the study as it is as a government hospital that caters exclusively to the gynecological needs of the city's population and also extends its services to the population in the district of Visakhapatnam. The sample consisted of 51 married adolescent girls in the age group of 13-19 years in their second and third trimesters of the antenatal phase, attending the Out-Patient Department of Gynecology in Government Victoria Hospital for Women.

Tools of Data Collection

The tools for collecting socio-economic and demographic data and reproductive health data included:

1. Personal data sheet with details of the respondents such as information on the age of the respondents, education; income; occupation; and type of family, caste and religion. Considering iron deficiency anaemia (Hemoglobin (Hb) < 12g/dl)* as the criteria physiological well-being of the sample was assessed. Information about these measures was taken from the hospital case sheets of the participants.
2. Information on reproductive concems such as age at marriage and conception; duration of marital life; consanguinity and use of fertility measures and HIV status.
3. Goldberg's General Health Questionnaire (GHQ-28) to screen for psychological wellness in the four dimensions of somatic symptoms, anxiety and insomnia, social dysfunction and depression. A cut off point

of 3/4 was used to identify cases with psychological illness. Since many of the respondents either had no formal education or did not know English, the Telugu version of GHQ-28 was used. This translated version had earlier been used by Sachi Devi (2003) and Mrudula and Vindhya (2005).

4. A semi structured interview schedule was used to assess reproductive and sexual health knowledge of the respondents. This included issues such as consent to marriage, dowry, preparedness for pregnancy, negotiation in fertility issues, contraceptive use dynamics, the context of induced abortions, sexually transmitted infections, including HIV and the infertility situation.
5. Information about coping strategies the respondents employed to deal with their reproductive concerns was also obtained through the semi-structured interview schedule.

Information for the socio-demographic sheet was obtained in the beginning of the interview. All interviews were in Telugu, the language of the respondents, and were transcribed verbatim and then translated into English. The medical staff at the hospital identified adolescent married girls in the Out Patient Department and referred them to the interviewer. Interviews were conducted in the space provided by the hospital authorities after obtaining consent from the respondents. Each respondent was interviewed in a single session lasting approximately an hour. Privacy was ensured during the session.

Hemoglobin concentration of less than 7.0g/dl is considered severe, 7.0-9.9 g/dl as moderate and 10.0-10.9 g/dl os mild if they are pregnant and 10.0-11.9 g/dl if they are not pregnant (Centre for Disease Control and Prevention, 1998).

Findings

Socio-demographic Characteristics of the Sample

Table 19.1 shows the socio-demographic profile of the sample in terms of age of the respondents, education, income, occupation, residence, caste, and religion.

Table 19.1 Socio-demographic Characteristics of the Sample

Demographic variables	Numbers	Per cent
1	2	3
Age of the respondent		
13-17	11	21.6
18-19	40	78.4

(Contd...)

1	2	3
Education		
No formal education	18	35.3
Primary	7	13.7
Secondary	9	17.6
High school and Inter	10	19.6
Intermediate	6	11.8
Graduation	1	2.0
Residence		
Rural	11	21.6
Semi-urban	15	29.4
Urban slum	19	37.3
Urban	6	11.8
Type of family		
Nuclear	13	25.5
Joint	38	74.5
Religion		
Hindus	48	94.1
Christians	1	2.0
Muslims	2	3.9
Caste		
Forward caste	13	29.5
Backward caste	30	68.2
Scheduled caste	1	2.3
Scheduled tribe	None	

This socio-demographic profile constructed from the sample of married adolescent girls is in line with research evidence that suggests that factors such as age at marriage; early child bearing; limited education, compounded with lack of gainful employment and limited income adversely affect the social well-being of adolescent girls. When education that can shape reproductive behavior leading to effective decision-making (Caldwell, 1979), is abridged due to early marriage, it has particularly detrimental implications for the empowerment opportunities of young girls.

Physical Well-being

Taking iron level in haemoglobin (Hb< 12g/dl indicates Anaemic status) as criteria for physical well-being, the study focussed on the presence of nutritional impairment during pregnancy. The present study found that a strikingly high percentage of the respondents (98%) were anaemic. Of them, 33 per cent were moderately anaemic and 65 per cent were mildly anaemic.

These results are in line with earlier research findings that one of every five ever-married adolescent women has moderate or severe anemic (NFHS - 2, 1998). It has been well documented by now that socio-economic factors such as poverty and gender discrimination affect the nutritional status of young girls (National Family Health Survey-2, 1998; Datta, 2003; Agarwal & Agarwal, 2006).

Reproductive Health Issues

Table 19.2 presents the findings on age at marriage, duration of marital life, consanguinity in marriage, fertility measures adopted by the respondents that include history of Medical termination of pregnancy (MTP) and HIV status.

Table 19.2: Reproductive Health Issues

Age at marriage		
< 18 yrs.	32	62.7
> 18 yrs.	19	37.3
Duration of marriage		
> 6 months	33	64.7
7-12 months	10	19.6
< 1 year	8	15.7
Type of marriage		
Consanguinity	13	25.5
Non-consanguinity	38	74.5

Age at Marriage

A significant finding is that nearly two-thirds of them (62.7%) were married before the legally sanctioned age for marriage i.e., 18 years while 37.3 per cent of them were married at 18 years or later. These figures drive home the fact that a large proportion of adolescent girls become wives and mothers before they become adults that are typically driven by poverty, parental concerns about premarital sex and economic and cultural reasons (Population Reference Bureau, 2006). This situation reflects adolescent girls' limited power to make their own marital and reproductive choices.

Duration of Marital Life

In this sample, 64.7 per cent of the girls were married and in the process of child-bearing within 6 months of marriage. A high proportion of married girls i.e., 85.3 per cent were pregnant within one year of marriage. In this regard Mensch, Bruce & Greene (2003) remark that in many developing countries "the females 'traditional mandate' to begin childbearing soon after marriage enhances their respectability and economic security" reflects the lack of reproductive choices for adolescent girls in marriage.

Fertility Measures

None of them reported use of any methods of contraception. Two of them currently pregnant resorted to termination of pregnancy using oral contraceptives, which however did not give the desired result, and they were continuing to full term.

Sexually Transmitted Infections — HIV

All the respondents in the sample had undergone HIV test, as it is mandatory in the hospital. None of the respondents in the sample were infected with HIV/AIDS. However, information on the modes of HIV transmission and measures required in protecting oneself from such infections were minimal.

Psychological Well-being

Table 19.3: Psychological Well-being in Relation to Demographic Characteristics

Background characteristics	Psychlogical well-being					
	Non cases		Cases		Total	
	Number	Percentage	Number	Percentage	Number	Percentage
1	2	3	4	5	6	7
	29		22		51	
Current Age						
Below 18	7	23.30	4	19.00	11	21.60
18 and above	23	76.70	17	81.00	40	78.4
Age at marriage						
Below the legal	23	76.70	9	42.90	32	62.70
Legal age for marriage	7	23.30	12	57.10	19	37.30
Marital life						
Below 6 months	19	63.30	14	66.70	33	64.70
7-12 months	5	16.70	5	23.80	5	10.00
Beyond 12 months	6	20.00	2	9.50	8	15.70
Education						
Illiterate	9	30.00	9	42.90	18	35.30
Primary	4	13.30	3	14.30	7	13.70
Middle school	6	20.00	3	14.30	9	17.60
High school	7	23.30	3	14.30	10	19.60
Intermediate	4	13.30	2	9.50	6	11.80
Graduation			1	4.80	1	2.00

(Contd...)

1	2	3	4	5	6	7
Residence						
Rural	7	23.30	4	19.00	11	21.60
Semi-urban	10	33.30	5	23.80	15	29.40
Urban slum	8	26.70	11	52.40	19	37.30
Urban	5	16.70	1	4.80	6	11.80
Type of family						
Nuclear	6	20.00	7	33.30	13	25.50
Joint	24	80.00	14	66.70	38	74.50
Consanguinity						
Consanguineous	6	20.00	7	33.30	13	25.50
Non-consanguineous	24	80.00	14	66.70	38	74.50
Religion						
Hindu	30	100.00	18	85.70	48	94.10
Christian			1	4.80	1	2.00
Muslim			2	6.50	2	3.90
Caste						
Forward caste	10	33.30	3	21.40	13	29.50
Backward caste	19	63.30	11	78.40	30	68.20
Scheduled caste	1	3.30			1	2.30
Anaemic status						
Moderate	21	70.00	12	57.10	33	64.70
Mild	8	26.70	9	42.90	17	33.30
Normal		3.30	1	2.00		

* Significant at $p < 0.05$

Of the 51 respondents, 22 could be identified as 'cases', that is, those who scored higher than the cut off point of 3/4 on the GHQ and 29 of them were considered as non-cases'. Interestingly respondents whose age at marriage was below the legal age of marriage (i.e. 18 years) were found to have adverse psychological health (x^2= 6.041, df = 1, $p< 0.05$). No other difference in socio demographic features of the 'cases' and 'non-cases' emerged in the analysis ofthe data. The findings of the present study show that early marriage does result in poor psychological health.

An item-wise analysis of GHQ data revealed a significant presence of somatic symptoms, and anxiety and insomnia. The respondents scored high on complaints that included pain, physical distress, headache and a general feeling of illness. Nearly one-third of the sample expressed a need for a good tonic for symptom reduction.

On the anxiety and insomnia dimension, one-fifth (10%) of respondents scored on the questions, "had difficulty in staying asleep once you are off" (item number 9 of GHQ). This is however to be expected since sleeplessness in later stages of pregnancy due to difficulty in finding a comfortable position is a common occurrence (Dutta, 1994).

The responses on the dimension of social dysfunction indicated that most of them were well adjusted. Since pregnancy and motherhood are valued positively, this was not surprising. However, all the respondents responded to the issue of decision making i.e., item 21 of GHQ, (felt capable of making decision about things) in the negative, reflecting lack of autonomy and personal choice in the realm of domestic and marital relationships.

Most of the respondents did not report any significant depressive and suicidal tendencies. Only one girl had elevated score on the depressive scale. Her husband abandoned her after marriage and she did not want to face her relatives in this state. It was in this condition that she contemplated suicide. However she reconciled with the situation, as she was pregnant and felt life was worth living for the sake of her unborn baby.

In the following sections, an exploration of sexual and reproductive health issues of adolescent girls such as consent to marriage, dowry, preparedness for pregnancy, negotiation in fertility issues, contraceptive use dynamics, the context of induced abortions, sexually transmitted infections, including HIV, and the infertility situation is done. Certain cross cutting issues such as gender inequities, power imbalances, exercise of informed choice, male involvement that are central to each topic have been addressed within the discussion of each subject rather than as separate sections.

Consent to Marriage

Choices in marriage are very much linked up with economic, demographic and cultural conditions. Fundamental to early marriages is the 'precariousness of girls status' and the fear of premarital sexual activity, which is linked to the 'honour' of the family. Thus attainment of menarche is mostly viewed as a sign of girls' readiness for marriage. In the present study most of the participants reported that they had no choice in deciding their partners. It was mostly the family members who chose the groom and the girls accepted irrespective of whether liked the boy or not. Poverty and gender roles expectations were prominent themes that were elicited in the interview data

- "...my parents decided on whom I should marry based on the means (wealth) they can give...".
- "...unmarried girl in the house calls for unnecessary attention .... doubts on character ... so parents incur debts and arrange for marriage...".

There has been enough evidence from demographic and health surveys in developing countries indicating adolescent girls' lack of control regarding choice of partners (Population Reference Bureau, 2006).

Dowry

An integral feature of marriage is the contract of taking dowry from the bride's family. Though none of the respondents evaded the issue of dowry they did not want to discuss the details of payment. In this regard respondents expressed their inability to go against the system. Excerpts from the respondents' interviews of how they felt are provided below:

- "...My in-laws were quite demanding, my parents yielded because I am the eldest and there are other siblings to be married after me...".
- "...If we refuse a proposal when the girl is young ... the older she grows it becomes difficult to arrange for the dowry...".

Preparedness for Pregnancy

Most of the respondents reported lack of preparedness and planning for pregnancy. They held the view that since they were married they were expected to fulfill the; eproductive role as an inevitable consequence. The respondents reported that the esser the gap between marriage and conception, the more they were accepted in the conjugal family. The findings reflect the restricted autonomy adolescent girls face in the sphere of marriage wherein child-bearing dominates their life choices.

Negotiation in Fertility Issues

It was evident from the responses of the respondents that they were unaware of their vulnerabılity as 'teenage mothers'. The adolescents had very low level of knowledge about several reproductive health matters and were not aware of the risks. of early sexual debut and other sexually transmitted diseases such as HIV In fact demographic and health surveys from 51 countries reveal that young age of girls hinders their capacity to negotiate sex and reproduction including aspects of domestic and public life (Nugent, 2006).

- "...My in-laws insisted that we have children immediately and not use any contraceptives...".
- "...As a woman one has to bear a child at some time or the other, the sooner the better, was what my husband said...".

Contraceptive Use Dynamics

In his report on the 'Youth in a Global World', (Nugent 2006) states that, "adolescents are less likely to use modern contraceptives because of lack of access to desired family planning methods" (p 149). Most respondents revealed that the elderly women in theirf family guided them and allayed their fears regarding pregnancy and childbirth, indicating that the main source of information about sexual and reproductive issues was the family. Excerpts from the respondents in the present study also suggest there was an unmet need for contraception because they did not have adequate knowledge of contraception. Even when they vaguely knew of contraception, all of them voiced their apprehensions regarding use of contraception. The misconceptions that these girls have regarding contraception are illustrated in these statements given below:

- "...I would consider abstinence as a better method of contraception...".
- "...My in-laws forewarned that using contraceptive pills might lead to infertility as a relative in our family never conceived after taking oral contraceptives...".

The Context of Induced Abortions

Interestingly almost all the respondents indicated that they were aware of ultrasound scan techniques that are used to detect fetal anomalies and a majority of them knew that this device can be used in determining the sex of the fetus. It is ironical that they do not know measures of contraception, while they were aware of technological developments used in detecting fetal anomalies and for sex determination of the fetus. This stark difference reinforces the fact that reproductive health issues have primarily been centered on fertility issues so far.

There is social approval for measures such as sex determination technology although knowing the sex of the child is legally banned now according to the Pre-natal Diagnostic Techniques Act (1996). While the girls expressed a desire for a healthy child they did report a desire for a male child as it is assumed that giving birth to a male child enhances the woman's social worth.

For some it was insignificant as it was their first pregnancy and the sex of the child was not a cause of concern. Some respondents attributed the sex of the child to the "will of God or divine providence".

Sexually Transmitted Infections, Including HIV

All the respondents had been tested for HIV and all of them tested exonerative indicating that there were no cases infected with HIV in the present sample. Most of the respondents had heard about HIV from the Parent to Child Transmission Counselling and Testing Centre (PPTC) located in the hospital premises, as it is mandatory for all registered cases in the hospital to undergo counseling and testing for HIV. A significant and alarming finding in this context was that married adolescents were not aware of the male contraceptive devices such as condoms that prevent transmission of HIV due to sexual contact. Owing to their low education levels, most of them were unable to comprehend the information given in the testing centre at the Hospital. The typical responses noted from the narratives are:

- "...HIV is an illness one gets if he/she indulges in relationships outside marriage...".

- "...I heard about this disease, it spreads through mosquito bite...".

These statements support the findings from Demographic and Health Survey in the recent years (from 2000 to 2003) that the knowledge of HIV risk is low among the adolescent group (ORC Macro, Measure DHS+, HIV/AIDS, cited in PRB 2006).

Stigma of Infertility

In the present study, for most of the girls pregnancy was welcomed as a means to avoid the stigma of infertility. The respondents placed a great value on motherhood and felt that infertility is primarily because of 'some defect' in the female reproductive system and that they were not aware of any other causes of infertility. From the narratives of the adolescent mothers it could be discerned that these girls had little negotiating power in child bearing and were mostly fraught with fears regarding their own fertility that are captured in the following statements:

- "...irrespective of young age I wanted to go through this stage for fear of being ostracized as an infertile woman...".
- "...not all women are blessed to be fertile and privileged for childbearing...".

Coping Strategies

Another important variable that was studied in the context of adolescent reproductive health was coping strategies. Though pregnancy and motherhood were viewed as positive life events they entail some amount of stress, considering the age of the mother, low level of education, lack of employment and lack of awareness about reproductive health and limited or no power in negotiating fertility issues. Most of the adolescent girls looked for external resources for coping, while few of them had internal resources of strength that had helped them to adjust to their situation. The predominant themes that emerged from the interview data included positive appraisal of pregnancy, existence of social support, faith in God and acceptance of their situation ungrudgingly.

Positive Appraisal of Pregnancy

An overwhelming majority of the respondents reported that they viewed pregnancy as a pleasant event. As one respondent puts it "pregnancy is a unique experience that every woman may not have the good fortune of receiving it". Though they had interpreted pregnancy as a positive event a majority of them accepted childbearing as an "inevitable experience in a married woman's life", and also indicated a strong external locus of control in matters related to fertility. It can be discerned from these responses as to how gender stereotypes of women as nurturers and care-givers are internalized.

Social Support

Support from natal families is not unusual and it is a prevalent cultural practice to bring girls to their natal family for childbirth. Traditional practices compel the girl's parents to shoulder the expenses for marriage, give dowry, and take the responsibility of her prenatal care and delivery of the child. Husbands were also considered as source of strength by some of the girls who would console them and also ease the tension between the girls and their in-laws. Some of the girls expressed that friends and other members in the family also provided support in adjusting to their life situations.

Viewed from the western models of family dynamics and gender roles, the current situation appears oppressive and stifling to the growth of the married adolescents with adverse effect on their well-being. Research has documented that despite the range of adversities experienced by women across the life span in Indio, women negotiate for spaces fort hemselves within the permissible range of deviation from norms, maneuvering their own fertility outcomes without overthrowing either patriarchy or the ideology of motherhood (Patel, 1999).

To conclude this discussion, the present study focused on the knowledge of reproductive health issues and on the physical health measures such as status of anaemia and BMI of 51 married adolescent girls consulting a local hospital. Although reproductive conditions are not life threatening, they do have a considerable impact on daily life (Sadhana, 2002) and in the case of India, mirror the vulnerabilities and disempowering conditions of lives of young women.

REFERENCES

Agarwal, K.N., & Agarwal, D.K.(2006). Prevalence al Anaemia in Pregnant and Lactating Women in India. *Indian Journal of Medical Research*, 124, August, 173-184.

Caldwell, M. (1979). Education as Factor 01 Mortality decline: An Expanded Examination 01 the Evidence in G.P. Kelly & CM. Elliot (Ed.), *Women's Education in the Third World: Comparitive Perspectives*. New York: SUNY Press.

Centre for Disease Control and Prevention. (1998). Recommendations to Prevent and Control Iron Deliciency in the United States. *Morbidity and Mortality Weekly Report*, 47 (RR-3): 1-29.

Datta, A. (2003). Articulation of An Integrated Women's Health Policy Using Life Cycle Approach. *Indian Journal of Gender Studies*, 10, 1, 25-43.

Dutta, D.C (1994). *Textbook of Obstetrics including Perinatology and Contraception*. Calcutta: New Central Book Agency.

Ganiger, S.B. (1992). Determinants 01 Age at Marriage in Karnataka During 1971-1981: A District Level Analysis. *Journal of Institutional Economic Research*, 27, 2, 13-23.

George, A. & Jaswal, S. (1995). Understanding Sexuality: Ethnographic Study 01 Poor Women in Bombay. *Women and AIDS Programme Research Report Series* No. 12. Washington D.C: International Centre for Research on Women.

Goldberg, D. (1978). *Manual of the General Health Questionnaire*. Windsor: NFER Publishing Co.

Hussain. S. (2003). Gender and Reproductive Behaviour. *Indian Journal of Gender Studies*, 10, 1,44-76.

International Institute lor Population Sciences, ORC MACRO (2000). National Family Health Survey -2 (1998-99). India, Mumbai, liPS, USA, ORC MACRO.

Jeieebhoy, S.J. (1998). Adolescent Sexual and Reproductive Behaviour: A Review 01 the Evidence from India. *Social Science and Medicine*. 46, 10: 275-90.

Karve, I. (1965). *Kinship Organization in India*. Bombay: Asia Publishing House.

Lloyd, CB., Mensch, S., & Clark, W. (1998). The Effects 01 Primary School Quality on the Educational Participation and Attainment 01 Kenyan Girls and Boys. Paper Presented at the Annual Meeting 01 the Population Association of America, 2-4 April, 1998. Chicago.

Mensch, B.S., & Lloyd, CB. (1998). Gender Differences in the Schooling Experiences of Adolescents in Low-income Countries: The Case 01 Kenya. *Studies in Family Planning*. 29, No. 2,167-184.

Mensch, B.S., Bruce, J., & Greene, M.E. (2003). The Uncharled Passage: *Girls' Adolescence in the Developing World*. New York: Population Council.

Mrudula, A, & Vindhya, U. (2005). *Using with HIV/AIDS: How do Widowed Women Cope?* Aaina, Bapu Trust.

Mukhoapdhyay, S., & Savithri, R. (1998). *Poverty, Gender and Reproductive Choice: An Analysis of Linkages*. New Delhi: Institute of Social Studies Trust.

Nugent, R. (2006). Youth in a Global World. *Population Reference Bureau*. Washington D.C.

Pachuari, S., & Santhya, K.G. (2002). Reproductive Choices for Asian Adolescents: A Focus on Contraceptive Behaviour. *International Family Planning Perspectives*. 28(4), 186-195. *Journal of Comparative Family Studies*, 30, 4, 429-451.

Petchesky, R.P. (1980). 'Reproductive Freedom: Beyond" A Woman's Right to Choose". *Signs: Journal of Women In Culture and Society*. (Special issues on '*Women and Sexuality*)', 5(4): 661-85.

Prakasam, C.P., & Upadhyay, R.B. (1985). Socio-economic Variables Influencing Mean Age at Marriage in Karnataka and Kerala. *Jansamkhya*, 3(1-2), 81-90.

Population Reference Bureau (2006). *Youth in a Global World*. Washington DC: PRB.

Ramsubban, R. (2000). Women's vulnerability: The Recent Evidence on Sexually Transmitted Infections. In R.Ramsubban, & S. Jejeebhoy, (Eds.), *Women's Reproductive Health in India*. Jaipur: Rawat Publications.

Sachi Devi. K. (2003). Study on the Prevalence of Common Mental Disorders in a Primary Health Centre in the District of Visakhapatnam. Unpublished Doctoral Thesis, Andhra University, Visakhapatnam.

Sadhana, R. (2002). *Definition and Measurement of Reproductive Health*. Bulletin of the World Health Organization. 80, 5, 408-409.

Sen, A (1997). *Editorial: Human Capital and Human Capability*. World Development. 25 (12) 1959-196l.

Tripathy, P.L., Roo, I. S., & Pradhan, P.N. (1992). An Integrated Path Analysis Approach to Study the Variation in the Age of Female Nuptiality of Orissa. *Janasamkhya*, 10 (1-2) 31-43.

A Study in Depression in Women with Pre and Post Menopause Stages in Tribal Area

N.V.V.S. Narayana[1]
Rupa Sevarai[1]

ABSTRACT

Depression has been found to be one of the main health concerns, especially in the case of women. A recent study by WHO found that depression will be the second important component in Global Burden of Disease (GBD) by the year 2020 in the case of women. Keeping this in view, the present study was carried out to see the depression levels and differences between women with pre and post menopause stages. The sample consists of 150 tribal women (84 in pre menopause stage and 66 in post menopause stage), with an age ranging from 30-60 years, taken from the Visakhapatnam agency area, Andhra Pradesh. A vernacular translation (into Telugu) of Beck's Depression Inventory (1978) was administered to the sample. The results indicate that 23 per cent of the tribal women were in 'Borderline Depression' or in 'Severe Depression' that needs clinical assistance. Significant difference was found between the pre and the post menopause stage groups with post menopause group being in borderline clinical depression. Results were also analyzed in terms of family type, period of menopause, husband body weight, health problems, hobbies and socio-economic status.

Depression is a disease that is caused by biological factors. Hormones in the brain, specifically serotonin, regulate your mood. Sometimes, serotonin levels can drop, causing fluctuations in mood and severe episodes of

1. **Department of Psychology and Parapsychology , Andhra University, Visakhapatnam, Andhra Pradesh (India).**

depression. Someone suffering from depression will experience intense feelings of sadness, hopelessness, and melancholy for prolonged periods of time (at least two weeks). Depression can lead to a variety of symptoms and can have disastrous effects on a person's life, including physical ailments, isolation, and even suicide. It is importantfora woman suffering from depression to realize that it is not her fault. The onset of depression cannot be controlled. As many of us know, depression is a common complaint during menopause.

The symptoms of depression vary from person to person, and the intensity of the symptoms depends on the severity of the depression. Depression causes changes in thinking, feeling, behavior, and physical well-being.

There are three primary types of depression Major Depression, Dysthymia, and Bipolar Depression. In addition to these primary depressions, many people also develop a 'reactive depression', which may be less severe, but still requires psychological treatment. A reactive depression occurs when you develop many of the symptoms of depression in response to the stress of a major life problem, but they are not severe enough to be considered a major depression. If these milder symptoms of depression occur without a clear life stress as the cause, and the depression has not lasted long enough to by considered dysthymia, then it is called an Unspecified Depression. Other depressions may be caused by the physiological effects of a medical condition, or by substance abuse. The specific depression label, beyond the three primary types of depression and reactive depression, will not be reviewed here.

Menopause, a normal and natural event, is the end of menstruation. It is usually confirmed when you have not had a period for 12 months in a row (with other causes forthis change ruled out). Menopause starts when your body's level of the hormone estrogen falls permanently to very low levels and your menstrual periods stop for good. Menopause is also known as "the change of life".

This change in your body usually doesn't happen all at once. There is a transition period before menopause called peri menopause, when your body starts making less of the female hormones estrogen and progesterone. During this time, you can have symptoms such as hot flashes and mood swings, and you mayor may not have a period. These changes usually begin between the ages of 45 and 55, with the average at about age 51. A few women reach natural menopause as early as their 30s (which is called premature menopause) and as late as their 60s. Women who smoke or who used to smoke can reach menopause one to two years earlier than non-smokers.

Many women wonder and worry about what will happen when they reach menopause, but in fact, it can be a positive experience! Even though some women have frustrating symptoms and health problems throughout peri menopause and after menopause, it is a chance for all women to focus more on themselves and make changes that will improve their health. The first step is to learn all you can about the physical and emotional changes that may be ahead of you.

Premature Menopause

Premature menopause is menopause that happens before the age of 40 — whether it is natural or induced. Some women have premature menopause because of:

- ❖ Family history (genes).
- ❖ Medical treatments, such as surgery to remove the ovaries.
- ❖ cancer treatments, such as chemotherapy or radiation to the pelvic area.

Having premature menopause puts a woman at more risk for osteoporosis later in her life. It also may be a source of great distress, since many women younger than 40 still want to have children. Women who still want to become pregnant can talk with their HCP about donor egg programmes.

Post Menopause

The term post menopause refers to all the years beyond menopause. It is the period past the time at which you have not had a period for 12 months in a row — whether your menopause was natural or induced.

Menopause and Perimenopause

Menopause is defined as the cessation of menstruation as a result of the normal decline in ovarian function. Technically, you enter menopause following 12 consecutive months without a period. Menopause has become increasingly medicalized, which means it is viewed as something that requires intervention and treatment rather than as a natural life transition that may benefit from support. Menopause signals the end of fertility and the beginning of a new and potentially rewarding time in a woman's life. Part of the stigma of menopause is its association with aging, but we age no more rapidly in our 50s than in any other decade of life.

Signs or Symptoms of Menopause

There have been a list of the "34 signs of menopause" circulating for years. The list originated with Judy Bayliss' wonderful newsgroup, The Menopause Listserv (That's Menopause without the 'e' at the end).

1. Hot flashes, flushes, night sweats and/or cold flashes, clammy feeling (related to increased activity in the autonomic/sympathetic nervous system).

2. Bouts of rapid heartbeat (related to increased activity in the autonomic/ sympathetic nervous system) along with rapid heartbeat (palpitations), women can experience skipped heartbeats, irregular heartbeats.
3. Irritability. Along with irritability, a host of 'anger' problems can develop during menopause.
4. Mood swings sudden tears. Mood swings can include anything from mood shifts (happy one moment, depressed the next) to sudden bouts of crying when nothing overt has occurred to cause the crying.
5. Trouble sleeping through the night (with or without night sweats). This can develop into insomnia or just waking at 2 in the morning for an hour. Relaxation and breathing exercises can be useful at this time.
6. Irregular periods: shorter, lighter or heavier periods, flooding, and phantom periods. A phantom period is when you experience all the symptoms you're accustomed to having before you menstruate — but ... no period comes. This is a common experience during peri menopause before a woman's period actually stops.
7. Loss of libido (sex drive).
8. Dry vagina (results in painful intercourse).
9. Crashing fatigue.
10. Anxiety, feeling ill at ease.
11. Feelings of dread, apprehension, and doom (includes thoughts of death, picturing one's own death).

Difficulty concentrating, disorientation and mental confusion. *Note:* Forgetfulness during peri menopause is often referred to lightly and humorously as 'brain fog'.

13. Disturbing memory lapses.
14. Incontinence — especially upon sneezing, laughing: urge incontinence (reflects a general loss of smooth muscle tone).
15. Itchy, crawly skin (feeling of ants crawling under the skin, not just dry, itchy.
16. Aching, sore joints, muscles and tendons. (may include such problems as carpal tunnel syndrome). Osteoarthritis can develop during perimenopause and those with existing arthritic and/or rheumatic pain may find it's exacerbated during the menopausal transition.
17. Increased tension in muscles.
18. Breast tenderness (Breast swelling, soreness, pain)

19. Headache change: increase or decrease. Many women develop migraine headaches during perimenopause. However, if one doesn't have a history of migraine headaches, they're generally a short-lived experience of perimenopause.
20. Gastrointestinal distress, indigestion, flatulence, gas pain, nausea.
21. Sudden bouts of bloat. *Note:* Acid reflux and heartburn are very common during perimenopause. Treat them as you would if you weren't going through menopause.
22. Depression (has a quality from other depression, the inability to cope is overwhelming, there is a feeling of a loss of self.
23. Exacerbation of any existing conditions. Often, conditions women had prior to entering perimenopause become exaggerated (worse) during the menopause transition.
24. Increase in allergies.
25. Weight gain (is often around the waist and thighs, resulting in "the disappearing waistline" and changes in body shape.)
26. Hair loss or thinning, head or whole body, increase in facial hair. There is often a loss of pubic hair during menopause. Many women are more comfortable simply shaving their pubic area instead of having patches of hair.
27. Diuiness, light-headedness, episodes of loss of balance. Although it's a common complaint during menopause, women can experience diuiness without having hypertension.
28. Changes in body odour. I wouldn't be too frightened about this one. It can happen, but in 11 years of running this site, there are relatively few cases of developing body odor during menopause.
29. Electric shock sensation under the skin and in the head.
30. Tingling in the extremities (can also be a symptom of B-12 deficiency, diabetes, or from an alteration in the flexibility of blood vessels in the extremities.)
31. Gum problems, increased bleeding.
32. Burning tongue.
33. Osteoporosis (after several years)
34. Brittle fingernails, which peel & break easily.

Menopause and Depression

If women live long enough, they will experience menopause, also known as 'the change of life'. Also menopause is a universal life transition for all women who live into their 50s, may know very little about what to expect, what is normal, how they might feel, and how to react to these changes (Maresh, 1998). Indeed in the survey by the north American menopause society, women reported that their main source of information regarding menopause was popular magazines, and that their physicians often failed to discuss how the menopausal transition would affect their emotions, partner relationships, well-being and health (Randall, 1993). Menopause often brings with it changes in the life of midlife women that can impact them physically and psychologically, therefore it is imperative that anyone working with midlife women in a therapeutic setting understand the complexity of this midlife phase can be ready to discuss it with concerned clients (Robinson Kurpius, Foley Nicpon, & Maresh, 2001).

You may find yourself feeling quite blue during menopause. It is not uncommon for women to feel frustrated with their bodies and sad at the loss of their ability to carry children. On top of that, menopause comes with a host of symptoms that can try any woman's patience. However, sometimes menopause can make you feel more than a little sad; often it can make you downright depressed.

Depression during Menopause

Menopause can trigger feelings of sadness and episodes of depression in a number of women. It is thought that somewhere between 8 per cent and 15 per cent of menopausal women experience some form of depression. Menopause depression is most likely to hit during peri menopause, the phase leading up to menopause. Causes of menopausal depression are under debate, but a variety of theories have been suggested as to why so many menopausal women experience mood disorders.

One theory asserts that the stress of menopause symptoms leads to depression. Women already have to deal with family, friends, work, and finances, let alone this huge physical change. Menopause may just be that straw that breaks the camel's back, causing the onset of depression.

Another theory links menopause depression with fluctuating levels of hormones in the body. Throughout menopause, levels of estrogen, progesterone, and androgen are constantly changing. These hormones are thought to be linked with the mood centers in women's brain. As hormones drop, especially estrogen, they can experience periods of sadness and hopelessness. Some women experience a severe drop in mood, resulting in depression.

Mood and Menopause

There is ongoing debate concerning the direction of the relationship between mood end the experience of the menopause. It is questionable whether mood influences menopause or whether menopause influences one's mood. Regardless of the causal direction, there is a strong relationship between the experience of menopause and mood. Two mood scales that are often attributed to the change are depression and anxiety. Woods and Mitchell (1996) suggested four explanations for the relationship of mood and menopause stage. Firstly it was suggested that depression in mid life is related to the depletion of estrogen. Therefore by stabilizing the hormonal changes through HRT depressed mood would be positively affected (Shaver; 1994; Vliet, 1995). Second it was proposed that depression and anxiety are a by-product of vasomotor symptoms such as sleep disturbance and hot flashes which can be treated with HRT (Haynes and Parry, 1998; Holte, 1998; Matthews, 1992). A third explanation posited that a woman's help history and current health status could be linked to depression in midlife (Woods and Mitchell, 1996). The fourth explanation linked stress experienced during menopause to more negative mood states (Woods and Mitchell, 1996); thus menopausal women who experienced more stress would report higher depression and anxiety.

Sexuality and Menopausal Transition

Many women experienced the menopausal transition also encounter changes in iheir sexual arousal desire, and satisfaction. Abernethy (1997) noted back many cssume that only biological components especially the naturally occur depletion of -crmones that signify the onset and course of menopause are responsible for the changes in midlife women's sexual behaviour and satisfaction. Evidence suggests —~women's sexual function is influenced by psychosocial factors as well as physical. Mansfield, Koch and Voda (1998) found that sexual difficulties during menopause stemmed more from dissatisfying marital relationships than from the physical symptoms can concomitant with menopause. Feilder and Robinsonkurpius (2001) also found that marital quality and sexual satisfaction were directly related to reported menopausal symptomatology.

Risk Factors

Women are at an increased risk for developing depression during menopause if they have a history of mood disorders. Women, who have been depressed before, especially during their 20s, are more likely to see their depression reoccur. Women who have gone through surgical menopause are also at increased risk for depression. Surgery causes a dramatic drop in estrogen levels not to mention increased anxiety and symptoms. If they have smoking habit, have young children, or are under a lot of stress, they are also more likely to develop some form of depression during this time.

Objective

To see the depression levels among pre-menopausal and post menopausal women.

Method

Sample

The study was conducted on a sample of 150 women. Out of which pre-menopausal women are 84 and 66 are post menopausal women. The age range of the sample is from 30 to 60 in Visakhapatnam tribal area.

Tools

Beck depression inventory developed by Aaron T. Beck (1978) was adopted forthis study. It consists of 21 items which measure depression in 6 levels (normal, mild, borderline, and moderate, severe, extreme). The scoring of the scale involves counting the number of answers ranging from 0 to 3. In this scale higher score indicates more depression. The depression scale was translated in Telugu version for the convenience.

Procedure

The researchers personally approached the subjects and administered the questionnaire individually. The subjects were also informed about the objective of the study. The menopausal group consists of 66 women and pre menopausal women.

Results

Table 20.1: Differences between the pre menopausal and post menopausal women on depression and sexual activity

Dimensions	Variable	N	M	S.D	t	Sig.
Depression	Pre menopause	84	12.62	6.53	2.733	0.007*
	Post menopause	66	16.61	10.34		
Sexual activity	Pre menopause	84	1.48	1.18	1.373	0.173
	Post menopause	66	1.74	1.18		

**p=0.05, **P=0.01

Table 20.1 shows the mean differences between the pre menopausal and post menopausal groups with respective to depression and sexual activity. A significance difference was found between these two groups and depression however post menopausal group reported being high on depression ($p<0.01$) when compared to pre menopausal group.

Table 20.2: Differences between the nuclear and joint family groups on depression and sexual

Dimensions	Variable	N	Mean	S.D	t	Sig.
Depression	Nuclear family	86	11.88	6.04	4.033	0.000**
	Joint family	64	17.72	10.33		
Sexual activity	Nuclear family	86	1.55	1.23	0.569	0.57
	Joint family	64	1.66	1.12		

*P=0.05, **P=0.01

Table 20.2 shows the mean differences between the nuclear family and joint family groups with respect to depression and sexual activity. Significance difference was found between these two groups on depression. However the joint family group reported significantly high score on depression when compared to the nuclear family group. There is no significant difference was found between the two groups on the sexual activity.

Table 20.3: Differences between the women with hobbies and no hobbies on depression and sexual activity

Dimensions	Variable	N	M	S.D	t	Sig.
Depression	Hobbies	52	21.10	10.79	6.640	0.000**
	No hobbies	98	10.81	3.99		
Sexual activity	Hobbies	52	1.46	1.16	1.002	0.318
	No hobbies	98	1.66	1.19		

*P=0.05, **P=0.01

Table 20.3 shows the mean differences between the women with hobbies like watching T.V and no hobbies group with respect to the depression and the sexual activity. Significant difference was found between the two groups on depression when compared to women without hobbies. No significant difference was found between these two groups on sexual activity.

Table 20.4: ANOVA results for the three period groups on depression and sexual activity

Dimensions	Variable	N	M	S.D.	F	Sig.
Depression	Group 1	84	12.62	6.53	4.201	0.017**
	Group 2	47	16.34	10.01		
	Group 3	19	17.26	11.38		
Sexual activity	Group 1	84	1.48	1.18	1.161	0.316
	Group 2	47	1.68	1.24		
	Group 3	19	1.89	1.05		

*P=0.05, **P=0.01

Table 20.4 shows the ANOVA results forthree period groups (group 1- pre menopause, group 2 -less than one year, group 3 - more than one year) across the depression and sexual activity. Significance difference was found on depression among the three groups. Group 3 reported high score on depression while group 1 reported low score on depression. No significance difference was found between these three groups.

Table 20.5: Levels of depression among the pre menopausal and post menopausal groups

Levels	Menstrual cycle		Total
	Continues	Stopped	
Nonnal	44	14	58
Mild	22	35	57
Border line	5	3	8
Moderate	11	2	13
Severe	2	9	11
Extreme	0	3	3

Table 20.5 shows the levels of depression among total sample. 36 people were in the minimal range.

An investigation into the level of depression for the sample 150 subjects revealed that 36 per cent out of the total sample have figured in the clinical range which amounts to 24 per cent. It shows that nearly 1/4 of women are undergoing psychological disturbance in the form of depression. Therefore the findings give direction towards organizing self awareness programmes and offering counseling services at group of individual levels so as to enable them to coup with the situation.

Discussion

Significant difference between pre menopausal and post menopausal groups on depression can be explained in the light of research findings pertaining post menopausal depression. Findings found that menopausal women suffer from depression present results to show them menopausal women as a significantly high scores and depression.

Further women coming from joint family was found to be significantly more depressed in comparison to those coming from the nuclear family backgrounds. It may be explained keeping in view the kind of adjustment required while interacting with each member of the family which may sometimes pose problems and conflicts to the individual.

Further significant observations regarding hobbies like watching T.V. serials was that women who were exposed to such programme were found to be depressed to a greater extent as compared to women who did not watch such programmes. This may be due to the fact that they feel more anxious, worried, and disturbed by identifying themselves with characters in the serials which portray themes relating to aging, family and work related issues, attractiveness, etc.

Conclusion

To sum up the findings it may be concluded that women in their post menopausal phase coming from joint families who are exposed to television serials were subjected to a significantly higher degree of depression as compared to women during their pre menopausal phase, nuclear family background who were not being exposed to television serials. Further about one quarter of the subjects seemed to suffer from depression causing psychological disturbance and hence may need professional help.

REFERENCES

Aaron IBeck, Beck Depression Inventory (1978).

Avis, Nancy E, *Psychology of Women Quarterly*. 27(2), Jun 2003, 91-100.

Benazzi, Franco, *Psychotherapy and Psychosomatics*. 70(3), May-June 2001, 167.

Becht, Marleen C .*Journal of Affective Disorders*. 63(1-3), Mar 2001, 209-213.

Cohen EM., d.e.McChargne & F.L.Collins,Jr; *'Health Psychology Hand Book'*, Sage Publications, New Delhi.

Kopala.M & M.Keitel *'Hand Book of Counselling Women; 2003'*, Sage Publications, New Delhi.

Venturino, G, *Medicina Psicosomatica*. 45(3), July-September 2000, 131-139.

en.wikipedia.org/wiki/Menopause

http://www.maytree.net

www.menopause.org

www.menopause-online.com

www.nlm.nih.gov/medlineplus/menopause.html

www.mayoclinic.com/health/menopause

www.allayurveda.com/ail_menopause.htm

www.minniepauz.com

www.healthandyoga.com/html/ppms.html

www.fbhc.org/patients/betterhealth/menopause

www.menopausejournal.com

www.medindia.net/patients/patientinfo/Menopause.htm

www.indianmenopausesociety.org

www.medicinenet.com/menopause/article.htm

www.safemenopausesolutions.com

www.menopausecanada.com

21

Shyness and Academic Achievement of Tribal Children and Adolescents
Some Preliminary Observations

Lancy D'Souza[1]
Ramaswamy[1]

ABSTRACT

The present study reports influence of shyness on academic achievement of children and adolescents with special reference to the tribal children. A total of 1220 students studying in classes I to X were employed in the present study of which 425 (171 boys + 254 girls) were children and remaining 795 (410 boys+ 385 girls) were adolescents. They were administered Shyness questionnaire (Crozier, 1995) and their academic achievement scores were collected from respective school records. Results revealed that for the overall sample shyness correlated significantly and negatively. Shyness had significant influence over academic achievement. Shyness affected the achievement negatively more for adolescents than children. Only physiological domain of shyness did not influence academic achievement of the sample selected. Treatment aspects of shyness also delineated.

Introduction

Shyness is a form of excessive self-focus, a preoccupation with one's thoughts, feelings and physical reactions. Shyness may vary from mild social awkwardness to totally inhibiting social phobia. It may be chronic and dispositional, serving as a personality trait that is central in one's self-

1. Department of Psychology, Maharaja's College, University of Mysore, Mysore-570 006, Karnataka (India).

definition. Situational shyness involves experiencing the symptoms of shyness in specific social performance situations but not incorporating it into one's self-concept.

The reactions for shyness can occur at any or all of the following levels: cognitive, affective, physiological and behavioral, and may be triggered by a wide variety of arousal cues (Henderson and Zimbardo, 1996).

Shyness in and itself is not a psychological disorder, and therefore doesn't warrant medication. But, if bashfulness prevents a person from functioning, or depression or anxiety accompanies it, then medication can be helpful. A common observation in most of the shyness research is that the consequences of shyness are deeply troubling. Shyness leads to higher levels of anxiety (D'Souza, 2003), decreased levels of happiness (Sreeshakumar, D'Souza & Nagalakshmi, 2007), neurotic tendency and lower academic performance (D'Souza, Urs & James (2000), lowered performance in physical education students (D'Souza, Singh, Basavarajappa, 1999), lowered self-esteem and decreased self concept (D'Souza, 2005; D'Souza, Urs & Ramaswamy, 2003), increased fear reactions (D'Souza, 2007, D'Souza, Gowda & Gowda, 2006) and social and emotional maladjustment (D'Souza & Urs, 2001). Some other studies revealed that (Bell *et al*, 1994) young adults with high shyness may be at risk for Parkinson disease later in life.

Childhood shyness is strongly related to the complex subtype of social phobia in the general population (Coyne, 1994).

A degree of shyness is normal whenever social expectations are new or ambiguous. Shyness begins to emerge as a problem if it becomes not merely situational but dispositional, so that the child is labeled as shy. The studies related to shyness and academic achievement in India is not very well documented specially on children and adolescents. In the present study an attempt is made to assess the influence of shyness on academic achievement and to see any influence of gender and age on shyness.

Method

Samples

Primary and high school children studying in classes I to X from tribal schools were selected for the present study. Of the total 1220 students included in the study 581 were boys and remaining 639 were girls. They were studying in 6 primary schools and 10 high schools in and around Mysore city. Of the total sample of 1220, they were further classified into children (425) and adolescents (795). Out of 425 children, 171 were boys and 254 girls and in 795 adolescents, 410 were boys and remaining 385 were girls. Stratified random sampling technique was used to select the sample. The sample involved students studying in both Kannada and English medium. Their age varied from 5 to 18 years.

Tool Used: Shyness Questionnaire

This questionnaire was developed by Crozier (1995) of University' College of Cardiff. It consists of 26 items and requires the subject to indicate his/her response by ticking "YES/NO" OR 'DON'T KNOW". The items of the questionnaire are based on situations or interactions like performing in front of the class, being made fun of, being told off, having one's photograph taken, and novel situations involving teachers, school-friends interaction and so on. The items pertain to three domains Physical, Psychological and Social. Of the 26 items, shyness is indicated by a 'YES' response for 21 items and a "NO" response for 5 items. Item analysis of the scale using SPSS programme resulted in Cronbach's alpha coefficient of 0.817. Further, in the present investigation the questions were further classified into three domains-social, psychological and physiological.

Procedure

The tests were administered to the subjects in groups of 6-10 subjects per group. Data collection was done in single session the session lasted for about 25-30 minutes. First, the researcher, established rapport with the subjects and they were asked to introduce themselves. The purpose of the study was made clear to them. Then they were administered the Shyness questionnaire. They were given appropriate instructions and the questions were read out to them. They were asked to indicate their responses in the respective sheets given to them. Whenever they had doubt in understanding questions, the test administrator made those questions very clear to them in their local language.

Scoring and Analysis

For the shyness questionnaire, items worded in the direction of shyness, responses were scored 2 for 'YES', 1 for 'DON'T KNOW' and 0 for 'NO' Scores were reversed for the items worded in the opposite direction. High scores indicate high level of shyness and low scores indicate low level of shyness. To find out the relationship between shyness and academic achievement, product moment correlation technique.

Results

Table 21.1 presents results of correlation coefficients between different domains of shyness and academic achievement of the total sample selected. From the table it is clear that shyness correlated negatively and significantly with all the domains and total shyness scores among male sample. However, in females shyness did not correlate with physiological domain of the shyness and correlated significantly and negatively with social domain, psychological domain, and for total shyness scores. When the total sample is considered, except for scores on physiological domain, all the scores on remaining domains and total shyness were correlated significantly and negatively with academic achievement scores.

Table 21.1: Gender-wise and total correlation coefficients of academic achievement with different domains of shyness for the entire sample

Domains of Shyness	Gender		Total
	Male	Female	
Social	-.191**	-.135**	-.159**
Psychological	-.195**	-.089*	-.134**
Physiological	-.095*	.028 NS	-.029 NS
Total shyness	-.233**	-.127**	-.172**
N	581	639	1220
df	579	637	1218

Note: * Sig at .05 level; ** Sig at .01 level; NS-Non-significant

Table 21.2 presents results of correlation coefficients between different domains of shyness and academic achievement of the children alone. From the Table it is clear that shyness correlated negatively and significantly only with physiological domain scores of shyness. All the remaining correlation coefficients obtained for different domains and total shyness scores with academic achievement scores were found to be non-significant.

Table 21.2: Gender-wise and total correlation coefficients of academic achievement with different domains of shyness for children

Domains of shyness	Gender		Total
	Male	Female	
Social	-.028 NS	-.092 NS	-.077 NS
Psychological	-.145 NS	-.015 NS	-.038 NS
Physiological	.196**	.082 NS	-.002 NS
Total shyness	-.125	-.045 NS	.121 NS
N	171	254	425
df	169	252	423

Note: ** Sig at .01 level; NS-Non-significant

Table 21.3 presents results of correlation coefficients between different domains of shyness and academic achievement of the adolescents alone. From the Table it is clear that shyness correlated negatively and significantly with all the domains and total shyness scores among male, female and total sample except for physiological domain.

Table 21.3: Gender-wise and total correlation coefficients of academic achievement with different domains of shyness for adolescents

Domains of Shyness	Gender		Total
	Male	Female	
Social	-.216**	-.234**	-.225**
Psychological	-.202**	-.263**	-.232**
Physiological	-.053 NS	-.057 NS	-.057 NS
Total shyness	-.248**	-.271**	-.258**
N	410	385	795
df	408	383	793

Note: ** Sig at .01 level; NS-Non-significant

Discussion

Main findings of the present study are:

1. For the overall sample shyness correlated significantly and negatively.
2. Shyness had significant influence over academic achievement.
3. Shyness affected the achievement negatively more for adolescents than children.
4. Only physiological domain of shyness did not influence academic achievement of the sample selected.

Higher levels of shyness resulted in lower academic achievement. The results of the present study with reference to shyness and academic achievement are in partially in agreement with studies done earlier. Lower academic performance (D'Souza, Urs & James (2000) was related to higher levels of shyness in one study; however in another study Shyness did not influence academic achievement. Shyness can also be acquired later on, instigated at times of developmental transition when children face new challenges in their relationships with their peers. For instance, entering the academic and social whirl of elementary school may leave them feeling awkward or inept with their peers. Teachers label them as shy and it sticks; they begin to see themselves that way and act it.

Adolescence is another hurdle that can kick off shyness. Not only are adolescents' bodies changing but their social and emotional playing fields are redefining them. Their challenge is to integrate sexuality and intimacy into a world of relationships that used to be defined only by friendship and relatives (Psychology today, 1995).

The treatment for shyness is multi-fold. In support of the benefits of the "tend-and-befriend" response, parents and teachers should encourage shy individuals to become more involved in social clubs and activities as a means of establishing a social support network. Service learning programmes through the school and other community volunteer activities have been proposed as offering shy individuals non-threatening opportunities for practicing and developing their social skills in a semi-structured social environment while minimizing feelings of social anxiety and self-consciousness (Carducci, 2000). In addition, to help shy individuals in their efforts to make conversation with others, teachers should consider including in the general curriculum information on such topics as the basic elements and protocol for approaching and engaging others in social conversation. Shy individuals tend to use alcohol and drugs to deal with their shyness, parents, teachers, and mental health professionals should also be sensitive to the possibility of substance abuse issues.

22

Psycho-cultural Factors Involved in Separation of the Couples

A Comparative Study Between Divorced Couples in Iran and India

Koaramollah Javanmard[1]
TBBSV Ramanaiah[1]

ABSTRACT

In the present study an attempt is mad study of divorce between youth in among couples from Mysore city of India in the year 2006-2007 and will also be gathered from the records maintained by the court.

A descriptive and a diagnostic design would be adopted in carrying out the study. The proposed study has the features of descriptive study as it elicits the baseline data and also the surface issues concerned with the study.

The study specific objectives to understand the extent or legal divorce in Mysore City of India — to know the socio-demographic profile of the divorced couple — to find out the factors associated with the divorce among marital couples — to understand the socio-economic and cultural life of both divorcer and divorcee. To find out the effects of divorce on the children of marital couple.

In the present study an attempt is made to study of divorce between youth in among couples from Khorramabad city of Iran in the year 2006-2007 and will also be gathered from the records maintained by the court.

A descriptive and a diagnostic design would be adopted in carrying out the study the proposal study has the features of descriptive study as it elicits the baseline data and also the surface issues concerned with the study.

1. **Ph.D. Student, Department of Social Work, University of Mysore, Mysore, Karnataka (India).**

The study specific objectives to understand the extent or legal divorce in Khorrmabad city of Iran to know the socio-demographic profile of the divorced couple to fin out the factors associated with the divorce among marital couples to understand the socio-economic and cultural list of both divorcer and divorcee to find out couple. The divorce rate is very high in Iran.

Review of Literature

India is a democratic country, India is a country of people belongs to different religions, languages and of cultural diversity, the marriage laws differ from religion to religion and Mysore city is chosen as the place of study in India. Divorce rate in India comparatively the lowest in the world, it is estimated that one out of 100 marriages ends up in divorce in India. However, the rate of divorce is higher in urban areas than the rural areas. However, it is estimated that number of legal divorces is around 400 in the preceding one year.

Divorce under the Hindu Marriage Act 1955, can be obtained by both the spouses on the basis of any of the following 9 groups: adultery, cruelty, leprosy, not heard for 7 year — No resumption, no restitution, rape, sodomy, bestiality, once the petition for divorce by mutual consent is filed.

The court gives the parties 6 months' times to reconsider (Junior, 2007). Divorce rate in India are amongst the lowest in the world 11 marriage out of 1,000 marriage end up to divorce in India. The divorce rate in India is even quite lower in the village in India and higher in urban parts of India (Journal Divorce rate in India, 2007).

The Hindu by and large practiced monogamy (one wife), however a small section of Hindu population consisting of princes and wealthy person marriage more than once.

The Hindu of Middle class married second time only if their wife proved to be barrel or died. This was also done with the consent of the Brahmans (Women and Law, p. 55, 2003).

Marriage is no longer sacred word and divorce no longer a taboo. With the passage of time a large number of Indians are flooding the divorce. Courts to escape from unhappy marriage and assert their independence (Violence against Women, p. 163, 2003). Almost 75 per cent of India population lives in village and the rural economy are agro based. Here the entire family goes to work. Both have band and wife earth for the whole family. The bond between the child and the mother cannot be refuted in any culture. This is the underlying principle of Indian family system (Violence against women, 2003).

In India, dowary problem is main reason for divorce in a weekly that most of the divorces in India are caused by financial reasons and mostly in urban areas. However, even today it is rate to find couples splitting up if they do not get along concern ally we Indians have a fairly practical view of marriage.

No one really expects to get along at all time, and overall I have seen in the marriages around me that both men and women tend to compromise (Mita, p. 1-4, 2007).

The divorce rate in India a bout twenty years ago was about 5 per cent. Now the divorce rate is about fewer than 5 per cent in an area called Haryana 5,000 divorces occur every year this is the highest in the country among state with comparable population (Mohan). This is quite alarming to many sociologists (www.exampleassays.com causes rise divorce rate in India, 2007). Until recently for Hindus marriage was obligatory and sacramental.

Hindus strongly believe that parent's should find rest only when the son performs the last rites. Initial marriage was considered equally binding to men and women, but later law givers admonished the wife to be completely devoted to her husband. The most important and effective legislation for divorce was the Hindu marriage and divorce at of 1955 which offered equal opportunity to the wife and comprising several major castes in city India.

The primary data was forum judicial files, supplemented by interviews, 9 per cent of the husbands and 17.5 per cent of the wives were illiterate or semi literate. Over 40 per cent of all divorces were among Brahmins, 25.5 per cent of the husband and 83.5 per cent of the wives were unemployed 50 per cent of the respondents felt that their marriage were arranged without through enquiry and planning 48 per cent of the wives were aged 16-20 when they got married; most men married between ages 21 and 25. Reason for divorce in this study includes:

1. cruelty;
2. interference by in-laws;
3. extra marital relations;
4. sexual dissatisfaction.

The Marriage Amendment of 1976 reduced the period of waiting for a divorce from the former average of 5-8 years to less than a year. The number of divorce increased suddenly in 1976 and continues to rise year.

65 per cent of the men divorced between ages 26 and 35, and 67.5 per cent of the women divorced between ages 21 and 30. Public opinion regarding divorce and divorces varies among communities. 2/3 of the mother in this study supported the children, 75.5 per cent of the men in the study had remarried by the time of the study, while only 35 per cent of the women had remarried (Journal, 1989).

Of all human groups the Family is the most important primary group it is a small social groups consisting of a 2 Father mother and on or more children (Bhushan, Vidya, the Family, 2005).

Family is a group defined by a sex relationship sufficiently precise and enduring to provide for the procreation and upbringing of children (Madver, p. 230). 1959.

Divorce is a complex and difficult experience for all family members. Anthropologist Paul Bo Hannah (1970) has identified six overlapping experiences which arise from divorce and which vary in intensity depending on the couple.

Divorce has become an unavailable (on sequin of martial dies harmony in certain cases. Divorce always brings adverse repercussions in the Family (Vance year not available, 2008).

According to Lee (2002) "children's well bring in post divorce situations is a highly complex interactive process that is influenced by a multitude of Factors. We would research that suggests that the effects of divorce extend to the college level of development and age already marked with high levels of change and personal development (AACAP, 1998).

Marriage is an important milestone in the life of the any it brings not only two individuals to gather but also two family together it is also found in a study made by Richardson and MCCABE (2001) that young person from divorced families display lower levels of life satisfaction and higher levels of anxiety than individuals from healthy families. The status of divorced women is much lower than divorced men.

Women encounter more problems from others and more likely to be socially ostracized. Some findings indicate that as a result of exciting atmosphere before divorce, violent quarrels and conflicts, step further deviation.

Parent's quarrels and conflicts, step further deviation. Parent's behaviour and father's negligence in socializing the criminal individual's faces in some difficulties (Masmehpar, 1999) in Islam divorce is a signature decree establish to rather than a constitutional on.

General speaking, in Islam it is tried to prevent divorce and to restrict its cases through various methods (Elmi Danaye, 1990).

Divorce for Iranians residing in foreign countries as divorce is a personal affair; it should be rules by national laws rather than a constitutional on.

Under the article 6 of civil law of Iran divorce and its related issues are subject to the rules and regulations of Iran and foreign courts must obey these rules, unless it is against their national order. Basically foreign court can investigate and judge divorce requests of Iranians residing in their country (Katuziayah, 1992). Through Iranian men can stain obtain a divorce.

One rate of marital dissolution is relatively law, hovering around to percent (Sanansariah, 1992).

Marital dissolution is particularly rare in rural and tribal communities in urban communities and metropolitan areas, the situation is different, and the rate of divorce is reported to be higher and rising (Naseehi Behnam 1985) Nevertheless, in a survey of simple of educated Iranians in Tehran, only a small minority of Women (24%) agreed that divorce should be made easier, despite their very limited right of obtaining it (Hojatetal, 1999).

This finding indicates the culture disagree associated with Divorce. Research on divorce in Iran, however shows that the rate of divorce is increasing among employed women, compared to women who are not employed outside the home (Aghjanaian 1986).

According to the figures, the divorce rate increased at the sometime. The revere 910/483 divorce registered intended March 2008. There was arising of 7.5 in the country divorce rate, compared with the last year. Divorce rates In Iran, 2008).

According to this conservative website, marriage and divorce rates have increased 8.4 and 6.58 respectively during the First nine months of this Iranian year (March-November), compared to the some period Last year. The number of marriage have been 459/568 cases during the first nine months of Last Iranian year was 49/694 cases reaching 52/928 cases over the same period this year (Journal Iran women, 2008).

Research Methodology

The researcher would approach the legal authorities with a request to accord permission to carry out the study. After getting permission, the list of all available cases of divorce will be prepared. The researcher would approach each case of divorce (divorced married couple) separately and explain the objectives of the study and assure confidentiality. The data will be collected mainly through informal records maintained by the Court in India. The profile of divorce cases in the preceding one year.

Sample

The sample of 100 consecutive cases (couple of divorce would be chosen for the study in Mysore city at India, a list of all settled cases of divorce from the court of Mysore city will be prepared from among the list of divorced couples, 100 consecutive cases adopting the ethical issues of research will be chosen.

Table 22.1: Distribution of the sample selected by country and age groups

Age groups (in years)		Country		Total
		Iran	India	
<20	Frequency	26	20	46
	%	13.0%	10.0%	11.5%
20-25	Frequency	57	62	119
	%	28.5%	31.0%	29.8%
26-30	Frequency	75	80	155
	%	37.5%	40.0%	38.8%
31-36	Frequency	42	38	80
	%	21.0%	19.0%	20.0%
Total	Frequency	200	200	400
	%	100.0%	100.0%	100.0%

Table 22.2: Distribution of the sample selected by country and educational levels

Educational level		Country		Total
		Iran	India	
Illiterate	Frequency	63	90	153
	%	31.5%	45.0%	38.3%
Diploma	Frequency	120	60	180
	%	60.0%	30.0%	45.0%
Bachelor	Frequency	15	28	43
	%	7.5%	14.0%	10.8%
Masters	Frequency	2	20	22
	%	1.0%	10.0%	5.5%
Ph.D.	Frequency	–	2	2
	%	–	1.0%	.5%
Total	Frequency	200	200	400
	%	100.0%	100.0%	100.0%

CC=.319; P=.000 (HS)

Table 22.3: Distribution of the sample selected by country and relationship others

Relationship with others		Country		Total
		Iran	India	
Husband with others	Frequency	2	25	27
	%	2.0%	25.0%	13.5%
Wife with other	Frequency	1	18	19
	%	1.0%	18.0%	9.5%
No such issue	Frequency	97	57	154
	%	97.0%	57.0%	77.0%
Total	Frequency	100	100	200
	%	100.0%	100.0%	100.0%

CC=.429; P=.000 (HS).

Table 22.4: Distribution of the sample selected by country and relationship others

Other reasons		Country		CC value	P value
		Iran	India		
Abuse (Physical/Sexual)	Frequency	18	75	.496	.000 (HS)
	%	18.0%	75.0%		
Domestic violance	Frequency	28	87	.512	.000 (HS)
	%	28.0%	87.0%		

CC=.496; P=.000 (HS).

Table 22.5: Distribution of the sample selected by country and support others

Support		Country		CC	P
		Iran	India		
Husband to pay	Frequency	81	65	.177	.011 (S)
	%	81.0%	65.0%		
Amount sent weekly	Frequency	0	5	.158	.024 (S)
	%	0	5.0%		
Paying reasonable amount	Frequency	47	53	.060	.396 (NS)
	%	47.0%	53.0%		

Conclusion

200 couples (100 couples from Iran and 100 couples from India) were randomly selected from cities of Khorramabad in Iran and Mysore in India. No significant association was observed between age groups and countries (CC=.058; P=.716). On the whole we find 38.8 per cent of the couples belonged to the age group of 26-30 years, followed by 29.8 per cent of the couples from the age group of 20-25 years.

It is very clear from the above table that number of children was a major issue for separation. In Iran it was childlessness (67%) as against 41 per cent in India. In India 49 per cent of the couple had single child at the time of divorce, as against only 13 per cent of the sample in Iran. Further, contingency coefficient test revealed a significant association between countries and number of children (CC=.387; P=.000). Overall we find that childlessness had maximum frequency (108), followed by single child (62) and four children least (5).

An interesting finding is that in India we find majority of the children live with mother (94.9%) as against 33.3 per cent in Iran. In Iran, 54.5 per cent of the children live with father as against only 5.1 per cent in India. Even statistically significant association was observed between stay of children and countries (CC=.555; P=.000). Overall we find majority of the children live with mothers and very few live with grandparents.

In Iran, majority of the sample opined drug abuse was a major concern (36%), followed by violence (21%) and sexual misconduct least or nil. However, in India, violence was the major concern (40%) for divorce followed by alcohol and drug abuse (10.5% and 10.0% respectively) and sexual misconduct least (CC=.418; P=.000). Overall, we find that violence had highest concern (30.5%), followed by drug abuse (23%) and sexual misconduct least (1.8%).

Main Findings

(a) 21-25 and 26-30 years are the high risk age groups for separation leading to divorce in both Iran and India.

(b) In Iran parent without children had higher proneness to divorce, where as in India parents with single child had more divorces.

(c) In India children live more with mothers and in Iran children live more with fathers.

(d) In Iran drug abuse was a major concern for divorce, where as in India, violence was a major concern.

REFERENCES

Anusha, Vidya; *Introduction to Sociology*, New Delhi, India, 2005.

MaClever R.M. C.H. *Society and Introduction Analysis*, London, MacMillan and Co., 1959.

P. Lamm, Robert, Sociology, New Forkst, Wester Illinois University, McGraw Hill Inc. 1992.

Vance, Andrew M. The Social Effects of Divorce File: D/THE%20social%20effects%20.of%divorce.htm

www.22cap.org/publications/factsfam/divorce,.htm (American Academy of Child and Adolescent Psychiatry, 1998)

Richardson, S. and McCabe M.P. Parental Divorce during Adolescence and Early Adulthood, Adolescence, 2001.

Masmehpar, Mohamad Reza, Study of the Relation Between Adventure and Social Deviances Among the Youth, 1999.

Danay Elmi Manijeh: Divorce Causes in Iran's Law, Tehran, 1990.

Katuziyan Naser: *Civil Law of Family*, Vol. I, University, 1992.

Aghajanian, A. Some Notes on Divorce in Iran, *Journal of Marriage and the Family*, Family and Family change in Iran D.S.F. University, 1986.

http://www.payrand.com/news/08/apr/1305.html; *Marriage and Divorce Rates in Iran*, 2008.

http://www.Iranian.wscgi-bin/iran-news/exec/view/cgi;iranian Rate on the Rise in Iran, *Persian Journal Iran Women*, 2008.

Junior, Ilite: *Hindu Marriage*, City Bangalore, State Karnataka, India, 2007.

www.Example Essays.com, DMCA; Divorce rate in India, 11/29.2007

Anjani Kant, Dr. *Women and the Law*, New Delhi, 2003.

Roy, As Hime, *Violence and the Law*, New Delhi, 2003.

Mita, Tameshraju, Divorce Rates of Word, April 4, 2007.

www.Example essays.com - Causes Rise Divorce Rate in India, 2007.

http://popline.org/close/0036/206834.htm Document Number 1, 206834: *Divorce in Hindu Society*, 1989.

Briec, Nekula: *Data Analysis Psychology and Sociology with Spss Translation to Ali Abadie*, Ali samadie, Tehran, University, 2005.

23

A Study on Psycho-socio Status of Child Labourers

Nanjunda DC.,[1] Mahadeviah CV.[2]
Dinesh PT.,[3] Siddaraju VG.[4]

ABSTRACT

This article presents an empirical view of the psycho-socio status of child labourers of safety Silk industries at Bangalore, in Karnataka. The study covered a sample of 200 child labourers belonging to different categories selected by stratified random sampling technique. Aaron's Socio-economic Status Scale developed by Aaron, Marihal and Malathesia (1976), the Self-Concept Scale developed by Harmohan Singh and Saraswathi Singh (1977) and Adjustment Inventory developed by the investigator were made use of in this study for collecting data from the respondents. The study showed that the child labourers did not differ significantly in terms of their family size and place of work. Their self-concept and significant association with their order or birth, parent's occupation and family income. Similarly, the SES of the respondents had significant association with their salary, parent's education and family income.

Introduction

Child labour remains a widespread problem in the world today. Although child labour can have positive effects, in some situations it has negative effects on health and development of the children. Child labour is a most vital, almost unavoidable and most serious problem throughout the world, especially in developing countries. India and Asia together account for over 90 per cent of total child employment. Child labour is especially prevalent in

3. CSSEIP, University of Mysore, Mysore, Karnataka, (India).

rural areas where the capacity to enforce minimum age requirements for schooling and work is lacking. Children work for a variety of reasons, the most important being poverty and the induced pressure upon them to escape from this plight. Though children are not well paid, they still serve as major contributors to family income in developing countries. Schooling problems also contribute to child labour, whether it is the inaccessibility of schools or the lack of quality education, which spurs parents to enter their children in more profitable pursuits (Becker, 1997).

The history of health concern with child labour significantly predates the industrial revolution, with some restriction prohibiting the employment of children in selective dangerous areas of work having been enacted as early as 13th century. However, the process of changing limited concern regarding child labour into a broad social consensus was a slow one, involving much public debate during which the perception of the child gradually moved from one of a vital wage earner to that of a vulnerable individual to be loved and protected. The issue of child labour has drawn increasing international attention and condemnation since the 1970s. Criticism has focussed on inhuman working conditions, impact on mental health, and lost educational opportunities. Even as practical consideration have been the central force behind the modified emphasis of international child labour rededication efforts, those efforts have also been pushed in new directions by growing social science critique of the philosophies underlying abolition oriented policies and the innovative approaches of some child welfare organisations. Their physical, mental and emotional growth needs are ignored. When caught up in clutches of the 'harsh reality'—child labour—they are deprived of their rights to development, education, medical care, recreation, leisure, play and the joys of childhood. The development of a nation depends on the attention and care bestowed upon the development of children. Hence an attempt is made to study the Adjustment, Self-concept and the SES of the child labourers (Reddy and Reddy, 2003).

The objectives of the present study were:

1. To find out the level of Adjustment of the child labourers working in Silk Industries.
2. To find out the level of Self-concept of the child labourers working in Silk Industries.
3. To find out the level of Self-economic Status of the child labourers working in Silk Industries.
4. To find out the relationship between Adjustment and Self-concept of the child labourers working in Silk Industries.
5. To find out the relation ship between Adjustment and Socio-economic Status of the child labourers working in Silk Industries.

6. To find out the relationship between Self-concept and Socio-economic Status of the child labourers working in Silk Industries.

Specific Objectives

1. To study the Adjustment, Self-concept and SES in terms of:
   - *(a)* Gender
   - *(b)* Order of birth
   - *(c)* Family size
   - *(d)* Education of the child
   - *(e)* Place of work
   - *(f)* Salary of the child
   - *(g)* Education of the parents
   - *(h)* Occupation of the parents, and
   - *(i)* Family income
2. To compare Adjustment and Self-concept
3. To compare Adjustment and SES
4. To compare Self-concept and SES

Method

Sample

The survey research strategy was used for carrying out the study. It was conducted on a select population of child labourers working in Silk Industries at Bangalore, Karnataka by Stratified Random Sampling technique. 150 child labourers were selected as sample. It included 75 boys and 75 girls belonging to the age group of below 14. Among them 53 were illiterate child labourers, 41 of them from Std.1 to 3. 36 of them from std. 4.to6. 20 of them from std. 7 to 9. 52 of them studying in schools and 98 of them out of school, 117 of them working in Silk Industries and the rest 33 of them working at their houses.

Tools

The details of the tools employed for collecting information from child labourers, were as follows:

1. Aaron's Socio-economic Status Scale developed by Aaron, Marihal and Malathesia (1976) was made use of in this tudy. This scale consists of five dimensions, viz.
   - *(a)* occupation of father;
   - *(b)* father's education;

(c) material possession;

(d) house; and

(e) shirts and blouses.

The reliability to-efficient and concurrent validity of the scale were found to be 0.77 and 0.61 respectively.

2. The Self-concept Scale development by Harmohan Singh and Saraswathi Singh (1977) was made use of in this study. The scale contains twenty two, trait descriptive adjectives. Nineteen were positive or socially desirable attributes (Friendly, happy, kind, brave, honest, likeable, trusted, good, proud, loyal, co-operative, cheerful, thoughtful, popular, courteous, obedient, polite, clean, and helpful) while there were negative (lazy, jealous and bashful). The rating categories, scored from 1 to 5, are entitled 'not at all', 'not very often', 'some of the time', 'most of the time', and 'all of the time'. The reliability co-efficient for this scale by test-retest method was found to be 0.83.

3. An Adjustment Inventory was developed by the investigator. This inventory consists of the following four dimensions:

   (a) Social Adjustment (SA)

   (b) Emotional Adjustment (EA)

   (c) Industrial Adjustment (IA); and

   (d) Home Adjustment (HA).

There were 10 items in each dimension totaling 40 items. The reliability co-efficient by test-retest method was found to be 0.74. To assess the validity, correlation co-efficent of scores obtained on these four dimensions with composite adjustment scores were calculated and found statistically significant at 0.01 level of significance (SA 0.71, EA 0.85 and HA 0.79).

Data Analysis

The collected data were analysed through computer. The statistical techniques employed in this analysis were mean, standard deviation, 't'-test, X^2-test, ANOVA and Pearson's product moment correlation. The findings of the study are presented below in four sub divisions:

Adjustment of child labourers working in Silk Industries

1. 14 per cent of the children were well adjusted.
2. There was no significant difference between the child labourers in terms of their gender in emotional, industrial and home adjustment but there was significant difference in their social adjustment.

3. There was no significant difference between the child labourers in the dimensions of adjustment-social, emotional, industrial and home in terms of their family size.
4. There was no significant difference between the child labourers studying in the schools and out of the schools in social and emotional adjustment but there was significant difference in their industrial and home adjustment.
5. There was no significant difference between the child labourers working in industries and working at houses in social, emotional, industrial, and home adjustment.
6. The order of birth of the child labourers had no significant association with their adjustment in the dimensions-social, industrial and home, but with their emotional adjustment.
7. Education of the child labourers had no significant association with the dimensions of adjustment-social, industrial and home, but with their emotional adjustment.
8. Salary of the child labourers had no significant association with their adjustment in the dimensions-emotional and home but with their adjustment in the dimensions-social and industrial.
9. Parents' education of the child labourers had no significant association with their adjustment in the dimensions-industrial and home but with their adjustment in the dimensions-social and emotional.
10. Parents' occupation of the child labourers had no significant association with their adjustment in the dimensions-social and industrial but with their adjustment in the dimensions-emotional and home.
11. Family income of the child labourers had no significant association with their adjustment in the dimensions-social and industrial but with their adjustment in the dimensions-emotional and home.

Self-concept of Child Labourers working in Silk Industries

1. 16 per cent of the child labourers had good self-concept.
2. In self-concept there was no significant difference between the child labourers in terms of their gender and family size.
   (i) There was significant difference between the child labourers studying in the schools and those out of schools in self-concept.
   (ii) There is significant difference between the child labourers working in Silk Industries and working at houses in self-concept.
   (iii) Self-concept of the child labourers had no significant association with their education but with their order of birth, salary, parent's education, parent's occupation and family income.

3. Socio-economic Status of child labourers working in Silk Industries
   - *(i)* 14 pe rcent of the child labourers had high level of socio-economic status.
   - *(ii)* In Socio-economic status, there was no significant difference between child labourers in terms their SES, family size and education.
   - *(iii)* There was significant difference between the child labourers studying in the schools and out of the schools in the SES.
   - *(iv)* There was no significant difference between child labourers working in industries and working at houses in the socio-economic status.
   - *(v)* Socio-economic Status of the child labourers had significant association with their salary, parents' education, parents' occupation and family income.
4. Relationship between psychological and sociological factors
   - *(i)* Self-concept of the child labourers had significant relationship with their social, emotional land home adjustment but not with their industrial adjustment.
   - *(ii)* SES of the labourers had significant relationship with their industrial adjustment but not with their social, emotional and home adjustment.
   - *(iii)* There was no significant relationship between the self-concept of the child labourers and their socio-economic status.

Conclusion

It is concluded from the study that the child labourers didn't show any difference between them in Adjustment (in general) in terms of their gender, place of work and family size. But, the respondent's emotional adjustment was influenced by their own education, parent's education, parent's occupation and family income. This might be due to the fact that the wealth of the family is one of the important factors in emotional stability.

The respondents didn't show any difference in self-concept in terms of their gender and family size. Also it was found that parent's education, parent's occupation and family income had influence the self-concept and socio-economic status of the respondents. It might be reasoned that the literate parents would provide more safe and comfortable life to their children than their illiterate counter-parts, which would covertly or overtly impact the self-concept of the children. Simply it is inferred from the study that Education is the only solution for elevating the psycho-socio status of any individual.

Universalization of Elementary Education is the minimum as, we Indians' have to implement to abolish the system of child labour and protect the right of children.

Although our findings indicate that child labour may be affecting the mental health of children, more data are needed to develop a better understanding of the short-and long-term mental health problems associated with child labour. Most important, longitudinal studies are required to understand the short and long-term mental health effects of child labour on the individual child.

REFERENCES

Akabayashi, H. and Psacharopoulos, G. (1999). Child Labour and Mental Health: A USA Case Study. *Journal of Health Studies* 35 (5). Vol. 4.

Assaad, Ragui, Deborah Levison, and Nadia Zibani (2001). "The Effect of Child Work on Mental Health". In Forum *Newsletter*, Vol. 8. No. 2. p 24.

Becker, Gary (1994). *Child Labour — A Theoretical and Empirical Analysis, with Special Reference to the Health*. New York: Columbia University Press.

Baland, Jean-Marie and James Robinson: Impact of Work on Child Health, *Journal of Political Economy*, 108(4): 663-679, 2000.

Becker, Gary S (1997). "Is There Any Way to Stop Child Labour Abuses?" *Health Week*, May 12, p. 22.

Morgan. C.T (1993). *Introduction to Psychology*, New Delhi: Tata McGraw-Hill Publication.

Women
The Psychology of Victims of Ambient Abuse

Surya Rekha[1]

ABSTRACT

Abuse as every one knows, is not only wife-beating or bride burning, it can take many forms. It is not confined to lower socioe-conomic levels of society. Women suffer emotional abuse at every level, even in so-called educated, 'cultured' houses. Psychological and emotional abuse is more common here. What is worse is that many times the victims themselves are not aware that they are being abused. Among the various types of psychological abuse, I wish to concentrate on 'Ambient Abuse' a very subtle form of abuse, where the victim is hardly aware that she is being abused. She believes that everything is normal and that it is her thoughts and behaviour that are at fault.

Introduction

In the words of Sam Vaknin. who introduced the concept, 'Ambient abuse' is the stealthy, subtle, underground currents of maltreatment that sometimes go unnoticed even by the victims themselves, until it is too late. It is by for the most dangerous kind of abuse here is". Ambient abuse, therefore, is the fostering, propagation, and enhancement of on atmosphere of fear, intimidation, instability, unpredictability and irritation. There are no acts of traceable explicit abuse, nor any manipulative settings of control. Yet, the irksome feeling remains, a disagreeable foreboding, a premonition, a bad omen. In the long term, such an environment erodes the victim's sense of

1. **Department of Psychology at V.V.N. Degree College, Bangalore, Karnataka (India).**

self-worth and self-esteem. Self-confidence is shaken badly. Often, the victim adopts a paranoid or schizoid stance and thus renders himself or herself exposed even more to criticism and judgement. The roles are thus reversed: the victim is considered mentally deranged and the abuser the suffering soul. There are five categories of ambient abuse and they are often combined in the conduct of a single abuser:

1. Inducing Disorientation
2. Incapacitating
3. Shared Psychosis
4. Abuse of Information
5. Control by Proxy.

The current paper explores the extent of awareness about ambient abuse prevalent in our society. A survey conducted in this area revealed the lack of knowledge about ambient abuse among women belonging to different walks of life.

Problem: To study the awareness of the existence of ambient abuse among women.

Sample: Women ranging in age between 20-50 years, belonging to different walks of life.

Method: A list of hypothetical situations representing the five categories of ambient abuse was given to each respondent. The respondent was asked to rate each as to whether the situation was abusive, and if so, to what degree. The respondents marked the degree of abuse on a Five-point rating scale.

Analysis: The average rating for each hypothetical situation was calculated, and the level of awareness of each type of abuse estimated.

Discussion: Results reveal that most respondents considered many of these situations acceptable and a part of life. They were not considered abusive. Could this be because of the gender role into which women are expected to fit, no matter what their social, economic or professional standing is? The woman is often expected to 'adjust', 'manage', 'comply', 'take it easy' etc. and perhaps these expectations are the ones that make them feel abuse is an acceptable, unchangeable part of life.

What can we do about it? Is it possible to sensitize men about this, and most importantly — women? Will women breathe easier when their husbands are at home, and have a normal, healthy, relaxed relationship? These are some important questions that could be addressed.

Strange as it sounds, many perfectly normal people get trapped in the cycle of abuse. We see it in the Stockholm syndrome, named from an incident in which hostages took the side of their captors and clung to them! Since the Middle Ages, inquisitors and torturers have known and capitalized on this bizarre phenomenon in the hapless victims at their mercy. The KGB's famed method of breaking people deliberately brought it about to establish mind control.

In 1993, the World Development Report of the World Bank estimated that "women aged 15 to 44 lose more Discounted Health Years of Life (DHYLs) to rape and domestic violence than to breast cancer, cervical cancer, obstructed labor, heart disease, AIDS, respiratory infections, motor vehicle accidents or war". Abuse as every one knows, is not only wife-beating or bride burning, it can take many forms. It is not confined to lower socio-economic levels. Women suffer abuse at every level, even in so called educated, 'cultured' houses.

Psychological and emotional abuse is more common here. What is worse is that many times the victims themselves are not aware that they are being abused. Among the various types of psychological abuse, I wish to concentrate on 'Ambient Abuse'—a very subtle form of abuse, where the victim is hardly aware that she is being abused. She believes that every thing is normal and that it is her thoughts and behaviour that are at fault.

The concept of 'Ambient Abuse' was introduced by Sam Vaknin (1997). According to him, 'Ambient abuse is the stealthy, subtle, underground currents of maltreatment that sometimes go unnoticed even by the victims themselves, until it is too late. Ambient abuse penetrates and permeates everything but is difficult to pinpoint and identify. It is ambiguous, atmospheric, and diffuse. Hence its insidious and pernicious effects. It is by far the most dangerous kind of abuse there is".

Ambient abuse, therefore, is the fostering, propagation, and enhancement of an atmosphere of fear, intimidation, instability, unpredictability and irritation. There are no acts of traceable explicit abuse, nor any manipulative settings of control. Yet, the irksome feeling remains, a disagreeable foreboding, a premonition, a bad omen.

In the long term, such an environment erodes the victim's sense of self-worth and self-esteem. Self-confidence is shaken badly. Often, the victim adopts a paranoid or schizoid stance and thus renders himself or herself exposed even more to criticism and judgment. The roles are thus reversed: the victim is considered mentally deranged and the abuser — the suffering soul.

There are five categories of ambient abuse and they are often combined in the conduct of a single abuser:

1. Inducing Disorientation

The abuser causes the victim to lose faith in her ability to manage and to cope with the world and its demands. She no longer trusts her senses, her skills, her strengths, her friends, her family, and the predictability and benevolence of her environment. The abuser subverts the target's focus by disagreeing with her way of perceiving the world, her judgment, the facts of her existence, by criticizing her incessantly and by offering plausible but specious alternatives. By constantly lying, he blurs the line between reality and nightmare. By recurrently disapproving of her choices and actions the abuser shreds the victim's self-confidence and shatters her self-esteem'. By reacting disproportionately to the slightest 'mistake' he intimidates her to the point of paralysis.

2. Incapacitating

The abuser gradually and surreptitiously takes over functions and chores previously adequately and skillfully performed by the victim. The prey finds itself isolated from the outer world, a hostage to the goodwill or, more often, ill-will of her captor. She is crippled by his encroachment and by the inexorable dissolution of her boundaries and ends up totally dependent on her tormentor's whims and desires, plans and stratagems. Moreover, the abuser engineers impossible, dangerous, unpredictable, unprecedented, or highly specific situations in which he is sorely needed. The abuser makes sure that his knowledge, his skills, his connections, or his traits are the only ones applicable and the most useful in the situations that he, himself, wrought. The abuser generates his own indispensability.

3. Shared Psychosis

The abuser creates a fantasy world, inhabited by the victim and himself and besieged by imaginary enemies. He allocates to the abused the role of defending this invented and unreal Universe. She must swear to secrecy, stand by her abuser no matter what, lie, fight, pretend, obfuscate and do whatever else it takes to preserve this oasis of inanity. Her membership in the abuser's 'kingdom' is cast as a privilege and a prize. But it is not to be taken for granted. She has to work hard to earn her continued affiliation. She is constantly being tested and evaluated. Inevitably, this interminable stress reduces the victim's resistance and her ability to 'see straight'.

4. Abuse of Information

From the first moments of an encounter with another person, the abuser is on the prowl. He collects information. The more he knows about his potential victim the better able he is to coerce, manipulate, charm, extort or convert it 'to the cause'. The abuser does not hesitate to misuse the information he gleans, regardless of its intimate nature or the circumstances in which he obtained it. This is a powerful tool in his armory.

5. Control by Proxy

If all else fails, the abuser recruits friends, colleagues, mates, family members, the authorities, institutions, neighbours, the media, teachers in short, third parties to do his bidding. He uses them to cajole, coerce, threaten, stalk, offer, retreat, tempt, convince, harass, communicate and otherwise manipulate his target. He controls these unaware instruments exactly as he plans to control his ultimate prey. He employs the same mechanisms and devices. And he dumps his props unceremoniously when the job is done. Another form of control by proxy is to engineer situations in which abuse is inflicted upon another person. Such carefully crafted scenarios of embarrassment and humiliation provoke social sanctions (condemnation, opprobrium, or even physical punishment) against the victim. Society or a social group becomes the instrument of the abuser. The current paper explores the extent of awareness about ambient abuse prevalent in our society.

Not much research has been done in this area, especially in our country. In fact, many people are ignorant of the term 'ambient Abuse'. In my experience I have seen a lot of women, who are in 'envious positions' in society, who have 'wonderful, caring husbands and families', living with a constant feeling of foreboding, wondering, what crisis will erupt in the family at what time, and always on tenterhooks when the husband is around, trying their level best not to 'upset him'. Hence this exploratory survey. If we are at least aware of what Ambient Abuse is, we can develop means of coping with it.

Method

Goal: To study the extent of awareness of Ambient Abuse in Indian women.

Problem: To study the awareness of the existence of ambient abuse, and the judged severity of such abuse among married and single women.

Participants: The sample was a 'convenience sample' and consisted of ninety six women ranging in age between 20 and 50 years, belonging to different walks of life. Of these, thirty-two respondents were married and sixty four single. Of the married respondents, two were divorced.

Procedure: This was an exploratory survey conducted with the help of hypothetical situations rated on a five-paint-scale. A list of hypothetical situations representing the five categories of ambient abuse was given to each respondent. In each category, three hypothetical situations were given, making a total of fifteen situations. The situations were based on experiences of women reported on various sites of the internet, experiences related by women who suffered such situations and news paper reports. The respondent was asked to rate each as to whether the situation was abusive, and if so, to what degree. The respondents marked the degree of abuse on a Five-point rating scale - Extremely Abusive, Highly Abusive, Mildly Abusive, Not Abusive and Normal Behaviour.

Each point was scored as follows:

Extremely abusive	–	5 points
Highly abusive	–	4 points
Mildly abusive	–	3 points
Not abusive	–	2 points
Normal behaviour	–	1 point

The total rating anyone type of abuse could get was 15 points. This included a rating of 'extremely abusive' to all three situations in one category. The minimum was three points.

Analysis

The judgment given for each type of abuse was calculated. This was done by computing the total rating given by each respondent to each type of abuse, and converting this into a percentage. Comparisons were made among different types of abuse for the whole group. Next, the judgement given by the respondents for each type of abuse was compared, on the basis of the marital status.

When the survey was thought of, it was expected that majority of the respondents would be unaware that the situations given for rating were abusive. But the results did not support this expectation. The comparison of ratings given for various types of abuse showed that the respondents judged all the five types of abuse described by Vaknin as either extremely abusive, highly abusive or mildly abusive. This is at least a cheering thought, because women in India are aware that abuse need not be overtly visible and physical.

In the words Hina and Benedictis, *et.al.*(2004) "In some cultures, control of women by men is accepted as the norm ... Today we see many cultures moving from the subordination of women to increased equality of women within relationships". Perhaps Indian women are among these women who are moving towards more equality.

Yet, reports in news papers about marital abuse do not allow us to believe this. An article by Mita Kapur — "Victims of Abuse" (2005) states that cross-border studies conducted by the International Centre for Research on Women (ICRWL in Rajasthan, Uttar Pradesh, Gujarat and Kerala, emphasizing that domestic violence cuts through caste, class, religion, age and education. These women are victims of physical, mental, sexual and emotional abuse regardless of their education and economic status.

20 per cent of the cases reported in Rajasthan are of working women. In Kerala, 30 per cent of women complained of physical abuse and 69 per cent of psychological torture. Two out of every five women in abusive relationships

suffer silently because 'of shame and family honour. The lack of viable options keeps such women trapped in violent situations. Nearly one-third of the women experiencing abuse have thought of running away but the fear of leaving their children behind and having no place to go restrained them. Social and economic constraints further compound their sense of isolation. Lack of awareness and how to seek help renders these women more vulnerable to continuing and escalating abuse.

Devyani Srivastava, (as cited by Mita Kapur—2005) who writes on gender issues said, "These women have been brain-washed into believing that they are responsible for the violence inflicted on them. They face so much brutality in the court, at the hands of their families and the police because gender violence is seen as a nonissue; a household affair at best". Domestic violence can't be stopped, she felt, but the women can seek help. Women have to refuse to become a mere statistic.

Few studies have been made of gender-based violence, partly because of the lack of accurate definitions, but also because it is so seldom reported to authorities. Women have many reasons for not reporting incidents of violence. Legal authorities often do not take appropriate action. Many women do not know their legal rights. Women have good reason to fear that they will be victimized again, either by insensitive, accusatory questions or by actual assault.

According to Meeta Rani Jha (2007) the western definition of domestic violence does not fit into the reality of women's lives in the context of India. Much of the violence that happens within the home (as private space) spills into public space depending upon the social group of the women. Women have very little ownership of any physical space they may inhabit, either private or public. For the majority of Indian women, violence crosses over into all spaces, not just designated private or public spaces.

Given the above results which show that there is an awareness in Indian women about Ambient Abuse, why is it that no one is talking about it? Violence within the family has always remained hidden and even now, women hesitate to speak of it for a variety of reasons. Family violence or 'family quarrel' is common to all classes, religions, and communities, all over India. In many families, particularly in the middle class, a woman's status is defined only in the context of a man's and the patriarchal family. Hence, it is difficult for women to give up their limited rights in an oppressive situation in order to break the pattern of abuse.

Conclusion

The survey showed greater awareness of violence than expected. These results are heartening, because Indian women are at least recognizing the different types of abuse to which they are being subjected. But now the question we face is what do we do about it? It is not natural for a person to take abuse. Our instincts prompt us to fight or flee. But society blocks this common sense in our genes by infesting our brains with the idea that divorce or fighting back is wrong. Especially when the abuser goes around putting on an act of how hurt he is. What choice does this idea leave the victim? She must choose whether to:

(a) be a bad person or

(b) submit to abuse.

Every person's most precious possession is her self-conceptthe picture of herself she carries inside, the image of herself as a good person. People will do anything to preserve it. They would rather die than lose it or have it taken from them. So, she usually chooses to go against nature and be a good girl (put up with the abuse and keep turning the other cheek).

Merely building greater awareness among women about abuse is not sufficient. We need to sensitize the men in the society, and the 'Social Rule Makers', who provide an image of the so called 'Ideal Woman'.

REFERENCES

Kathleen Krajco (2007) "*The Essence of Narcissism*" http://www.operationdoubles.com/ na rei eycleola buse. htm.

Meeta Rani Jha (2007) 'Global Frontlines: India' endabuse.org/programs

Mita Kapur (2005) "Victims of Abuse" www.countercurrenls.org/gender-kapurD80305.htm

Sam Vaknin (1998) "Malignant Self Love—Narcissism Revisited" http://samvak.tripod.com; palma@unet.com.mk

Shelly Marshall (2006) "Defining the Abuser and Abuse" www.youareatarget.com/deline.

Tina de Benedictis, Ph.D., Jaelline Jaffe, Ph.D., and Jeanne Segal, Ph.D., (2007) "Domestic Violence and Abuse: Types, Signs, Symptoms, Causes, and Effects.

Relationship Between Adjustment and Self-esteem Among Adolescents

Ningamma C Betsur[1]
Armin Mahmoudi[2]

ABSTRACT

In the present study an attempt is made to see whether self-esteem is related to adjustment among adolescents studying in class 9 in Mysore city. A total of 100 adolescent students studying in Mysore city were randomly selected. They were administered Bell's Adjustment Inventory (1968) (which measured adjustment of an individual in 4 areas—Home, health, social and emotional) and Self-esteem inventory developed by Cooper and Smith (1987), which measured self-esteem of an individual in five areas—general self, social self, home parents, lie scale and school academic. Further, the students were classified into low and high self-esteem groups. Independent samples 't' test was applied to see the differences between students having high and low self-esteem in their adjustment scores. Results indicated that Home parents self-esteem had positive influence over emotional adjustment of the students, where the analysis revealed that higher the self-esteem better the adjustment. School academic self-esteem had positive influence over health adjustment of the students, where the analysis revealed that higher the self-esteem better the adjustment. Lastly, in other areas of self-esteem, there was no significant of self-esteem over adjustment of the students in individual areas as well as in total adjustment scores.

1. Reader, Department of Studies in Education, University of Mysore, Manasagangothri, Mysore - 570 006, Karnataka (India).
2. Department of Studies in Education, University of Mysore, Mysore, Karnataka (India).

Introduction

Adolescence is a transitional period of one's life between childhood and adulthood, during which some important biological, psychological and social changes take place. It is a period of storm and stress. Adolescents have to adjust with their own changes in personality on one side and the changing socio-economic environment on the other side. Some adolescents find it difficult to adjust normally with these changes and experience some problems, which are characteristic of this developing stage.

The adolescence boy or girl may be faced with serious problem of adjustment when there is a difference of opinions, ideas and attitudes with their parents. Conflicts may arise between the adolescent and the parents that are difficult to resolve if both of them want to willing compromise. It takes all the tact and understanding of parents to handle their adolescent. (Coleman, 1974). Families of delinquent or uncontrollable adolescents are characterized by poorer family relationships and less social connectedness and adjustment. In general, these families are lower on cohesion and independence and higher on conflict and control (Fox, 1998).

Necessity is the most remarkable element in making all people have various needs including biological adjustment and mental ones. The former comprises the needs such as sleep, subsidiaries which cause the survival and satisfy the basic human demands, and the latter contributes to making a healthy personality and growth and removing the mental illness or breakdown. The needs can be named as self-esteem, security and invention.

Indicating the importance of a healthy environment. On the whole, satisfying the needs leads to every single individual adjustment. Man lives in a world full of challenges resulted in depression and conflict as hindrances in achieving the goals. In other words, when a man's needs are not satisfied, he she suffer mental breakdown and tension. Thus, removing disappointment, shortcomings and life challenges ends in adjustment.

Self-esteem is the judgment we make about our own worth and the feelings associated with those judgments. According to Rosenberg (1979) a person with high self-esteem is fundamentally satisfied with the type of person he is yet he, may acknowledge his faults while hoping to overcome them. High self-esteem implies a realistic evaluation of the self's characteristics and competencies, coupled with an attitude of self-acceptance and self-respect. The persons with high self-esteem which shoulder more responsibilities can be more resistant and steadfast against mental pressure and the rest of ups and downs. High self-esteem causes prosperity, flourishing the hidden talents, initiative and economic, social and cultural achievements.

Self and peripheral adjustments are the bare necessities for every creature. Lack of due attention to the adjustment reactions amongst the youth will be gradually disguised as mental disorders, then it is significant to pay considerable and equal attention to the youth affairs as it is done to the adults to prevent from further consequences. Stank (2001) in his study demonstrated that there is a positive relationship between self-esteem and a given person's assumptions or of his/her capabilities; in other words, if the ratio of self-esteem in a person is lowered, the person feels debility. Conversely, high self-esteem will resuscitate empowerment feeling in a person. If a person feels that his/her self-esteem is exposed to instability, he/she preserves and defends from his self-worth by various behaviours and strategies.

Therefore, the adolescence with the same age group who are present at school can feel the tangibility of Pedagogical changes. Since school is a social environment, it is fundamental that every single individual keeps in touch with his/her peer groups Besides, the adjustment conflict can be posited in terms of the manner of adjustment to the school atmosphere, principals, teachers and subject matters is incorrect behaviours and will be pessimist to the future. Douglas (1968).

Objectives

1. To find whether there is a significant difference between the adjustments of Standard (IX) students having different levels of General self-esteem.
2. To find whether there is a significant differences between the adjustments of Standard (IX) students having different levels of Social self-esteem.
3. To find whether there is a significant differences between the adjustments of Standard (IX) students having different levels of Home, Parents self-esteem.
4. To find whether there is a significant differences between the adjustment of Standard (IX) students having different levels of School Academic self-esteem.

Methodology

Population and Sample

Population: The population of the study consisted of all the Standard (IX) student in Mysore city. The present study was conducted on the random sample of 100 Standard (IX) students ($N = 100$), male ($N_1 = 50$) and female ($N_2 = 50$) of secondary schools of Mysore city. The age of the subjects of class (IX) ranged between 14 and 15 years.

Tools

1. Adjustment Inventory for adolescent Students (BAI) developed by Bell's Adjustment (1968). The inventory comprises of 140 items in relation to five areas of adjustment (Home 35, Health 35, Social 35, and Emotional 35 items). The test is helpful in screening the poorly adjusted students who may need further psycho-diagnostic study and counseling for their adjustment problems. The reliability co-efficients were determined by spilt half and test retest methods, where the reliability co-efficients varied from .81 to .89 for various areas of adjustment through split half and reliability co-efficients varied from .89 to .92 through test retest method for different areas of adjustment. Cross validation of the scale with K.Kumar's adjustment inventory resulted in Pearson's *r* of .72, .79, .82 and .81 for home, health, social and emotional areas respectively.
2. Self-esteem Inventory for adolescent Students developed by Cooper smith(1987).The Inventory comprises of 58 items in relation to five areas of Self-esteem.(General self 25, Social self 8, Home parents 8, Lie scale 8, School Academic 8). The alpha co-efficient for the total self-esteem scale was .88 and .79 for the Anglo-Indian and Vietnamese-Australian samples respectively. The validity of the scale was ascertained by Convergent and discriminate validity using EPQ (Eyesenck Personality Questionnaire), where negative and significant correlations were obtained for neuroticism scale and positive and significant correlations were obtained for extroversion dimension.

Procedure

The inventories were administered on the sample of 100 adolescent subjects. The data collection was one in two sessions. Before administering the scale proper rapport was established with the students. In the first session data were collected on personal information and self-esteem scale was administered. In the second session after a gap of 2-3 days the sample was administered Bells Adjustment Inventory. The questionnaires were administered in a batch of 2-3 students. They were given instructions for answering as prescribed in the respective manuals. The items in the answer sheet were scored with the help of scoring keys for four different areas for self-esteem and adjustment.

The obtained scores were recorded on master sheet and later fed to the computer using SPSS for Windows software (version 16.0). Depending on the scores the subjects were classified into two levels of self-esteem-low and High. Using Independent samples 't' test, influence of self-esteem was verified on 4 areas of adjustment and total adjustment scores, taking self-esteem as independent variable (varied at 2 levels-low and high) and adjustment scores as dependent variables.

Analysis and Interpretation of Data

Tables 25.1 to 25.5 show influence of self-esteem on adjustment scores and results of independent samples 't' test.

(a) General self-esteem and adjustment

Table 25.1: Mean adjustment scores (on various areas) of the sample having low and high general self-esteem with the results of Independent samples 't' test

Areas of Adjustment	Level of Self-esteem	Mean	S.D	't' Value	P Value
Home	Low	12.81	4.49	1.205	.231
	High	11.70	3.58		
Health	Low	8.90	5.12	.637	.526
	High	8.20	4.84		
Social	Low	16.69	4.82	.593	.555
	High	16.03	5.54		
Emotional	Low	13.69	5.69	1.129	.262
	High	12.40	3.86		
Total	Low	51.83	14.57	1.136	.259
	High	48.60	8.25		

From Table 25.1, it is evident that in all the areas of adjustment, self-esteem did not have significant influence as all the obtained 't' values found to be non-significant. In other words students with low and high levels of general self-esteem had statistically equal scores on different areas of adjustment. Self-esteem was independent of adjustment in various areas as well as total adjustment scores.

(b) Social self-peer self-esteem and adjustment

As in the case of social adjustment, the students with low and high Self-esteem did not differ significantly in their adjustment scores in various areas and total adjustment scores. Here also, self-esteem did not have significant influence over adjustment scores. In the areas of home, health, social & emotional, the students with low and high Self-esteem did not differ significantly in their adjustment scores. Even with respect to total adjustment students with high and low Self-esteem didn't differs significantly. That means, Self-esteem didn't have significant influence over adjustment scores.

Table 25.2: Mean adjustment scores (on various areas) of the sample having low and high social self peer self-esteem with the results of Independent samples 't' test

Areas of Adjustment	Level of Self-esteem	Mean	S.D	't' Value	P Value
Home	Low	12.69	4.53	.649	.518
	High	12.11	3.73		
Health	Low	8.45	4.91	.627	.532
	High	9.11	5.27		
Social	Low	17.11	4.79	1.657	.101
	High	15.39	5.30		
Emotional	Low	12.80	5.32	1.288	.201
	High	14.19	5.00		
Total	Low	51.08	14.00	.222	.825
	High	50.47	11.31		

***(c)* Home parents self-esteem and adjustment**

Table 25.3: Mean adjustment scores (on various areas) of the sample having low and high home parents self-esteem with the results of Independent samples 't' test

Areas of Adjustment	Level of Self-esteem	Mean	S.D	't' Value	P Value
Home	Low	13.16	4.76	1.613	.110
	High	11.80	3.59		
Health	Low	9.16	5.26	.935	.352
	High	8.22	4.78		
Social	Low	17.10	4.66	1.217	.227
	High	15.88	5.35		
Emotional	Low	14.36	5.66	2.061	.042
	High	12.24	4.57		
Total	Low	53.22	14.95	1.831	.070
	High	48.50	10.44		

In the case of parents self-esteem only in the case of emotional adjustment, those with low self-esteem had higher emotional maladjustment (mean 14.36), and those with higher self-esteem (mean 12.24) had better adjustment and the obtained 't' value of 2.061 was found to be significant at .042 level. In other words self-esteem had positive influence over emotional adjustment and not on other areas and in total adjustment.

(d) Academic self-esteem and adjustment

Table 25.4: Mean adjustment scores (on various areas) of the sample having low and high school academic self-esteem with the results of Independent samples 't' test

Areas of Adjustment	Level of Self-esteem	Mean	S.D	't' Value	P Value
Home	Low	13.03	4.42	1.786	.077
	High	11.46	3.75		
Health	Low	9.42	5.36	1.998	.049
	High	7.34	4.06		
Social	Low	16.69	5.16	.547	.586
	High	16.11	4.83		
Emotional	Low	13.32	5.47	.060	.952
	High	13.26	4.82		
Total	Low	52.43	14.45	1.655	.101

In the case of school academic self-esteem only in the case of health adjustment, those with low self-esteem had higher health maladjustment (mean 9.42), and those with higher self-esteem (mean 7.34) had better adjustment and the obtained 't' value of 1.998 was found to be significant at .049 level. In other words self-esteem had positive influence over health adjustment and not on other areas and in total adjustment.

(e) Total self-esteem and adjustment

In all the areas of adjustment, self-esteem did not have significant influence as all the obtained 't' values found to be non-significant. In other words students with low and high levels of total self-esteem had statistically equal scores on different areas of adjustment. Self-esteem was independent of adjustment in various areas as well as total adjustment scores.

Table 25.5: Mean adjustment scores (on various areas) of the sample having low and high self-esteem with the results of Independent samples 't' test

Areas of Adjustment	Level of Adjustment	Mean	S.D	't' Value	P Value
Home	Low	13.18	4.80	1.662	.100
	High	11.78	3.53		
Health	Low	8.42	4.97	.536	.593
	High	8.96	5.11		
Social	Low	17.08	4.57	1.176	.242
	High	15.90	5.43		
Emotional	Low	13.74	5.90	.841	.403
	High	12.86	4.48		
Total	Low	51.86	15.01	.765	.446
	High	49.86	10.79		

Main Findings of the Study

1. Home parents self-esteem had positive influence over emotional adjustment of the students, because students with higher Self-esteem had better emotional adjustment.
2. School academic self-esteem had positive influence over health adjustment of the students, because students with higher Self-esteem had better health adjustment.
3. In other areas of self-esteem, there was no significant influence of it over adjustment of the students in individual areas as well as in total adjustment scores.

   (Except, in the above mentioned two uses).

The results obtained in the present study are some what in agreement with the studies done aboard. In a study on advantaged and disabled groups, self-esteem correlated positively with general self-efficacy. Both variables correlated positively with adjustment (Berenice Saracoglu, Harold Minden, Marc Wilchesky, 1989). David, L. DuBois, Catherine, A. Bull, Michelle, D. Sherman & Magie, Roberts. (1998) investigated *(a)* global self-esteem and *(b)* social-contextual incongruity in factors contributing to the development and maintenance of self-esteem as predictors of the emotional, behavioural, and academic adjustment and found that higher reported levels of global self-esteem were associated with more favorable scores on most measures of adjustment. Incremental predictive contributions also were found, however, for indices of social-contextual incongruity in factors contributing to the development and maintenance of self-esteem. Incongruity in the direction of domain-specific self-evaluations being relatively stronger for peer-oriented domains in comparison to the domains of school and family was linked consistently with less positive adjustment.

Study by Duncan (1949) adopts a multi-dimensional construct of self-esteem to examine the relationship between self-perception and psychological adjustment in order to identify specific dimensions that discriminate between disturbed and non-disturbed groups. Results indicate that dimensional self-concept scores are significantly lower for clinical subjects while there are no significant differences between groups on the mathematics, honesty, and physical ability dimensions. These findings provide a more fine grained understanding of the relationship between self-esteem and psychological adjustment and emphasize the need to examine self-esteem in terms of its particular dimensions.

Descriptive views of the self and standards for self-evaluation will be more favorable and lenient than parental views and standards in corresponding areas results in poorer adjustment. Results indicate the importance of social-contextual factors for understanding the role of self-esteem in adaptation during adolescence. Implications for esteem enhancement as a prevention and health promotion strategy with this age group should be focussed.

REFERENCES

Bell, R.K. Ojha. (1968). *Bell's Adjustment Inventory.*

David, L. DuBois, Catherine A. Bull, Michelle D. Sherman & Magie Roberts (1998). Self-esteem and Adjustment in Early Adolescence: A Social-contextual Perspective. *Journal of Youth and Adolescence*, 27, 557-583.

Duncan, M.H. (1949). Home Adjustment of Stutterers Versus Non-stutterers. *Journal of Speech and Hearing Disorders*, 14, 225-259.

Berenice Saracoglu, Harold Minden, Marc Wilchesky (1989). The Adjustment of Students with Learning Disabilities to University and Its Relationship to Self-esteem and Self-Efficacy. *Journal of Learning Disabilities*, 22, 9, 590-592.

Coleman, J. (1974). *Personality Psychology, Theories and Researches.* Translated by Javad Jafari, Parvin Kadivar (1993): Rasa Publicarion.

Coopersmith. (1987). *Self-esteem Inventory.*

Douglas.C. Kimmel Irving.B. Weiner (1968). *Adolescence Developmental Transition.*

Fox, M. (1998). *Adjustment Psychology*. Bonyad Press.

Rosenberg, M. (1979). *Conceiving the Self.* New York: Basic Books.

Stank, J.D. (2001): *"Conformity, Ability and Self-esteem"*, Representative New Search in Social Psychology, Vol. 30 No. 2.

26

Influences Gender on Adjustment Among Adolescents

Armin Mahmoudi[1]

ABSTRACT

In the present study an attempt is made to see whether male and female adolescents studying in standard 9 differ in their level adjustment. A total of 100 adolescent students studying in Mysore city were randomly selected. They were administered Bell's Adjustment Inventory (1968) (which measured adjustment of an individual in 4 areas—Home, health, social and emotional). Independent samples 't' test was applied to see the differences between male and female students. Further, Gender had no differential influence over adjustment scores in home, health, emotional, and social areas.

Introduction

Adolescence is the Physiological learning period and the Physical adaptation which varies from person to the other (Alan, 2000). Adolescence will start with puberty and end with growth and general development termination. Both periods of adolescence and puberty start at the same periods; however, adolescence lasts 8 years and includes pubescence changes in the body along with mental, drive, tendency, interaction, emotional development, job satisfactory and moral and religious purification. The adolescence period lasts about 7 to 8 years and ranges from 12 to 20 years old (Weissman, 1975).

1. **Department of Studies in Education University of Mysore, Mysore, Karnataka (India).**

Adjustment refers to adoption of the organism to demands of the environment. Human being not only adapts to their environment but through the use of intelligence changes the environment to meet the needs more effectively. He learns to develop his self by exchanging the demands and influence of his environment. In the process of meeting the demands of life on may be encountered with problems of health. Duncan (1949). Many studies have been conducted on problems of adolescents and various factors influencing adolescents' behaviour. Conflict between parents, mother's low level of education, lack of support from parents, negligence by parents, adverse affect of television viewing giving rise to unfulfilled unrealistic demands, exposure to peers who smoke, drink or use drugs, their social status in modern society etc. were some of the important factors found to be responsible for development of problem behaviour in adolescents. Problem behaviour in adolescent gives rise to symptoms such as frustration, obstinacy, aggressiveness, impulsiveness, violent behaviour, anti-social behaviour, etc. Faulty lifestyle is responsible for some behavioural problems in adolescents and it increases prevalence of psychosomatic disorders during this stage of development indicating the importance of a healthy environment. On the whole, satisfying the needs leads to every single individual adjustment. Man lives in a world full of challenges resulted in depression and conflict as hindrances in achieving the goals. In other words, when a man's needs are not satisfied, he she suffer mental breakdown and tension. Thus, removing disappointment, shortcomings and life challenges ends in adjustment.

In recent years there has been increasing interest in gender-related influences on adolescence adjustment and academic achievement. There is growing appreciation that a better understanding of concerns in these areas will be necessary not only for promoting optimal individual development, but also for meeting the nation's social and economic needs (Browen & Finkelhor, 1986). Contemporary theory and research reflects a shift from studying gender as static, relatively isolated indicator to examining their mutual implications for adolescence adjustment within more process-oriented, integrative frameworks. (Chandy & Blum, 1996). Using this approach. Contextual and psychological experience of group members can be considered in relation to normative processes of adaptation within specific periods or stage of development. Several factors point to early adolescence as a period of particular importance for issue pertaining to gender (Cohen & etc, 1996). These include increased exposure to others of differing backgrounds at this age stage-specific concerns such as puberty and dating and the emerging salience of group identity in processes of self-understanding (Cohen & Willis, 1985).

Therefore, the adolescence with the same age group who are present at school can feel the tangibility of Pedagogical changes. Since school is a social environment, it is fundamental that every single individual keeps in touch with his/her peer groups Besides, the adjustment conflict can be posited in terms of the manner of adjustment to the school atmosphere, principals, teachers and subject matters is incorrect behaviours and will be pessimist to the future (Douglas, 1968).

Satisfactory adjustments in adolescents are very important because it can exert powerful influence on their developing personality. According to Adler (1953) normal adjusted individual has both energy and courage to meet the problems and difficulties as they come along. They are socially and psychologically adjusted to the daily tasks of life. The maladjusted individuals like neurotics, psychotics, criminals, drunkards, problem children, suicides and perverts and failures because of lack of social skills and interest. To adjust and not to adjust includes both inner and overt changes that individual experience during their growing-up years.

According to Skinner (1952), adjustment involves the organization of personality, which leads to stability of the individual to his social and physical environment. Erickson's (1968) statement on individual development, state the ability to accommodate oneself to changing circumstances is a mark of maturity could easily be interpreted as a definition of adjustment.

Adjustment is a process that takes a person to lead a happy and well-contented life. It helps in keeping balance between need and the capacity to meet these needs. It persuades to change the way of life according to the demands of the situation. Adjustment gives strength and ability to bring desirable changes in the conditions of our environment.

Objectives

The purpose of the present study is to investigate.

1. To find whether there is a significant differences between the adjustment of Standard (IX) boys and girls.
2. To study the influence of gender on levels of adjustment in home, health, emotional and social areas.

Methodology

Population and Sample

Population: The population of the study consisted of the entire Standard (IX) student in Mysore city. The present study was conducted on the random sample of 100 Standard (IX) students (N = 100), male (N_1 = 50) and female (N_2 =50) of secondary schools of Mysore city. The age of the subjects of class (IX) ranged between 14 and 15 years.

Tools

Adjustment Inventory for adolescent Students (BAI) developed by Bell's Adjustment (1968). The inventory comprises of 140 items in relation to five areas of adjustment (Home 35, Health 35, Social 35, and Emotional 35 items). The test is helpful in screening the poorly adjusted students who may need further psycho-diagnostic study and counseling for their adjustment problems. The reliability coefficients were determined by spilt half and test retest methods, where the reliability coefficients varied from .81 to .89 for various areas of adjustment through split half and reliability co-efficients varied from .89 to .92 through test retest method for different areas of adjustment. Cross validation of the scale with K.Kumar's adjustment inventory resulted in Pearson's *r* of .72, .79, .82 and .81 for home, health, social and emotional areas respectively.

Procedure

The Tools were administered on the sample of 100 selected adolescent subjects. The items in the answer sheet were scored according to of scoring keys for four different areas. (Home, Health, Social, and Emotional).The data thus obtained was analyzed and interpreted using various statistical techniques.

The obtained scores were recorded on master sheet and later fed to the computer using SPSS for Windows software (version 16.0). Using Independent samples 't' test.

Analysis and Interpretation of Data

Table 26.1: Mean adjustment scores (on various areas) of male and female students with the results of Independent samples 't' test

Areas of Adjustment	Gender	Mean	S.D	't' Value	P Value
Home	Male	12.72	4.71	.563	.575
	Female	12.24	3.77		
Health	Male	8.80	5.25	.218	.828
	Female	8.58	4.84		
Social	Male	16.98	5.40	.975	.332
	Female	16.00	4.63		
Emotional	Male	13.70	6.11	.764	.447
	Female	12.90	4.20		
Total	Male	52.24	15.31	1.059	.292
	Female	49.48	10.28		

In all the areas of adjustment, gender did not have significant influence as all the obtained 't' values found to be non-significant. In other words male and female students did not differ significantly in their adjustment scores. In areas like home, health, social, emotional and in total adjustment scores, male and female students had statistically similar scores.

Main Findings

1. Gender had no differential influence over adjustment scores in home, health, emotional, and social areas.

The relationship among gender identity, sex typing, and adjustment has attracted the attention of social and developmental psychologists for many years. However, they have explored this issue with different assumptions and different approaches. Generally the approaches differ regarding whether sex typing is considered adaptive versus maladaptive, measured as an individual or normative difference, and whether gender identity is regarded as a unit-dimensional or multidimensional construct. In this context, Lurye, Zosuls, & Ruble (2008) consider both perspectives and suggest that the developmental timing and degree of sex typing, as well as the multidimensionality of gender identity, be considered when examining their relationship to adjustment.

Boys and men also live by social pressures to behave in the prescribed roles that define manhood. Boys and men are also subject to inauthentic feelings of self if they do not fulfill the definition of being 'male'. In research and policy design, gender issues need to be addressed more explicitly, rather than as a sub-category of the poor. Modeling and planning tools, such as Social Accounting Matrices should incorporate gender disaggregated data where available.

The use of rapid, qualitative, participatory and action oriented research techniques may be of more value than top down quantitative exercises in identifying the implications of adjustment for women. Resources might be usefully geared to community level monitoring and evaluation, for example of service provision, with the involvement of women who are the users of services. This should be tied to some form of accountability of service providers.

To conclude, adolescent age is being considered as stress and storm full age, where there will be rapid transition both psychologically and physically among adolescents. This in turn affect the adjustment process of the adolescent in different settings too.

REFERENCES

Alan, Slater & Drawing, Mair (2000) *The Blackwel Reader in Developmental Phychology.*

Browne, A., & Finkelhor, D. (1986). Impact of Child Sexual Abuse: A Review of the Research. *Psychological Bulletin*, 99, 66-77.

Chandy, J.M., Blum, R. W., & Resnick, M. D. (1996). Gender-specific Outcomes for Sexually Abused Adolescents. *Child Abuse and Neglect*, 20, 1219-1231.

Cohen, Y., Spirito, A, Sterling, C., Donaldson, D., Seifer, R., Plummer, B., Avila, R., & Ferrer, K. (1996). Physical and Sexual Abuse and Their Relation to Psychiatric Disorder and Suicidal Behaviour Among Adolescents Who are Psychiatrically Hospitalized? *Child Psychiatry and Psychology*, 37, 989-993.

Cohen, S., & Willis, T. (1985). Stress, Social Support, and the Buffering Hypothesis. *Psychological Bulletin*, 98, 310-357.

Duncan, M.H. (1949). Home Adjustment of Stutterers *Versus* Non-Stutterers. *Journal of Speech and Hearing Disorders*, 14, 225-259.

Douglas, C. & Kimmel, Irving. B. (1968). *Adolescence Develpmental Transition.*

Lurye, Leah. E., & Zosuls, Kristina, M., & Ruble, Diane , N. (2008). Gender Identity and Adjustment: Understanding the Impact of Individual and Normative Differences in Sex Typing. *New Directions for Child and Adolescent Development*, 120, 31-46.

Shamlou, Saeed. (2005). *Mental Health*. Tehran: Rosh Publication.

Rosenberg, M. (1979). *Conceiving the Self.* New York: Basic Books.

Weissman.M.M.(1975). *The Assessment of Social Adjustment a Review of Techniques in care.* Gen. Psychiatry.

27

Psychological Intervention in Anxiety of Patients with Major Thalassemia

Forough Mahigir[1]

ABSTRACT

The aim of the study is to find out the effect of psychological intervention (cognitive-behavioural therapy) on anxiety of patients with Major Thalassaemia. The sample consisted of 40 subjects in talasemia centre of Bangalore in India. After the pre test of two groups, the intervention by CBT was given to the experimental group for 45 days and the scores measured by Zung Self-rating Anxiety scale.

The Two independent sample Test and paired sample T test methods is used to find out the differences between experimental and control groups and it has shown that there is significant difference between two groups after intervention. More over the differences between pre test and post test of experimental group also is significant.

Introduction

By the beginning of the 20th century, European clinicians had become aware of an anemia syndrome in infancy associated with enlargement of the spleen (Wasi, 1981). In the American literature the first clinical description of thalassemia is attributed to the Detroit pediatricians Thomas B. Cooley and Pearl Lee and the actual term thalassemia was coined by George Whipple at 1936 (Weatherall, 1980).

---

1. **Department of Studies in Psychology, University of Mysore, Manasagangothri, Mysore - 570 006, Karnataka (India).**

The thalassemias are a group of anaemias that result from inherited defects in the production of hemoglobin and among the most common genetic disorders worldwide, occurring more frequently in the Mediterranean region (Fawdry,1998), the Indian subcontinent, Southeast Asia, and West Africa (Weatherall, 2001).

The child with Thalassaemia Major will be treated for life. This treatment consists of regular blood transfusions every 3-5 weeks throughout life. The red blood cells given during a transfusion contain a lot of iron. This iron tends to accumulate in the body as the red cells get older and are destroyed. The iron accumulates in many parts such as the heart and liver and causes many complications. Since it is iron that is the major problem in Thalassaemia, a drug called Desferal is given by subcutaneous infusion, from a small portable syringe driver for 8 -12 hours on at least 5 nights per week. The future of patients with the correct treatment looks very promising. Children with Thalassaemia Major may need to take time off school to attend clinic appointments and for blood transfusions (World Health Organization, 1977).

Thalassemia can occur as either alpha thalassemia or beta thalassemia, and take the form of major, minor or intermediate. Thalassemia minor means that the person is a carrier of the disease, or has the 'trait'. This is not very serious, and the patient can lead a more or less normal life. If the patient has thalassemia major, this can be very serious indeed, and even life-threatening. Thalassemia intermediary is a milder form. It is vitally important for our country for people to understand that thalassemia can be prevented.

In the study of depression and anxiety in patients with thalassemias, it is well documented that persons with thalassemias tolerate a high amount of psychological problems (Anderson *et al.*, 2002) and few studies have considered the use of psychological interventions in the treatment of depression following thalassaemia.

Cognitive behavioural therapy (CBT) is an effective treatment of anxiety and depression in the general population (Wasi, 1981), and there is some indication that it may be effective for people with thalassaemia. According to Lustman, CBT for depression in adults with thalassemias has been shown to be effective in reducing depressive symptoms (Lustman, *et al.*, 1998). Moreover Lincoln compared a 4-week baseline period with 10 sessions of CBT and found that there was a tendency for improvement in mood of the 19 patients with thalassaemia.

Despite of the many studies about effectiveness of CBT on different forms of anxiety, there is scarce if any documentation of the influence of CBT on anxiety in patients with thalassaemia Major. This presents study therefore focuses on these issues and if the CBT treatment has a significant affect in reducing anxiety in patients with major thalassemia.

Aims

The aim of the present study is to evaluate CBGT as a treatment for anxiety in the patients with major thalassemia in the center of blood donation and we want to find that if CBGT as a treatment can reduce the anxiety of patients with major thalassemia.

Method

Sample Participants

Participants were 32 patients (By the age range of 13-23 years) and randomly divided to two groups. The control group consisted of 16 subjects (8 girls and 8 boys) and the experimental group also consisted of 16 subjects (8 girls and 8 boys).

Measures

Zung Self-rating Anxiety Scale (*ZAS*): The Zung Self-rating Anxiety Scale (SAS) was designed by Zung (1971) to quantify the level of anxiety. The self-administered test has 20 questions. Each question is scored on a scale of 1-4 (none or a little of the time, some of the time, good part of the time, most of the time).There are fifteen questions worded towards increasing anxiety levels and five questions worded towards decreasing anxiety levels. Saito & Garza (1999) found the significant reliability and validity of this scale (0.77 for Cronbach Alpha and .85 for test retest). The scores range from 20-80.

- 20-44 Normal Range
- 45-59 Mild to Moderate Anxiety Levels
- 60-74 Marked to Severe Anxiety Levels
- 75-80 Extreme Anxiety Levels

Procedure

The study carried out in 3 phases:

Phase 1, (pre test): In this phase Zung Self-Rating Anxiety Scale (ZAS) were administered to 36 selected patients with major thalassemia and the level of anxiety in two groups computed.

Phase 2, (Intervention): The second phase of this study consisted of adapting a Cognitive-Behavioural Therapy (CBT) treatment manual which has evacuated to reduce anxiety. The CBGT therapy contains 15 sessions in 35 days and was co-led by two doctoral level psychologists using the adapted CBT treatment manual. Participants were given a workbook with a summary of the material presented in each session and worksheets used in sessions and for home practice assignments. All sessions were carried out on Monday, Wednesday and Friday at the center of blood donation. In the intervention plan, the purpose of the programme and CBT was explained for patients in 3 sessions, identified negative automatic thoughts (N.A.T) and trained the patients on how to cope with (N.A.T) has done in 6 sessions and also used assertiveness training and modelling methods in 6 sessions.

Phase 3, (post test): After 5 days from phase 2, Zung Self-rating Anxiety Scale (ZAS) were administered on two groups and data has given for computing by SPSS. In this study, testing was done in a quiet atmosphere. The instruction was given clearly without any ambiguity and there was no time limit for answering the questionnaire.

Results and Discussion

Results

Table 27.1 presents the scores of anxiety between control and experimental groups in pre test and post test.

Table 27.1: Two independent sample 'T' test between control and experimental groups

Group	Pre				Post			
	N	M	SD	T	N	M	SD	T
Experimental	16	55.7500	3.78594		16	37.8750	5.99861	
Control	16	58.25	5.27	1.541	16	58.0625	5.02618	*10.318
Total	**32**	**57.005**	**4.52**		**32**	**48.23**	**5.56**	

df= 30

* Correlation is significant at the 0.01 level (1-tailed).

As it has shown, there is no significant differences between Experimental group and control group before intervention (T = 1.58, p>0.05). But the scores of patients in post test has shown that there is a significant differences between Experimental group and control group after intervention (T = 10.318, p <. 01). In the Experimental group the scores of sample had mean = 37.87 and for control group it was mean = 58.06.

Moreover with respect to the scores in pre test and post test, in Experimental group there is a significant decrease from pretest to post test. In the pre test the total sample had mean 55.75 which had reduced to 37.8750. But in control group the reduction of anxiety between per test and post test was not significant.

Discussions and Recommendations

The objective of the study was to explore the effectiveness of CBGT therapy on anxiety among patients with Major thalassaemia in Iran. The finding revealed that CBGT was highly effective in reducing anxiety in the

Experimental group. The results of this study have approved the current hypothesis and are agreement with previous studies.

These findings corroborate pervious studies which have considered the use of psychological interventions in the treatment of anxiety following thalassaemia. (Lustman, *et al.*, 1 998).

According to the above-mentioned results:

(a) The average scores of patients with Major thalassaemia is more than normal Range (the normal Range is between 20-44 , but it was 57.01 for patient with Major thalassaemia).

(b) CBGT is highly effective in reducing anxiety in the Experimental group and we can use of this treatment for patient with Major thalassaemia.

With regard to mentioned results it is recommended that this groups of patients should be prepared in counseling and interventional classes as a group therapy.

REFERENCES

Anderson, J., Freedland, K., Clouse, R., & Lustman, P. (2002). The Prevalence of Comorbid Depression in Adults with Diabetes. *Diabetes Care*, 24(6), 1069-1077.

Fawdry, A.L. (1998). Erythroblast Anaemia of Childhood in Cyprus. *Lancet 1*: 171-176.

Lustman, P., Griffith, L., Freedland, K., Kissel, S. S., & Clouse, R. (1998). Cognitive Behaviour Therapy for Depression in Type 2 Diabetes Mellitus. *Annals of Internal Medicine*, 129(8), 613.

Saito, Y. & Garza, T.J. (1999). Foreign Language Reading Anxiety. *Modern Language Journal*, 83, 202-218.

Wasi P, (1981). Haemoglobin Apathies including Thalassaemia. Part 1: Tropical Asia. *Clin Haematol*; 10(3): 707-729.

Weatherall DJ. In Wintrobe MM, ed. (1980). *Blood, Pure and Eloquent: A Story of Discovery, of People, and of Ideas*. New York: McGraw-Hill, 378.

Weatherall DJ. (2001). *The Thalassemias*. 6th Ed. New York: McGraw-Hill: 562-564.

Whipple G. H, (1936). Bradford WL. Mediterranean Disease — 'Thalassemia' Associated Pigment Abnormalities Simulating Hemochromatosis. *J Pediatr*; 9: 279-311.

World Health Organization. (1977). *World Health Report*. Geneva: United Nations.

Zung, W. K, (1971). A Rating Instrument for Anxiety. *Disorders Psychosomatics*. 12: 371-379.

28

The Effect of Shyness Through the Life Cycle View

Daryoush Ghasemian[1]

Introduction

Shyness is a form of excessive self-focus, a pre-occupation with one's thoughts, feelings and physical reactions. It may vary from mild social awkwardness to totally inhibiting social phobia. Shyness may be chronic and dispositional, serving as a personality trait that is central in one's self definition. Situational shyness involves experiencing the symptoms of shyness in specific social performance situations but not incorporating it into one's self-concept. We experience a personality trait as important as shyness in different ways at various points throughout our lives. As babies, we cannot rightly be said to be shy, but we may have been burn with a brain that is highly reactive to novelty. As young children, we must learn to make friends and play with others in the sometimes chaotic school environment. As adolescents, we may feel stigmatized by our shyness and seek ways to hide it. As adults, we struggle for strategies to connect with others — friends, lovers, co-workers — and assuage our loneliness. But although different issues arise at each of these life stages, the same underlying principles apply; in dealing with shyness of the body, mind and self we grapple with our slow-to-warm-up tendencies, the approach/avoidance conflict and restrictive comfort zones.

Bernardo J. Carducci and Lisa Kaiser described her baby grand daughter to them:

1. **Research Scholar, Department of Psychology, University of Mysore, Mysore, Karnataka (India).**

> If Kelly were at my house and you walked in — no matter how much fun we were having — she would just stop and crawl over to where her mom and dad were sitting. When she was a year old, if anyone would go to her or talk to her, she would break out in tears. On her first birthday, the whole family was at her house. She was playing and was just fine. Then we sat her down in her high chair to have cake. Everyone gathered around to sing 'Happy Birthday', and she looked at us with an expression like, "What are you doing to me?" She went from a happy lit the girl to one in tears in seconds!

Even now, when we first come into her house, she doesn't run up to us and give us a kiss. It takes five or ten minutes before you can approach her, and then she's loving.

The research of Paul Pilkonis has identified different types of shy people: shy and those who are privately shy. Publicly shy people express distress as a consequence of more overt manifestation of their shyness, such as a through being too quiet, behaving awkwardly , and failing to respond appropriately in social situation (e.g., not acknowledging a compliment) (Pilkonis,1977). Privately shy people express distress as a consequence of more covert manifestations of their shyness, such as a through intense psycho physiological arousal (e.g., pounding heart, muscle tension, and anxiety reactions) (Pilkonis, 1977). Socially anxious shy people express distress as a consequence of more cognitive manifestations of their shyness, such as being excessively self-concious (e.g., do my clothes fit right) and overly concerned about being evaluated socially by others (e.g., I wonder what she thinks of my comment) (Carducci & Clark, 1994; Melchior& Cheek, 1990).

According to Charducci (1999), there are five types of shyness: those who are publicly shy and those who are privately shy. One is more concerned about behaving badly, the other about feeling badly. The chronically shy people often lead a pained existence. They experience shyness more frequently than other shy people and report being shy in significantly more situations. They perceive themselves as being more shy than their peers. They experience shyness as a personal problem more frequently and believe that they are less capable of overcoming their shyness than other people. The other type is transitionally shy, these individual act and feel shy during certain periods of their lives, usually when they leave one phase and being an other, such as entering college, starting a new job, or beginning to date after divorce. This is a common and normal response to uncertain, insecure, and unpredictable situations. In these threatening circumstance, they display all of the characteristics of the publicly shy, but once they have habituated and are able to cope with their new challenges, they become less shy and more confident about themselves and their abilities.

Are we born shy?

Temperament does not act alone to create shyness. Your biological make up, along with your life experiences and how you interpret those experiences, help to create shyness. D. Arcus and J. Kagan states:

> Biology influences your body's reactivity. You have been born with the capacity to handle a certain level of threatening stimulation. But biology is just a starting point, an influence you can surrender to or control through determination and wisdom. Its power will manifest throughout your life but will be most obvious when you are young — before experience and intellect come into play.

If you were born with a highly reactive system, your inhibited temperament may have been instrumental during the first two years of life because you had neither the mental capacity nor the experience upon which to rely. Consequently, like Kelly, you might have clung to your parents, cried when you were separated and fussed when strangers came near.

But after the age of two, biology ceases to be the most important factor. A. Caspi explains, "environmental experiences come to the fore during the second year of childhood and beyond. How your parents and teachers treat you, the friendships you form, your relationship with your siblings, the classroom environment—all of these factors and the memories they evoke may instigate or extinguish shy behaviour".

During adolescence the mind becomes the most potent force, and it will hold sway into adulthood. But it need not ordain a life of shyness. The shy adolescent, attempting to interpret his experiences as a highly reactive child, can begin to make appropriate choices that will calm his nervous system. He can select friends who support those choices by sparing him from overwhelmingly stimulating situations. He can build a strong identity based on his strengths and decide how he will use those strengths in the business and social world. Using his higher brain, he will be able to take charge of his life.

Almost half of the adult population claims to be shy, yet only 20 per cent of babies are born inhibited. So, many of these adults must have acquired their shyness — through mental and emotional experiences and using their higher minds.

Just as parental care and experience influence temperamentally inhibited children, so are temperamentally uninhibited children shaped by these factors. But their shy minds interpret these circumstances and create shyness, scoring it into the brain's wiring with repetition and reinforcement. Their shyness comes from without. The shy mind is critical to this course.

Some people are born with bodies that make them highly reactive, but this does not mean they will become shy. In the next chapter we will explore how these biological processes are important during childhood, before we acquire learned shyness or the experience and wisdom to combat it.

Shyness in Preschooler

"I remember feeling mortified if someone noticed me", explained Jenny, a film maker in New York. And H. Triandis expresses:

> When I was very young, before kindergarten, I remember hanging on to the back of my mother's skirt and trying to keep her between me and anybody whom I didn't want to notice me wile we were shopping or out in the world.
>
> I couldn't meet other children. The only kids I knew were my next-door neighbours. My parents tell me I wouldn't associate with anybody but my immediate family and the kids next door. I was terrified of my grandparents: I didn't even like to go to their house. With other relatives or family friends, I'd just hide in my room and hope that they'd leave me alone. I thought people could see through me — that burning sensation I still get occasionally — and I wanted to disappear through a hole in the floor. I'd even hide behind the furniture.

In addition to temperament, experiences within the family have a profound impact on the development of your child's personality traits, including shyness. The family is his first social environment; it teaches him how to cope with relationships. What he learns there will be reproduced in adulthood.

Siblings

A Pennsylvania college student explained to me why she believed she was shy. "I have a brother who is three years older than me", she wrote, "and as long as I can remember, he dominated the conversations where I was present, whether it be with our parents, relatives or friends. Because he did all the talking, I never had to. I could just fade into the background. To this day it continues".

Siblings are our first peers. How we interact with them often affects how we deal with others later in life. It may be a cliché, but its still true that older siblings seem to be overly responsible and mature, middle children want to be noticed as individuals and youngest, the 'babies of the family', can shirk responsibility because their parents are permissive with them.

Intense sibling rivalries often affect how people see themselves and the world. J.B. Asendopf wrote:

> I don't know if I am genetically predisposed to being shy, but I do know that, while growing up, I always felt like I was second best to my six-years-older sister. I was nothing, and my opinions didn't matter to anybody. Maybe that wasn't the case in reality, but I always felt like it.

The Father's Role

Most dads teach their youngsters about power and self-expression through their style of play. They toss their kids into the air, give piggyback rides, scare and chase them, wrestle with them, or hold them tightly until they cry 'uncle'.

Your child learns many life lessons from this rowdiness. First, he sees that you and adults in general are stronger and more powerful than he is. He also must tolerate a certain level of frustration in a world that is rough, tough and scary; He carefully watches your moods and nonverbal cues, your face and body language, to predict what will happen next. He also learns to clearly communicate his emotions by giggling, crying, struggling, asking you to stop, or wandering away from the uncomfortable situation. This forces him to listen to his emotions, which may signal that the roughhousing is getting out of hand.

In short, through play, you train your children to hold their own in the world by teaching them to tolerate frustration, solve problems and interpret and communicate emotions.

The Impact of Divorce

Divorce is hard on children in general and can be especially difficult for a shy child, who reacts more to change, is more sensitive, and has less social support than his outgoing siblings. Even when the breakup is relatively painless for the spouses, it is a trauma that can bring about shyness in temperamentally uninhibited children or make an inhibited child withdraw even further.

According to J.B. Asendopf:

> Indeed, withdrawal is merely one sign of adjustment to the new situation. To cope with their confusion about divorce, young children may also become depressed, blame themselves, develop intense fears, create reconciliation fantasies, and even become aggressive and hostile. If you divorce, keep in mind that your children will be profoundly affected by the loss. Be sure that both of you are communicating with them clearly, compassionately and honestly.

You and your family members will have the first and most fundamental influence on your child's shyness. But this may wane as your youngster discovers other children in the neighborhood, at play centers, and at school. IN fact, children naturally turn to playmates at the age of six or seven and enter what is called the latency period, during which they become sociable.

The latency period is a dress rehearsal for the roles children play as adults. Youngsters care for their dolls to practice parenting, play catch to mimic professional athletes, prepare tea parties to feel like hosts, and play war games to experience powerfulness. IN the process, they learn valuable lessons about cooperation, sharing, friendship, leadership and negotiation. Not only do they want to play with each other, but they must in order to grow.

The latency period can be the most critical in the development of shyness. Children need to learn social lessons during this time but cannot do so if they isolate themselves by watching television, playing computer games, or reading. They need to be with friends and to explore the world.

The Growing Impact of Shyness in Latency

During the first few years of elementary school, young children seem oblivious to the fact that some of their peers are more reticent, but their attitudes change as they get older. Gradually, almost inevitably, the more dominant children begin to shun, reject and bully their shyer classmates. Sadly, those who are naturally less vocal and assertive and who do not benefit from a network of supportive friends can suffer for it.

Although they may emerge from their cocoons when among new children who don't label them, children tend to become stuck in their shyness with those who are familiar. If classmates believe a child is shy, no matter how much he wants to make overtures, he may be unable to break out and create a new persona.

This bias against shy children soon takes its toll. As early as the fourth or fifth grade, they realize bashfulness and anxiety are problems for them. In fact, surveys of shy fifth-graders show they have lower self-esteem than their more gregarious classmates.

Shyness in Adolescence

The development task of adolescence is to decide who we are and where we fit in the community that extends beyond our families. Teenagers must make these important decisions based on their needs and talents, not what others want them to be. Whether it's choosing a major, how to behave at a party, or how to dress, these decisions should reflect their true selves.

This is particularly true for shy teens who don't want their lives to reflect their shyness. They may try to deny that they feel insecure, socially anxious, and fearful. Consequently, they may follow the paths of others [and conform] rebel, or withdraw. Unfortunately, all of these choices work against self-awareness.

Shy teens need to come to terms with themselves and their shyness. If they are successfully shy at a young age, they will be prepared for the tasks of adulthood: expressing themselves through intimate relationships and work. We all discover who we are by interacting with others at work or at home. But if adolescents are uncertain about or quell their emotions and opinions, they will feel shackled by shy myths that can impede their growth.

In order to become successfully shy adults, teenagers must understand themselves and how shyness influences the many important choices they make. In fact, shyness in adulthood can become not just a personality trait but a quality-of-life issue. Researchers have correlated it with loneliness, depression, substance abuse, limited career advancement, low self-esteem, self-doubt, poor coping skills, the inability to solve problems, lack of community involvement, and poor health. Shy people view challenges as threats to their sense of self rather than sources of personal growth. Consequently, they are apt to shrink from them and live in a state of social and emotional stagnation.

Shyness in Adulthood

Shyness can be an issue at all stages of your life. Indeed, research has shown that adults who have been shy may have more difficulties as they age. They tend to be lonelier; have smaller and more unpredictable social and caregiving networks; have more difficulty replacing friends lost to retirement, illness, or death; and are more likely to be institutionalized. In many cases, adults grow into shyness and lose their old comfort zones following a divorce or the death of a spouse. The shy response alters as expectations and life circumstances evolve.

Conclusion

The many tasks of adulthood include developing a sense of community, discovering your place in society, finding and keeping love, raising a family, and engaging in meaningful work. Sadly, many of these tasks are difficult to achieve if your shyness makes you feel like a second-class citizen. Researchers have shown that shy people know what to do to make their lives more enjoyable but doubt their ability to carry through. For example, you may recognize that you must take a risk to begin a relationship but still worry excessively about self-disclosure, becoming the focus of attention, or rejection. You may want to make eye contact when talking with someone but feel too cautious and believe that you can't rise to the challenge. You may refrain from asking others questions because you fear you may be prying even though you know it just means you are showing an interest. You may have unreasonable expectations — you want immediate intimacy and paradoxically still expect others to draw you out.

Scientists have found that some shy people are highly anxious and may have poor emotional coping skills. They allow their feelings to run amok because they don't open up to others to seek reality checks or advice. They even deny themselves the comfort that comes from knowing that others have had the same experience. They feel lonely in new or challenging situations. When you don't rely on friends, social anxiety and self-doubt can fester, decreasing your ability to handle problems constructively. When you're anxious, you may find yourself unable to break problems into manageable components. Overwhelmed by your troubles, you soon fall into a vicious cycle. You constantly evaluate yourself negatively but never give yourself a chance to succeed. Indeed, a in times of challenge you may engage in catastrophic, negative thinking and social avoidance and may fail to recognize opportunities for growth. Rather than solving your problems creatively, you become passive and just dwell on them. You may believe that other people can't relate to you because, unlike you, they seem so confident and able to work through their difficulties. The result is plummeting self-esteem. Shy people constantly fail in their own eyes. They know what's expected, don't try, don't succeed, and feel miserable that they cant accomplish what they know they're supposed to. It is easy to see how shyness, unhappiness and loneliness are rightly interwoven. Social support is imperative for happiness. It affects the way you think about the world and your place in it. It gives you hope and the belief in your ability to change your circumstances. It enhances problem-solving skills and motivation. O. Allen is reputed to have said, "99 per cent of life is just showing up". In Part IV, I will help you learn how to 'show up' in your own life as a successfully shy lover, worker and citizen of the world.

REFERENCES

Allen, O. (1994) Gender Differences in Selected Psychological Characteristics of Adolescent Smokers and Non-smokers. *Health Values*, 18, 34-39.

Arcus, D., and Kegan, J. (1995). *Temperament and Craniofacial Variation in the First Two Years.* Child Development , 33, 250-259.

Asendopf, J.B. (1993). Abnormal Shyness in Children. *Journal of Child Psychology and Psychiatry*, 34, 1069-1081.

— (1990) *Beyond Social Withdrawal: Shyness, Unsociability, and Peer Avoidance*. Human Development, 33, 250-259.

Carducci, Bernardo J. and Kaiser, Lisa (2002). *Shyness: A Bold New Approach.* Harper Collins Publishers: New York.

Caspi, A. Bem, D. J., and Elder, G.H. Jr. (1988). *Moving Away from the World: Life-course Pattern of Shy Children.* Developmental Psychology, 24, 824-831.

Pilkonis, P.A. (1977). Shyness, Public and Private, and Its Relationship to Other Measures of Social Behaviour. *Journal of Pesonalty*, 45, 585-595.

29

Marital Adjustment in Rural Women Identified With HIV/AIDS and Undergoing Anti-Retro Viral Drug Therapy

Sudarshan[1]

ABSTRACT

Since 'Human Immunodeficiency Virus' (HIV) was first reported, 'Acquired Immunodeficiency Syndrome (AIDS) has now become a major public health issue all over the country. The typical rural Indian woman is often a hapless victim of this deadly disease infected by her philandering spouse. There is growing evidence that the pandemic is spreading into the country's rural areas, wherein marital relationships and gender equations are generally on a different platform as compared to those in towns and large cities. It is one thing to know about the disease and quite another thing to be guaranteed a protected sex life. Against this background, this study chose to investigate into nature or characteristics of reported marital adjustment in rural women identified with HIV/AIDS and undergoing anti-retro viral drug therapy. This study uses a cross sectional small group survey design to elicit details on marital adjustment in the target population. Data collection involved the use of two tools:

(a) Demographic Profile Sheet; and

(b) Ten Item Marital Adjustment Inventory (Singh, 1987).

On the whole, results show that the rural Indian women respondents identified or diagnosed as affected by HIV/AIDS have qualitatively an

1. **Research Scholar, Department of PG Studies in Psychology.**

attitude on marital adjustment which falls in the interpretable range of 'More than Least Favourable'. Significant differences are seen in their scores on marital adjustment in relation to their age, non-nuclear type of family backgrounds, higher SES, and type of occupation. However, associated variables like route of infection, ongoing stage of their affliction and their educational status do not emerge as significant in their report on marital adjustment. These findings are presented and discussed along with their implications for the ongoing social-cultural movement advocacy and empowerment of affected rural women in raising their voice against HIV/AIDS in the country.

Introduction

Since 1986, when the first case of Human Immunodeficiency Virus (HIV) was reported in India, Acquired Immunodeficiency Syndrome (AIDS) has now become a major public health issue (Maniar, 2000; Pais, 1996). The Indian National AIDS Control Organization estimates 2.31 million HIV cases in the country for 2007 with significant variations across the states (NACO, 2007). There are clearly identified low risk groups (like housewives, college students or teenagers) (Jejeebhoy, 1998; Apte, 1997; Singh *et al*, 1997) and high risk groups (like sex workers or intravenous drug users) (Newmann *et al*, 2000). Infected husbands form the main source of infection for housewives (George *et al*, 1997). Thus, the route of transmission via sex workers and long distance truck drivers has slowly penetrated and endangered marital sexual relationships (Bryan, Jeffrey and Joseph, 2001; Venkataramana and Sarada, 2001; Rao *et al*, 1999; Singh and Malaviya, 1994).

There is growing evidence that the pandemic is spreading into rural areas of the country, wherein marital relationships and gender equations are generally on a different platform as compared to those in towns and larger cities. Since women have little say or autonomy in rural areas, HIV poses a greater burden on infected rural women, than in their men or similar women folk from urban areas. Further, rural women have different needs, impacts and consequences of the disease. Additional factors like lack of knowledge about HIV and its prevention, age, illiteracy, nature of family system or available supports places the average rural women in greater jeopardy. In a related survey, it was reported that only 30 per cent of a population of over 90,000 married women in reproductive age from rural areas were aware of HIV (NACO, 2007); but reported that they could not do much about it.

It is one thing to have awareness or knowledge (even though it may be incomplete) and it is quite another thing that the available information guarantees women to lead a protected sex life (Sharma *et al*, 1997). Sexual behaviours are central to any marital relationship. In the traditional Indian settings, by and large, people have conservative attitudes towards sex. On many occasions, it is a taboo subject for open or public discussion (Bang *et al*,

1989). An understanding of sexuality and gender based power relations within the marital context is an important issue of reproductive health (Balmer *et al*, 1995; Dixon-Muller, 1993). Female sexuality is seen as needed to be channeled into marriage at an early age in the rural Indian culture.

The traditional Indian ideal or stereotype is marital fidelity, premarital chastity, submission and near total absence of homosexuality in women although these notions are now changing under the influence of mass media, increased mobility and late age of marriage (Nag, 1996; Savara and Shridhar, 1996). There are reports to believe that unlike in Africa (Boerma *et al*, 2002), for example, HIV/AIDS maybe higher in rural India than in urban areas (Banerjee, Deaton and Duflo, 2004; Bang *et al*, 1989). This may be because such cases go under reported and are kept secret. Or it may be that awareness is higher in urban areas and rural women may not be culturally in a position to refuse sexual relations with their infected husband. Many rural uneducated women (this is true of urban educated women also) may have little or no control over choice in marriage (Singh and Samara, 1996), abstinence (Sharma, Sujay and Sharma, 1998) or condom use at home or about the extra marital activities of their husbands (Bhattacharjee *et al*, 2000; Bharat and Aggleton, 1999). Many times, their basic right to safe motherhood is deprived or infringed (Baylies, 2001). These cultural and economic inequities increase the vulnerability of rural women (Dube, 1997). Against this background, this study attempts to investigate the nature or characteristics of marital adjustment in rural women identified with HIV/AIDS and undergoing anti retro viral drug therapy.

Methodology

The present study makes use of a cross sectional small group survey design to elicit information on the self reported nature or characteristics marital adjustment in rural women identified with HIV/AIDS and undergoing anti-retro viral drug therapy.

Participants

The sample in the present investigation comprised of 60 rural women identified or diagnosed as affected by HIV/AIDS and those who were regularly attending as out patients in the Department of ART Clinics at Krishna Raja Hospital, Mysore Medical College, Mysore, Karnataka, as well as those who visited the VCTC in the districts of Mysore and Chamrajnagar, Karnataka, during April-December, 2009.

Procedure

After obtaining informed permission from competent authorities, participating subjects and by following the ethical guidelines stipulated for such research activities (Venkatesan, 2009), data collection involved individual interview of 60 target women respondents using a semi-structured questionnaire in their native tongue. The interviews were carried out in a quiet, undisturbed, private and confidential milieu. Wherein women respondents were unwilling to discuss related issues with the male investigator, a female interviewer was used to ease inter-personal communication and data collection. Home visits and interviews were not undertaken because of the risk of a breach in confidentiality. On an average, each interview took about half an hour. Some respondents, especially, women who were recently widowed, became distressed, wept, or tended to remain silent at certain points during the interviewing process. Such situations were handled tactfully by not precipitating greater grief or distress in the subjects. Where ever possible, an alternative line of questioning was adopted for the remainder of the interview. The areas or topics covered in the questionnaire or interview schedule included demographic details, age, number of years of marriage and those related to interpersonal relationships and adjustment with their husband as perceived by the infected sample of women in this study (Helitzer-Allen, Makhambera and Wangel, 1994).

Operational Definitions

Marital adjustment as operationally defined in this study refers to 'sexual satisfaction, verbal and non-verbal communication'. Marital satisfaction, different from marital adjustment, refers to ones level of agreement, liking and approval towards ones own marriage. It is an attitude of greater or lesser favourability towards ones own marital relationship. It is a measurement on the perception of ones marriage by means of an attitude scale which is at the same time objective uncontaminated by marital conventionalization and social desirability; and, which could also provide items that would reflect attitudinal change likely to occur as a result of marital intervention. Some well known marital adjustment scales, inventories or measures available for use are: 'The Locke Wallace Marital Adjustment Test' (1959) (Cocoran and Fischer, 1987), 'The Dyadic Adjustment Scale' (Spanier, 1976), 'The Kansas Marital Satisfaction Scale' (Schumm *et al.*, 1986), 'Marital Satisfaction Scale' (Fowers and Olson, 1993), 'The Comprehensive Marital Satisfaction Scale' (Blum and Mehrabian, 1999; Arthur, Frazier and Bowden, 1981), 'Marital Adjustment Inventory' (Singh, 1987) and others.

Tools and Materials

The two tools used in this study are:

1. *Demographic Profile*

   This tool was developed for the purpose of this study to elicit details of the respondents on their current age, the age or years of their marriage, number and ages of children, the family housing standards, etc.

2. *Marital Adjustment Inventory*

   The 10-item Marital Adjustment Inventory (Singh, 1987) developed on the basis of factor analysis was used for data collection in this study.

This tool comprises of two forms A and B separately to be filled about the husband by the wives or about the wife by their husband respectively. However, in this study, only the form containing ten statements to be answered by the wives was used. The procedure of administration for this inventory involved the respondents to answer each of ten statements as either 'yes' or 'no'. After giving the direction of their response as consent for 'yes' (+ sign) or 'no' (- sign); they were also expected to circle any number between +1 to +10 or -1 to -10 to indicate the strength of their response by circling the number which best explained their opinion towards the issue. The rating scale ranges from +10 (most favorable) to +10 (least favourable). All doubtful situations were to be avoided. The specific items in the inventory included statements on the kind or amount of freedom given to their husbands, regarding upkeep of the homes, preparation of menus, intellectual participation or grasp on their business or occupational activities, sharing of leisure and recreation time or matters of common interests, relationships with his friends and relatives, dressing and appearance according to his tastes or likings, etc. Scoring for individual respondents for each item on this scale involves the corresponding integer (+) or (-) the number for 'Most Favourable' (10), 'Significantly Favourable' (9), 'More than Slightly Favourable' (8), 'Slightly Favourable' (7), 'Just Favourable' (6), 'Favourable' (5), 'Definitely Favourable' (4), 'Comparatively Favourable' (3), 'More than Least Favourable' (2) and 'Least Favourable' (1) respectively. Thus, higher scores on this scale for an individual respondent indicates attitudes towards favourable direction as low scores denote less favourable valence. The maximum possible score for the most favourable attitude on this scale is +100 and the minimum score for the most unfavourable attitude towards marital adjustment of an individual respondent on this scale is -100. The scale has been shown to have a co-efficient of reliability for the general population to the order of 0.94. The discriminant validity of the instrument to separate the lower and upper fifteen per cent of the persons in a distribution of scores has been demonstrated.

Results and Discussion

The marital adjustment score (by considering their integers) as derived for the overall sample of 60 rural women respondents identified or diagnosed as affected by HIV/AIDS is 1384 out of a maximum-minimum possible score range between +/- 6000 (N: 60; Score: 1384; Mean: 23.07) for all the ten items on this scale. This implies that qualitatively their attitude falls in the interpretable range of 'more than least favourable' for the whole group.

When these overall trends are analyzed in terms of *age variable,* it is seen that respondent rural women in age 30-35 years (N: 14; Score: 110; Mean:

7.86) show least marital adjustment scores followed by women in age range 20-25 years (N: 11; Score: 212; Mean: 19.28), those above 35 years (N: 12; Score: 330; Mean: 27.50) and last by women between 25-30 years (N: 23; Score: 732; Mean: 31.83) respectively. Therefore, age of the rural women appears to be significant variable in influencing their report of more or less marital adjustment in this sample (f: 3.29; p: 0.03). Studies have linked several psycho-social determinants like flexibility, dyadic consensus, interest sharing between the married couple, and higher standard of living as correlated with women reports on their positive marital adjustment (Kitamura *et al*, 2006). Others have connected perceived emotional intelligence, or the mediating role of personality and social desirability in marital adjustment (Joshi and Thingujam, 2009). Still others have found factors like loneliness (Demir and Fislolu, 1999), sexual satisfaction, verbal and non-verbal communication, expressiveness (Lamke, 1989) as well as demographic variables like age and number of years of marriage (Tucker and Horowitz, 1981) as critical in marital adjustment for women.

With regard to *education variable*, all levels of the rural women respondents in this sample report similar trend of marital adjustment irrespective of their illiteracy (N: 15; Score: 449; Mean: 29.93), education up to primary level (N: 9; Score: 205; Mean: 22.78), middle school level (N: 8; Score: 64; Mean: 8.00) and/or high school level (N: 28; Score: 669; Mean: 23.89)(f: 1.88; p: 0.15). There are indications to show that Indian women tend to generally report adequate marital adjustment and positive subjective well-being irrespective of their occupation and/or levels of education (Nathawat and Mathur, 1993) as also otherwise (Dubey, 1999). These findings have implications for the ongoing social-cultural movements, advocacy and empowerment of rural women in raising their voice against HIV/AIDS (Kishore and Gupta, 2004; Hawkes and Santhya, 2002). Mere knowledge or awareness about the disease condition in the rural Indian women does not appear to automatically translate into positive social action (Pallikadavath, Jayachandran and Stones, 2003; Hirve and Sathe, 1999; Kunte *et al*, 1999).

The *type of family* background of the rural women respondents in this study emerges as a significant variable in their report on marital adjustment depending upon whether they hail from nuclear (N: 40; Score: 1148; Mean: 28.70) or non-nuclear settings (N: 20; Score: 236; Mean: 11.80). There is greater marital maladjustment reported by HIV/AIDS affected rural women from non-nuclear type of family milieu than women from nuclear families (f: 1.4699; p: 0.002). These trends are in consonance with similar findings on greater psychological depression, dissatisfaction in life and mental health issues in rural Indian women from such family backgrounds (Patil, Somasundaram and Goyal, 2002; Patel and Oomman, 1999).

Table 29.1: Distribution of Marital Adjustment Scores across Various Variables

	N	Test Item Numbers										Total		Probability
		I	II	III	IV	V	VI	VII	VIII	IX	X	Actual	Maximum	
Overall	60	162	424	239	172	216	313	-178	29	-128	135	1384	6000	
Age:														
20-25	11	43	77	60	53	30	31	-38	-7	-40	1	212	1100	
25-30	23	50	184	127	86	122	134	-79	48	-57	87	732	2300	F: 3.29; p: <0.0315
30-35	14	31	75	9	-6	17	73	-16	-40	-38	5	110	1400	df: 3, 36, 39
35+	12	38	88	43	39	47	45	-47	28	7	42	330	1200	
Education														
Nil	15	79	113	37	43	64	68	-40	49	-13	49	449	1500	
Primary	9	21	59	59	-8	12	30	-8	13	10	17	205	900	
Middle	8	-4	20	35	3	21	40	-27	-5	-36	14	64	800	F: 1.88; p: <0.1504
High	28	66	232	108	134	119	175	-103	-28	-89	55	669	2800	df: 3, 36, 39
Family														
Nuclear	40	134	302	210	121	144	165	-77	91	-31	89	1148	4000	t: 4.699; p: <0.0022
Joint	20	28	122	29	52	72	148	-101	-62	-97	46	236	2000	df: 9

(Contd…)

	N	Test Item Numbers										Total		Probability
		I	II	III	IV	V	VI	VII	VIII	IX	X	Actual	Maximum	
Occupation:														
Skilled	16	128	309	216	145	194	240	-123	88	-58	122	1261	1600	t: 4.272; p: <0.0034
Unskilled	44	34	115	23	27	22	73	-55	-59	-70	13	123	4400	df: 9
Income														
High	33	136	254	192	100	163	166	-81	54	-55	51	980	3300	t: 3.256; p: <0.0120
Low	27	26	170	47	72	53	147	-97	-25	-73	84	404	2700	df: 9
Route														
Sexual	48	149	312	189	91	125	228	-165	-23	-144	48	810	4800	t: 0.5785; p: <0.577
Non-sexual	12	13	112	50	81	91	85	-13	52	16	87	574	1200	df: 9
Stage														
I	13	0	59	28	17	49	64	-33	3	-18	5	205	1300	
II	26	83	205	102	93	89	156	-87	11	-38	67	681	2600	F: 2.58; p: <0.6861
III	13	46	99	96	62	64	44	-23	27	-22	33	424	1300	df: 3, 36, 39
IV	8	2	61	13	2	14	49	-35	-12	-50	30	74	800	

(Contd…)

	N	Test Item Numbers										Total		Probability
		I	II	III	IV	V	VI	VII	VIII	IX	X	Actual	Maximum	
Treatment:														
ARV I	43	139	295	201	141	154	190	-144	53	-87	86	1028	4300	
ARV II	4	-13	30	21	17	21	30	1	16	6	17	146	400	F: 4.15; p: <0.0127
ARV III	11	20	81	3	-3	26	77	-25	-40	-48	42	133	1100	df: 3, 36, 39
ARV IV	2	16	18	14	17	15	16	-10	0	1	-10	77	200	

Likewise, *the type of occupation* held by the rural respondent women in this study also surfaces as significant variable in their report on marital adjustment depending on whether they are skilled (N: 16; Score: 1261; Mean: 78.81), or unskilled workers (N: 44; Score: 123; Mean: 2.80). The unskilled workers experience greater marital maladjustment than their skilled counterparts (f: 4.272; p: 0.0032). Related studies on working females in rural and urban India have shown that outdoor work orientation, and urbanization increases masculinity levels of females and debilitates the marital adjustment of the females in contrast to lower masculinity level facilitates marital adjustment in females (Dubey, 2009; Agarwal, 1971).

The women respondents from *high income groups* (N: 33; Score: 980; Mean: 29.70) show statistically significant differences by reporting higher scores on marital adjustment compared to their counterparts from low income groups (N: 27; Score: 404; Mean: 14.96)(f: 3.256; p: <0.012). A few studies have reported the presence or prevalence of sexual harassment and domestic violence in families with husbands afflicted by HIV/AIDS (Khan *et al*, 1992). This gives the predilection especially for affected rural women from low income groups to reflect lower marital adjustments (Kumar *et al*, 1995) in contrast to their counterparts from urban settlements (Nayar and Chawla, 1996).

The *route of infection* for HIV/AIDS either sexual (N: 48; Score: 810; Mean: 16.87) and/or non-sexual (N: 12; Score: 574; Mean: 47.83) does not surface as an influential variable for determining marital adjustment in this study (f: 0.5785; p: 0.577). Available literature suggests that spread of HIV to rural women is mostly from their infected husbands and/or their irregular use of condoms to ensure safe sex (George *et al*, 1997). Despite this observation, the typical rural Indian infected woman offers neither resistance nor reports of severe marital maladjustment in the companionship of the infected or risky spouse.

Data was analyzed based on *stage of the infection* ranging between I-IV. For the rural women respondents in stage IV (N: 8; Score: 74; Mean: 9.25), the marital adjustment scores are the least compared to women in stage I (N: 13; Score: 205; Mean: 15.77), stage II (N: 26; Score: 681; Mean: 26.19), and stage III (N: 13; Score: 424; Mean: 32.62). Even though these differences on the basis of stage of infection are not statistically significant (f: 2.58; p: 0.6861), there are differences based on the level or type of ARV treatments being taken by the infected respondents of rural women (f: 4.15; p: 0.013). The highest marital adjustment being reported by infected rural women who are at ARV IV (N: 2; Score: 77; Mean: 38.5), followed by those women who are at ARV II (N: 4; Score: 146; Mean: 36.5), ARV I (N: 43; Score: 1028; Mean: 23.91), and ARV III (N: 11; Score: 133; Mean: 12.09) respectively.

Item Analysis

At another level, an analysis on the 10-item Marital Adjustment Scale showed that majority of the respondents gave negative markings to item seven and nine related to questions like 'Do you not care in dressing according to the likes or dislikes of your husband?', *'Do you not care about the interests of your husband and so be an hindrance to him during leisure hours?', etc.* In related studies, it was reported that women can impose authority within the husband's household only after she gives birth to a live child, particularly a son. Her status in the family rises with the number of healthy children that she gives birth for the family (Karve, 1965). In patrilocal societies the status of widows in the family is low (Dreze and Sen, 2002). Dube (1997) notes the husband's exclusive right over the wife's sexuality is unquestioned. Women have no power to make men use barrier contraceptive methods, such as, the condom which could prevent both pregnancy and sexually transmitted infections (Sharma, Sujay and Sharma, 1998).

In sum, the present study has highlighted the adverse position and predicament of a typical Indian rural woman afflicted by HIV/AIDS and undergoing anti retro viral drug therapy. The derived profile of an affected typical rural Indian woman as one who, irrespective of her knowledge or awareness about HIV/AIDS in the spouse, is monogamous, uncomplaining, adjusting, accepting of the spouses vagrant sexual behaviours, etc. (Flanigan *et al*, 2000). These findings have tremendous implications for the ongoing social-cultural movement on advocacy and empowerment of affected rural women in raising their voice against HIV/AIDS in the country.

REFERENCES

Agarwal, A.K. (1971). Patterns of Marital Disharmonies. *Indian Journal of Psychiatry*. 14. 48. 186-194.

Apte, H. (1997). Adolescent Sexuality and Fertility: A Study in Western Maharashtra. *International Centre for Research on Women, Information Bulletin*, January.

Arthur J.R., Frazier, L.P., and Bowden, S.R. (1981). The Marital Satisfaction Scale: Development of a Measure for Intervention Research, *Journal of Marriage and the Family*. 43, 3: 537-546.

Balmer, D.H., Gikundi, E., Kanyotu, M., and Waithaka, R. (1995). The Negotiating Strategies Determining Coitus in Stable Heterosexual Relationships. *Health Transition Review*, 5: 85-95.

Banerjee, A., Deaton, A. and Duflo, E. (2004). Health Care Delivery in Rural Rajasthan. *Economic and Political Weekly*, 39: 944-949.

Bang, R.A., Bang, A.T., Baitule, M., Chaudhary, Y., Sarmukaddam, S., and Tale, O. (1989). High Prevalence of Gynaecological Diseases in Rural Indian Women *The Lancet*, 8 (29): 85-88.

Baylies, C. (2001). Safe Motherhood in the Time of AIDS: The Illusion of Reproductive Choice. In Sweetman, C.G. (Ed.). *Development and Health*. Oxford: Oxfam.

Bharat, S., and Aggleton, P. (1999). Facing the Challenge: Household Responses to HIV/AIDS in Mumbai, India. AIDS Care, 11, 31-44.

Bhattacharjee, J., Gupta, R.S., Kumar, A., and Jain, D.C. (2000). Pre- and Extra-marital Heterosexual Behaviour of an Urban Community in Rajasthan, India. *Journal of Communicative Diseases*. 32: 33-42.

Blum, J.S., and Mehrabian, A. (1999). Personality and Temperament Correlates of Marital Satisfaction. *Journal of Personality*, 67: 93-125.

Boerma, J.T., Urassa, M., Nnko, S., Ng'weshemi, J., Isingo, R., Zaba, B. and Mwaluko, G. (2002). Socio-demographic Context of the AIDS Epidemic in a Rural Area in Tanzania with a Focus on People's Mobility and Marriage. *Sexually Transmitted Infections*. 78. I97-I105 Suppl. 1.

Bryan, A.D., Jeffrey, D.F. and Joseph, B. (2001). Determinants of HIV Risk Among Indian Truck Drivers. *Social Science and Medicine*. 53, 1413-1426.

Corcoran, K., and Fischer, J. (1987). *Measures for Clinical Practice: A Sourcebook*. New York: Free Press.

Demir, A., and Fislolu, H. (1999). Loneliness and Marital Adjustment of Turkish Couples. *Journal of Psychology*. 133.

Dube, L. (1997). *Women and Kinship: Comparative Perspectives on Gender in South and South-East Asia*. Tokyo: United Nations University Press.

Dubey, S.K. (2009). Marital Adjustment of Masculine Working Families. *Proceedings of Ninth Annual IBER & TLC Conference*. USA: Las Vegas.

Dixon-Muller, D. (1993). The Sexuality Connection in Reproductive Health. *Studies in Family Planning*, 24 (5): 269-82.

Fowers, B.J., and Olson, D.H. (1993). ENRICH (Evaluation and Nurturing Relationship Issues, Communication and Happiness) Marital Satisfaction (EMS) Scale. *Journal of Family Psychology*, 7.2: 176-185.

George, S., Jacob, M., John, T.J., Jain, M.K., Nathan, N., Rao, P.S., Richard, J. and Antonisamy, B. (1997). A Case-control Analysis of Risk Factors in HIV Transmission in South India. *Journal of Acquired Immune Deficiency Syndromes*, 14, 290-293.

Hawkes, S., and Santhya, K.G. (2002). Diverse Realities: Sexually Transmitted Infections and HIV in India. *Sexually Transmitted Infections*. 78, 131-139 Suppl. 1.31.

Helitzer-Allen, D., Makhambera, M., and Wangel, A.M. (1994). Obtaining Sensitive Information: The Need for More Than Focus Groups Reproductive Health Matters. 3:75-81.

Hirve, S.S., and Sathe, P.V. (1999). AIDS Awareness Among Married Women in Reproductive Age Group from Rural Areas of Three Coastal Districts. *AIDS Research and Review*. 2, 156-160.

Jejeebhoy, S.J. (1998). Adolescent Sexual and Reproductive Behaviour: A Review of the Evidence from Social Science and Medicine 46(10): 1275-1290.

Joshi, S., and Thingujam, N.S. (2009). Perceived Emotional Intelligence and Marital Adjustment Examining the Mediating Role of Personality and Social Desirability. *Journal of Indian Academy of Applied Psychology*. 35.1.79-86.

Khan, M.E., Townsend, J., Sinha, R., and Lakhanpal, S. (1992). *Sexual Violence within Marriage Seminar* 447 (11): 32-35.

Kishor, S. and Gupta, K. (2004). Women's Empowerment in India and Its States: Evidence from the FHS. *Economic and Political Weekly*. 39, 694-712.

Kitamura, T., Watanabe, M., Fujino, M., Aoki, M., Ura, C., and Fujihara, S. (2006). Factorial Structure and Correlates of Marital Adjustment in a Japanese Population: A Community Study. *Journal of Community Psychology*. 23, 2, 117-126.

Knodel, J., Van Landingham, M., Saengtienchai, C., and Pramualratana, A. (1996). *Thai Views of Sexuality and Sexual Behaviour Health Transition Review* 6: 179-201.

Kumar, R., Singh, M.M., Kaur, A., and Kaur, M. (1995). Reproductive Health Behaviour of Rural Women. *Journal of Indian Medical Association*. 93: 129-31.

Kunte, A., Misra, V., Paranjape, R., Mansukhani, N., Padbidri, V., Gonjari, S., Kakrani, V., Thakar, M. and Mehendale, S. (1999). HIV Sero-prevalence and Awareness about AIDS Among Pregnant Women in Rural Areas of Pune District, Maharashtra, India. *Indian Journal of Medical Research* 110, 115-122.

Lamke, L.K. (1989). Marital Adjustment Among Rural Couples: The Role of Expressiveness. *Sex Roles*. 21, 9-10, 579-590.

Maniar JK(2000), Health Care Systems in Transition III, India. Part II. Current Status of HIV/AIDS in India, *Journal of Public Health Medicine*. 22:33-37.

Nag, M. (1996). *Sexual Behaviour and AIDS*. New Delhi, Vikas Publishing House.

Nathawat, S.S., and Mathur; A. (1993). Marital Adjustment and Subjective Well-being in Indian Educated Housewives and Working Women. *Journal of Psychology*. 127.

National AIDS Control Organization. (2007). National AIDS Control Programme, HIV/AIDS Sentinel Survey of the India scenario. File: http://www.naco.nic.in/indianscene/esthiv.htm

Nayar, T. and Chawla, S.C. (1996). Sexual Behaviour of Women in an Urban Resettlement Colony of Delhi *The Radical Journal of Health*. 11. 2/3: 113-32.

Newmann, S., Sarin, P., Kumarasamy, N., Amalraj, E., Rogers, M., Madhivanan, P., Flanigan, T., Cu-Uvin, S., Mc Garvey, S., Mayer, K. and Solomon, S. (2000). Marriage, Monogamy and HIV: A Profile of HIV-infected Women in South India. *International Journal of STD and AIDS*. 11, 250-253.

Pais, P. (1996). *HIV and India: Looking into the Abyss*. Tropical Medicine and International Health. 1, 295-304.

Pallikadavath, S., Jayachandran, A.A. and Stones, R.W. (2003). Women's Reproductive Health, Socio-cultural Context and AIDS Knowledge in Northern India, Abstracts of the Population Association of America Meeting, Minneapolis.

Patel, V. and Oomman, N. (1999). *Mental Health Matters Too: Gynaecological Symptoms and Depression in South Asia Reproductive Health Matters* 7. 14: 30-38.

Patil A.V., Somasundaram K.M., and Goyal, R.C. (2002). Current Health Scenario in Rural India. *Australian Journal of Rural Health*, 10 129-135.

Rao, K.S., Pilli, R.D., Rao, A.S. and Chalam, P.S. (1999). Sexual Lifestyle of Long Distance Lorry Drivers in Questionnaire Survey, *British Medical Journal* 318, 162-163.

Savara, M. and Shridhar, C.R. (1996). Sexuality: Differing Perceptions Survey in Maharashtra, *The Radical Journal of Health* (New Series) 11. 2/3: 133-39.

Schumm, W.R., Paff-Bergen, L.A., Hatch, R.C., Obiorah, EC., Copeland. J.M., Meens, L. D., and Bugaighis, M.A. (1986). Concurrent and Discriminant Validity of the Kansas Marital Satisfaction Scale. *Journal of Marriage and the Family*, 48, 381-87.

30

A New Perspective on Successfully Shy Life

Sedigheh Ebrahimi[1]

Introduction

Shyness could be defined experientially as discomfort and inhibition in interpersonal situations that interferes with pursuing one's interpersonal or professional goals. It is a form of excessive self-focus, a preoccupation with one's thoughts, feelings and physical reactions. It may vary from mild social awkwardness to totally inhibiting social phobia. Shyness reactions can occur at any or all of the following levels: cognitive, affective, physiological and behavioural, and may be triggered by a wide variety of arousal cues (Henderson and Zimbardo, 1996). Most of them are: authorities, one-on-one opposite sex interactions, intimacy, strangers, having to take individuating action in a group setting, and initiating social actions in unstructured, spontaneous behavioural settings. According to Charducci (1999), there are five types of shyness: those who are publicly shy and those who are privately shy. One is more concerned about behaving badly, the other about feeling badly. The successfully shy also take steps at the transpersonal level, getting involved in the lives of others. They start small, making sure their day-to-day exchanges involve contact with other people. when they pick up a newspaper, for instance, they don't just put their money on counter. they focus on the seller, thanking him or her for the service. This creates a social environment favourable to positive interactions. On a larger scale, I encourage volunteering. Once the shy are more outwardly focussed on the lives of other people, shyness no longer controls them.

1. Research Scholar, Department of Psychology ,University of Mysore, Mysore, Karnataka (India).

The successfully shy don't change who they are. They change the way thy think and actions they make. There is nothing wrong with being shy. In fact, we have come to believe that what out society needs is not less shyness but a little more. Bernardo J. Carducci and Lisa Kaiser state that:

> When I speak to someone, I usually get nervous and uncomfortable. I talk very fast, mumble my words, stutter. I don't talk loud enough for others to hear, so I'm constantly repeating myself. "I egotistically take other people to be noticing and criticizing my behaviour much more than they probably do. I set excessively high standards for myself, expecting a smoothness, quality and ease of interaction that a non-shy person wouldn't dream of expecting".
>
> When I was younger, I was very quiet with strangers and in social situations. I was a completely different person when I was with my family and friends. I have a great sense of humour and a lot of personality that seemed to disappear in public. Today there is an ongoing struggle and inner badgering during social situations'.
>
> "Life is hell, when you cannot even talk because of fear of saying something dumb".

If you are shy, you're not alone. One of the tricks shyness plays on the mind is that it creates feelings of isolation. But shy people are not alone. They make up almost half of the population, and about 95 per cent of us know first-hand what it means to be shy in some situations. We also know that shyness is not simply defined as "the failure to respond appropriately in social situations," as it once had. It's not introversion, being tongue-tied, having stage fright, or being a wall flower. Shyness addresses these and many other myths and misinformation about shyness by examining and synthesizing what is known about shyness in a practical manner that will make it possible for your to use this information in our own every day living experiences. By providing a deep understanding of shyness and explaining now to use this information. Shyness will enlighten and empower people who feel they're cut off from the world.

The Successfully Shy Lover:

W.H. Jones states that:

> "I do not attend social events like weddings or parties", a college student wrote to me. "I have never really had a boyfriend because I shy away from men when they attempt to talk to me. This is really bothering me because all of my friends are dating and I am not, due to my shyness. This is ridiculous"!

According to P.A. Pilkonis:

> "all of these people have had difficulties initiating social interactions. Paradoxically, less than 7 per cent of the more than 150 letters I analyzed for a recent study claimed that shyness interfered with their intimate relationships. Unfortunately, the problem lies not in getting along once the connection is cemented but in getting close to someone in the first place".

You may struggle to meet new people, summon the courage to ask someone for a date, and behave naturally and openly on the first few dates with a new partner. Since you may have trouble approaching and making small talk with new acquaintances, this is easy to understand. But making romantic connections is not as complicated as you may believe. I will share with you the relatively few rules you'll need to remember in order to do so successfully. Some people seem to do this intuitively, but others profit from practice, patience and persistence.

Successfully Shy Manager

Management requires you to have delicate people skills while conveying a sense of authority. At the heart of a good management style is communication, which you use to exchange information in a constructive manner. You obtain what you need and explain what you want from your employees and how your company's objectives can be met. These skills help you give and receive feedback, delegate assignments, deal effectively with authority figures, mediate disputes and foster creative expression among your supervisees.

Your position puts you squarely between higher-ups and subordinates. With those above you in the hierarchy, you must make your needs and accomplishments known, obtain the resources you require to get the job done, receive and apply feedback, and get credit where it is due. With those below, you must become comfortable making requests and giving orders, conveying authority and being assertive, providing feedback and building camaraderie. You must approach your employees often to ensure that they do their jobs and to maintain morale. For a shy person, that's tall order indeed (Philips & Bruch, 1988).

Management is one of the most difficult jobs a shy employee can undertake. You can be handicapped by underdeveloped social skills, which may erode the output and the esprit de corps of your team. You may reinforce quietness in your department. This can create a harmful model for your subordinates; denying them the opportunity to interact can lead to poor morale (Triandis, 1994). Negotiation and tact can also be difficult for you. If you're negatively preoccupied with yourself, it's hard to be socially sensitive and to discern others' feelings — musts in skillful managing.

If you're inclined to lock yourself in your office, you won't get good results from your employees because you seem aloof. You may be oblivious to what's going on in your department (both the good and the bad). You may miss your employees' strengths and limitations, and others may perceive you as harsh. Finishing projects may be difficult for you either because you're poor at delegating or because your employees make empty promises. They resent being asked to put out for someone they see as uncaring and who doesn't engage in small talk with them.

Filled with your own self-doubts, negative evaluations, and uncertainties, you may also have trouble exercising authority over others. You may worry too much about your employees' feelings and not enough about the job at hand. You don't want them to take criticism personally or be offended in any way because you know how bad that feels, but if you're submissive; your employees may take advantage of you (Zimbardo, 1977).

To be a good manager, you must concern yourself not just with the bottom line but also with building rapport in your department. You may believe that its acceptable to communicate only through Email, but your workers need human contact. Inaugurate after-hours gatherings, social events and retreats. Be sure to use your small-talk skills at these events. Try in-house training seminars at which you do the training or rotate assignments so everyone gets a chance to be in authority or in a subordinate position. Provide regular performance reviews — every few weeks rather than every six months. This helps with the warm up process and allows supervisees to accept feedback more readily because they are used to it. Frequent performance reviews are easier for you because they're shorter.

How to Handle a Shy Employee

As a shy person yourself, you may recognize shyness in an employee. Be sensitive to the many issues he must cope with. As a result of his approach/ avoidance conflict, he may hesitate to talk to you or speak up in meetings. He may need guidance but not seek it.

According to R.M. Page, there are ways you can help:

❖ Ask for opinions from employees who are rarely vocal, and let them know that you value them and that they can trust you.

❖ Vary the modes of communication. Don't just rely on written comments. Use E-mail, phone and memo messages, but also meet with shy employees one-on-one. Vary the location—your office, her cubicle, over lunch. This shows you're willing to talk at any time and in almost any circumstance. Follow verbal feedback with written or electronic confirmation or written feedback with a phone call or personal contact. This helps get shy employees out of the habit of communicating via E-mail exclusively. You are modelling new behaviours.

- Be respectful of the warm up period. A shy employee may initially resist change. Persist, and give him time to adjust.
- Open the lines of communication. Encourage shy employees to make their needs known to you.
- Be a mentor — take a shy employee along on sales calls so he will have an example to emulate.
- Recognize how shyness may affect an employee's performance. His people skills and not his work skills may be holding him back.

Positive reinforcement does wonders for shy employees—eventually. They rate themselves more favorably after a success. However, research has shown that they need more than a single success and more encouragement than their nonshy colleagues to feel confident. Perhaps they see the first achievement as a fluke or good luck. Perhaps they are slow to warm to the idea of doing well. Continue to encourage shy employees with positive feedback, and in time you will both reap the rewards.

Successfully Shy Workers

Work interactions are no different from interactions in other areas of your life. The same rules apply. As you become more successful socially, your skills will easily translate to the work place. If you're shy at work but relaxed with friends and family, make your co-workers friends. By the same token, the lessons you learn at work can transfer to your personal life. If you're confident at work but not at a party, think of the party as a job. Learn what's expected, prepare, ask questions, make contacts.

Allen found a way out of his shyness in the work place. With the advice of a psychologist, he used 'positive cognition activities'. Whenever I had a negative thought I wrote it down, and then I would write a positive thought to replace it. At first it didn't work—actually it would have, but I didn't do it enough. Then I persevered and became consistent and it finally worked. I forced myself into situations that I wouldn't have been in before. The more I did it, the easier it got. As I did this, my confidence grew".

Today Allen has an engineering sales position. "Not only do I have to go out and get new customers, but I have to keep the customers we already have". That takes people skills and Allen seems to have acquired them.

"A lot of people think that there is no cure for shyness", he continued. "But a lot of people don't realize that it takes time to get over this problem. Shyness and anxiety are habits that form over years and years. You can't change that overnight. It takes years to unlearn. I'm proud that I've come as far as I have" (Kagan, 1994).

Successfully Shy Global Citizen

When people find themselves among those of different cultures and races, they begin to feel more salient, more self-conscious, as if they are sticking out like a sore thumb. In fact, their behaviour becomes more guarded and reserved. Those in the majority seem to watch what they do and attribute more responsibility to them for negative outcomes. Indeed, whether shy or not, once perceived as part of a minority, people become situationally shy. They leave their comfort zones and feel disquieted.

This was brought home to me recently when a friend told me about her experience at a Los Angeles manicurist's shop staffed by a group of young Vietnamese women. As Louise and another client—a stranger—sat waiting for their nails to dry, the six manicurists chatted excitedly among themselves in their native tongue. They seemed relaxed and happy in their small enclave. The other customer turned to Louise and said in hushed tones, "You know, I feel like I'm in a foreign country here". Her discomfort was evident.

Rubin points out, gesturing toward the Asian women, "I'll bet most of the time they feel the way you do right now".

Understanding how people of different cultures interface become increasingly important as communication and mobility have opened us all to contact with those of many lands. But we need not look to intercultural domains to grasp these issues. If you are the only female engineer in an office filled with men, the only disabled person in a class of able-bodied, the only black person in a restaurant full of Hispanics or whites, the only teenager in a group of your grandparents;' friends, you to are likely to feel uncomfortable and situationally shy. You will believe, perhaps rightly so, that all eyes are on you, and you will react accordingly by becoming self-conscious, self-evaluative and guarded. It's human nature to do so, but these are also the characteristics of a shy person.

According to Davis, social psychologist Kay Deaux at City University of New York found that in such situations people practice the art of remooring — connecting to other like-minded individuals to create a new comfort zone. A Mexican-American student attending a predominantly white college, for example, might join a Latino club. An employee transferred to another city might seek out his religious community or a chapter of his service organization. Recent immigrants live in proximity to others from their homeland, forming ethnic pockets — Little Italy, Chinatown, Germantown, Little Saigon, the Lower East Side in Manhattan.

These associations are not ends in themselves, but serve as stepping stones in the adjustment process toward further assimilation. They help individuals make the transition into the larger culture and speed the warm up process. Those who have come before explain the rules of the dominant society to the newcomers and show them how to accommodate. Soon the émigrés begin to blend in. The student in the Latino Club, for instance, may eventually feel comfortable enough to join a nonethnically oriented political science or writing group and move into the culture at large.

These intercultural dynamics — the need to feel comfortable in awkward, shyness-provoking situations — help us understand why people limit their comfort zones and become clannish. All of us should be aware of these natural human impulses. If you find yourself in the majority, be sensitive to others' discomfort. And if you are in the minority, give yourself time to adjust. A successfully shy person of the world is able to move with relative ease from one cultural context to the next based on this awareness.

As the world gets faster, people tend naturally to withdraw and avoid. But as a successfully shy global citizen, you may have no need to do that. Because you grasp the basic concepts of your shy personality—approach/avoidance, the comfort zone, and slow to warm up — you are in a better position than most to deal with all of these changes personally as well as in your culture. And you will recognize how to incorporate these fundamentals into the ever-changing world around you.

Conclusion

Shyness is not just about shyness. It's about living a successful and full life brimming with self-awareness, self-acceptance and self-confidence. Rather than turning you into an extrovert, my goal has been to ensure that the negative side of your shyness no longer limits your choices. I never said you had to change, only that you needed to make better choices that will open to you many potential rewards.

The successfully shy life should be no different from any other. All of the processes that we've talked about - shyness of the mind, body, self; slowness to warm up, limited comfort zones, and the approach/avoidance conflict — are fundamental principles of human nature. They just seem to be more salient issues for shy people.

These processes are fluid and dynamic. They are constantly changing within you and your world. But now, because you understand the underlying dynamics of shyness, you're well prepared for these changes. In fact, because you have self-awareness, self-acceptance and self-confidence you may be better off than many nonshy people who lack these strengths.

I hope Shyness will make is possible for you to greet the world on your own terms. I cannot stress enough the value of social skills, social graces, and small talk. They help you relate to others more gracefully, but they also help society function more smoothly. They make people feel more comfortable.

When they aren't anxious or distressed, they can behave much more naturally instead of reactively. Living a successfully shy life is good for you and for those around you. It makes the world a better place.

REFERENCES

Carducci, Bernardo J. and Kaiser, Lisa (2002). Shyness: *A Bold New Approach*. Harper Collins Publishers: New York.

Jones, W.H. (1986). *Shyness: Perspectives on Research and Treatment*. New York: Plenum.

Pilkonis, P.A. (1977). *Shyness, Public and Private , and Its Relationship to Other Measures of Social Behaviour*. Journal of Pesonalty, 45, 585-595.

Philips, S.D. and Bruch, M.A. (1988). *Shyness and Dysfunction in Career Development*. Journal of Counselling Psychology, 2, 159-165.

Triandis, H.C. (1994). *Culture and Social Behaviour*. New York: McGraw- Hill.

Zimbardo, P.G. (1977). *Shyness: What It Is, What to Do About It. Reading*, MA: Addison-Wesley.

Page, R.M. (1990). Shyness and Sociability: A Dangerous Combination for Illicit Substance Use in Adolescence Males? *Adolescence*, 25, 803-806.

Kagan, J. (1994). *Galen's Prophecy: Temperament in Human Nature*. New York: Westview Press.

Rubin, K.H. (1982). *Non-social Play in Pre-schoolers: Necessary Evil*? Child Development, 53, 651-657.

Davis,M. (1994). *The Role of the Amygdala in Emotional Learning*. International Review of Neurobiology, 36,225-266.

Carducci, Bernardo J. and Kaiser, Lisa (2002). *Shyness: A Bold New Approach*. Harper Collins Publishers : New York.

Index